Frommer's® 2000

P O R T A B L E

Sydney

by Marc Llewellyn
with Natalie Kruger

Macmillan • USA

ABOUT THE AUTHOR

Sydney resident **Marc Llewellyn** is one of Australia's premier travel writers and a regular contributor to all of Australia's leading newspaper travel sections and travel magazines. As a member of the Australian Travel Writers' Association, he keeps his suitcase ready-packed beneath his bed. He is also the co-author of *Frommer's Australia* and *Frommer's Australia from $50 a Day*.

MACMILLAN TRAVEL

Macmillan General Reference USA, Inc.
1633 Broadway
New York, NY 10019

Find us online at **www.frommers.com**

ISBN 0-02-863419-5
ISSN 1097-654X

Editor: Suzanne Jannetta
Production Editor: Suzanne Snyder
Photo Editor: Richard Fox
Design by Michele Laseau
Staff Cartographers: John Decamillis and Roberta Stockwell
Page Creation: John Bitter, Natalie Evans, and Judith McMullen

SPECIAL SALES

Bulk purchases (10+ copies) of Frommer's and selected Macmillan travel guides are available to corporations, organizations, mail-order catalogs, institutions, and charities at special discounts, and can be customized to suit individual needs. For more information, write to Special Sales, Macmillan General Reference, 1633 Broadway, New York, NY 10019.

Manufactured in the United States of America

5   4   3   2   1

Contents

List of Maps

AN INVITATION TO THE READER

In researching this book, we discovered many wonderful places—resorts, inns, restaurants, shops, and more. We're sure you'll find others. Please tell us about them, so we can share the information with your fellow travelers in upcoming editions. If you were disappointed with a recommendation, we'd love to know that, too. Please write to:

Frommer's Portable Sydney 2000
1633 Broadway
New York, NY 10019

AN ADDITIONAL NOTE

Please be advised that travel information is subject to change at any time—and this is especially true of prices. We therefore suggest that you write or call ahead for confirmation when making your travel plans. The authors, editors, and publisher cannot be held responsible for the experiences of readers while traveling. Your safety is important to us, however, so we encourage you to stay alert and be aware of your surroundings. Keep a close eye on cameras, purses, and wallets, all favorite targets of thieves and pickpockets.

WHAT THE SYMBOLS MEAN
✪ Frommer's Favorites

Our favorite places and experiences—outstanding for quality, value, or both.

The following abbreviations are used for credit cards:

AE	American Express	EU	Eurocard
CB	Carte Blanche	JCB	Japan Credit Bank
DC	Diners Club	MC	MasterCard
DISC	Discover	V	Visa
ER	enRoute		

FIND FROMMER'S ONLINE

Arthur Frommer's Budget Travel Online (**www.frommers.com**) offers more than 6,000 pages of up-to-the-minute travel information—including the latest bargains and candid, personal articles updated daily by Arthur Frommer himself. No other Web site offers such comprehensive and timely coverage of the world of travel.

Planning a Trip to Sydney

By Natalie Kruger
Natalie is the co-author of *Frommer's Australia*
and *Frommer's Australia from $50 a Day.*

*S*ydney, the "Emerald City," sits majestically around the greenest, most beautiful urban harbor in the world. It's at its best approached at night from the air, when you'll see a million twinkling lights, a vast swath of fluorescent spreading across the water, and the Sydney Opera House and Harbour Bridge lit up like Christmas. And this is not just one Sydneysider's opinion of the city, either. In recent years, the readers of both *Condé Nast Traveler* and *Travel & Leisure* have voted Sydney the World's Best City. Beat that Paris, or Venice, or Melbourne, or myriad other hopefuls.

Sydney has something for everyone: miles of beaches, from world-famous Bondi to pretty little Shelly Beach on the North Shore; world-class cuisine that combines the very best of many cultures; historic pubs where you can buy a "shout" for your new Aussie mates; city strolls; Harbour cruises; and more. Sydney is also, of course, gearing up for the 2000 Olympic Games, when the city will be the focus of the world's attention. See chapter 3 for everything you need to know about the games: what events are where, how to get tickets, and how to find a place to stay.

No matter what your interests, or what your reason for journeying to Sydney, this handy guide will give you everything you need to get you on your way, and tell you how to get around, where to stay, and where to dine once you arrive.

1 Visitor Information, Entry Requirements & Customs

VISITOR INFORMATION

The **Australian Tourist Commission (ATC)** offers several ways to help you plan your trip Down Under, which are laid out below. You can also write to the Australian Tourist Commission at Level 4, 80 William St., Woolloomooloo, Sydney NSW 2011 (☎ **02/ 9360 1111;** fax 02/9331 2538).

Australia

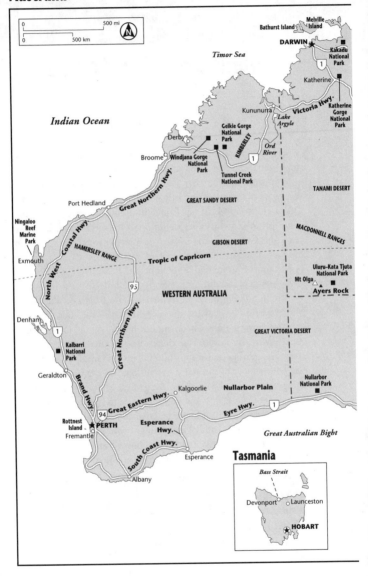

0 500 mi
0 500 km

Timor Sea

Bathurst Island
Melville Island
DARWIN
Kakadu National Park
Katherine
Katherine Gorge National Park
Kununurra
Lake Argyle
Victoria Hwy.

Indian Ocean

Geikie Gorge National Park
Derby
KIMBERLEY
Ord River
Broome
Windjana Gorge National Park
Tunnel Creek National Park

TANAMI DESERT

Port Hedland
Great Northern Hwy.
GREAT SANDY DESERT

Ningaloo Reef Marine Park
North West Coastal Hwy.
HAMERSLEY RANGE
GIBSON DESERT
MACDONNELL RANGES

Exmouth
Tropic of Capricorn

Uluru-Kata Tjuta National Park
Mt Olga
Ayers Rock

WESTERN AUSTRALIA

Denham
Great Northern Hwy.
GREAT VICTORIA DESERT

Kalbarri National Park

Geraldton
Brand Hwy.
Kalgoorlie
Nullarbor Plain
Nullarbor National Park

Rottnest Island
PERTH
Great Eastern Hwy.
Eyre Hwy.

Fremantle
Esperance Hwy.
Great Australian Bight

South Coast Hwy.
Esperance

Albany

Tasmania

Bass Strait
Devonport
Launceston
HOBART

2

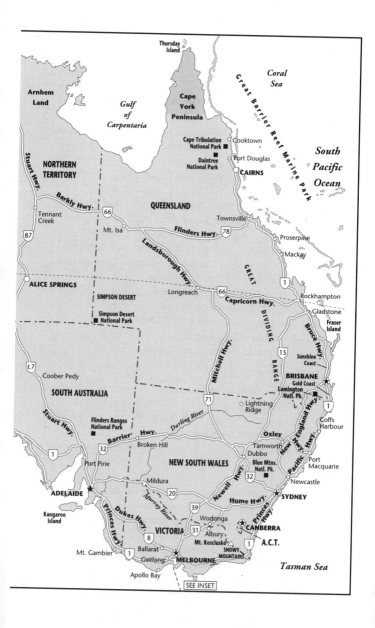

For help with piecing together an itinerary, or to find out more about any aspect of traveling in Australia, contact the ATC's **Aussie Helpline** at ☎ 805/775-2000 or fax 805/775-4448 in the United States and Canada; ☎ 0990/022 000 or fax 0171/940 5221 in the United Kingdom and Ireland, or to simply order brochures call ☎ 0990/561 434 in the U.K. and 01/402 6896 in Ireland; and 0800/65 0303 or fax 09/377 9562 in New Zealand. When you call, request a copy of the ATC's comprehensive brochure, the *Australian Vacation Planner*. The ATC also publishes *Australia Unplugged,* an excellent, hip guide to the country's coolest offerings.

The ATC also maintains a network of **"Aussie Specialist"** travel agents in several hundred cities across North America, Canada, the United Kingdom, New Zealand, and many other countries. These agents are committed to a continuous training program on the best destinations, hotels, deals, and tours in Oz. They will know better than most general travel agents on how to package an itinerary that's right for you. To find the Aussie Specialist nearest you, call the Aussie Helpline or the ATC in Sydney, or check the ATC Web site.

The Australian Tourist Commission's excellent Web site, **www.australia.com,** has more than 10,000 pages of listings for tour operators, hotels, car-rental companies, specialist travel outfitters, public holidays, maps, distance charts, and much more.

OTHER USEFUL WEB SITES

- The **Australian Embassy** in Washington, D.C., has a handy Web site at **www.austemb.org**. The site posts loads of links to sites on tourism; cultural and educational matters; briefings on the economy, trade, sport, geography, and the people; and events listings. It's written with North Americans in mind, though much of the information is relevant no matter where you are traveling from.
- All Australian telephone numbers are listed in the **Telstra White Pages** (search by name) and Yellow Pages (search by subject)—**www.whitepages.com.au** and **www.yellowpages. com.au**.
- For the latest on the **Sydney 2000 Olympic Games,** visit the official site at **www.sydney.olympic.org**.
- Check out the latest weather forecasts and research average temperature, rainfall, and humidity on the **Australian Bureau of Meteorology's** site at **www.bom.gov.au**.
- Pick up cool suggestions on sporting activities, restaurants, shops, attractions, and festivals as well as current film and other

cultural listings, an extensive accommodation directory, and lifestyle feature stories on Sydney at **www.sydney.citysearch. com.au**.

ENTRY REQUIREMENTS

Along with a current passport valid for the duration of your stay, the Australian government requires a visa from visitors of every nation (New Zealand citizens are issued a visa on arrival in Australia). This gets up the noses of the United States and other countries who do not make reciprocal demands on Australians, so the Australian government has introduced the **Electronic Travel Authority (ETA)**— an electronic or "paperless" visa that takes the place of a rubber stamp in your passport.

This is how the ETA works: you give your passport details in person or over the phone to your travel agent or when you book your plane ticket. This information will be entered into the travel agent's or airline's reservations system, which is linked to the Australian Department of Immigration and Multicultural Affairs' computer system. Assuming you are not wanted by Interpol, your ETA should be approved in about 6 to 8 seconds while you wait. You can also apply for an ETA at Australian embassies, high commissions, and consulates (see below).

Tourists should apply for a **Tourist ETA.** It's free and is valid for as many visits to Australia as you like of up to three months each within a one-year period. Tourists may not work in Australia, so if you are visiting for business, you must pay A$50 (U.S.$35) for a **Long Validity Business ETA,** which entitles you to as many three-month stays in Australia as you like for the life of your passport. Business travelers who are U.S., Canadian, French, or Spanish citizens can apply for a free **Short Validity Business ETA,** which is valid for a single visit of three months within a one-year period.

There are still some situations in which you will need to apply for a visa the old-fashioned way—by taking or mailing your passport, a completed visa application form, and the appropriate payment to your nearest Australian embassy or consulate. This will be the case if your travel agent, airline, or cruise ship (if you plan to arrive in Australia by boat) is not connected to the ETA system. In the United States, Canada, the United Kingdom, and many other countries, most agents and major airlines are ETA-compatible, but few cruise lines are. There is a A$60 (U.S. $42) processing fee for non-ETA visas for stays of up to three months and A$145 (U.S.$101.50) for business visas for stays between three months and four years.

You will also need to apply for a visa the old-fashioned way if you plan to enter Australia as something other than a tourist or a business traveler—for example, as a full-time, long-term student; a long-term resident; a sportsperson; a performer; or a member of a social group or cultural exchange. If you fall into one of these categories, you will need to apply for a **Temporary Residence visa.**

You can apply for non-ETA visas at Australian embassies, consulates, and high commissions. In the **United States,** contact the Australian Embassy, 1601 Massachusetts Ave. NW, Washington, D.C. 20036-2273 (☎ **202/797-3000**); or the Australian Consulate-General, 2049 Century Park East, Level 19, Los Angeles, CA 90067-3238 (☎ **310/229-4840**). In **Canada,** contact the Australian High Commission, 50 O'Connor St., #710, Ottawa, ON K1P6L2 (☎ **613/783-7619**). For business visa inquiries in the United States and Canada call ☎ **800/579-7664.** In the **United Kingdom,** contact the Australian High Commission, Australia House, The Strand, London WC2B 4LA (☎ **0171/379 4334** or 0891/600 333 for 24-hour recorded information); or the Australian Consulate, Chatsworth House, Lever St., Manchester M1 2QL (☎ **0161/228 1344**). In **Ireland,** contact the Australian Embassy, Fitzwilton House, Wilton Terrace, Dublin 2, Ireland (☎ **1/676 1517**).

You can obtain an application form for a non-ETA visa via the Internet at the **Australian Department of Immigration and Multicultural Affair's Web site** (www.immi.gov.au). This site also has a good explanation of the ETA system.

Allow at least a month for processing of non-ETA visas.

CUSTOMS

Anyone over 18 can bring in to Australia no more than 250 cigarettes or 250g of cigars or other tobacco products, 1.125 liters (41 fl. oz.) of alcohol, and "dutiable goods" to the value of A$400 (U.S.$280), or A$200 (U.S.$140) if you are under 18. Broadly speaking, "dutiable goods" are luxury items like perfume concentrate, watches, jewelry, furs, plus gifts of any kind. Keep this in mind if you intend to come bearing presents for family and friends in Australia. If the items are your own personal goods and you're taking them with you when you leave, they are usually exempt from duty. If you are not sure what is dutiable and what's not, contact the nearest Australian embassy or consulate (see above).

Because Australia is an island, it is free of many agricultural and livestock diseases. To keep it that way, strict quarantine applies to importing plants, animals, and their products, including food. Don't be alarmed if, just before landing, the flight attendants spray the aircraft cabin (with products approved by the World Health Organization) to kill flying insects that entered the plane in a foreign country. For more information on what is and is not allowed entry, contact the nearest Australian embassy or the **Australian Quarantine and Inspection Service** in Sydney (☎ **02/9364 7222**).

For U.S. Citizens   Returning U.S. citizens who have been away for 48 hours or more are allowed to bring back, once every 30 days, U.S.$400 worth of merchandise duty-free. You'll be charged a flat rate of 10% duty on the next U.S.$1,000 worth of purchases. Be sure to have your receipts handy. On gifts, the duty-free limit is U.S.$100. You cannot bring fresh foodstuffs into the United States; tinned foods, however, are allowed. There are a few restrictions on amount: 1 liter of alcohol (you must be over 21), 200 cigarettes, and 100 cigars. Antiques over 100 years old and works of art are exempt from the U.S.$400 limit, as are gifts you mail home. Once per day, you can mail U.S.$100 worth of gifts duty-free; label each package "unsolicited gift." Any package must state on the exterior a description of the contents and their values. You cannot mail alcohol, perfume (it contains alcohol), or tobacco products as duty-free gifts. For more information, contact the **U.S. Customs Service,** 1301 Constitution Ave. (P.O. Box 7407), Washington, DC 20044 (☎ **202/927-1000**) and request the free pamphlet *Know Before You Go.* It's also available on the Web at **www.customs.ustreas.gov**.

For U.K. Citizens   British citizens returning from a non-EC country have a customs allowance of 200 cigarettes, 50 cigars or 250g of smoking tobacco; 2 liters of still table wine; 1 liter of spirits or strong liqueurs (over 22% volume) or 2 liters of fortified wine, sparkling wine or other liqueurs; 60cc (ml) perfume; 250cc (ml) of toilet water; and £145 worth of all other goods, including gifts and souvenirs. People under 17 are not entitled to the tobacco or alcohol allowance. Meat and poultry products and some plants are also banned or restricted. For more information, contact **Her Majesty's Customs & Excise, Passenger Enquiries** (☎ **0181/910 3744; from outside the U.K. 44/181 910 3744**), or consult their Web site at **www.open.gov.uk**.

For Canadian Citizens   For a clear summary of Canadian rules, write for the free booklet *I Declare,* issued by **Revenue Canada** (☎ **800/461-9999; www.rc.gc.ca**). Canada allows its citizens a

Can$500 exemption after an absence of seven days, and you're allowed to bring back duty-free 200 cigarettes, 200g of tobacco, 1.14 liters (40 imperial ounces) of liquor, and 50 cigars. In addition, you're allowed to mail gifts to Canada from abroad at the rate of Can$60 a day, provided they are not alcohol or tobacco (write on the package "Unsolicited gift, under $60 value"). Restrictions apply to animal, plant and biological products.

For New Zealand Citizens The duty-free allowance for New Zealand citizens is NZ$700. Citizens over 17 can also bring in 200 cigarettes, or 50 cigars, or 250 grams of tobacco (or a mixture of all three if their combined weight doesn't exceed 250 grams); plus 4.5 liters of wine and beer, or 1.125 liters of liquor. Foodstuffs, plant material, and even used sporting goods, such as golf clubs and camping equipment, must be declared. Most questions are answered in a free pamphlet available at New Zealand consulates and Customs offices: *New Zealand Customs Guide for Travellers, Notice no. 4.* For more information, contact **New Zealand Customs (☎ 0800/ 428 786; www.customs.govt.nz).**

2 Money

CASH & CURRENCY The Australian dollar is divided into 100 cents. Coins come in 5¢, 10¢, 20¢ and 50¢ pieces (all silver in color) and $1 and $2 pieces (gold in color). The 50-cent piece is 12-sided. Prices in Australia often end in a variant of 1¢ and 2¢ (for example, 78 cents or $2.71), a relic from the days before 1-cent and 2-cent pieces were phased out (prices are rounded to the nearest 5¢). Bank notes come in denominations of $5, $10, $20, $50 and $100.

ATMs One of the fastest, safest, and easiest methods of managing money Down Under is to withdraw money direct from your home bank account at an Australian automatic-teller machine (ATM). That way you can get cash when banks and currency exchanges are closed, and your money is safely residing in your bank account back home until you withdraw it. It also means you get the bank exchange rate, not the higher commercial rate charged at currency exchanges. You will be charged a fee for each withdrawal, usually A$4 (U.S.$2.80) or so. It's your bank that charges this, not the Aussie bank, so ask your bank what it is.

All of the biggest banks in Australia—ANZ, Commonwealth, National, and Westpac—are connected to the Cirrus network. ANZ, Commonwealth, and National are also connected to Maestro. Only ANZ and National take Plus. Ask your bank at home for a directory of international ATM locations where your card is accepted. Both **Cirrus** (☎ **800/424-7787**; www.mastercard.com/atm) and **Plus** (☎ **800/843-7587**; www.visa.com) networks have automated ATM locators that list the banks in each country that will accept your card. Most ATMs in Australia accept both 4- and 6-digit PINs (personal identification numbers), but it's a good idea to request a 4-digit PIN from your bank, as these are the most common, not just in Australia, but the rest of the world.

Few ATMs have letters on the keypads, so memorize your PIN by number.

CREDIT CARDS   **Visa** and **MasterCard** are universally accepted in Australia, but American Express and Diners Club are accepted less often. Always have some cash on your person, as many merchants in Australia will not take cards for purchases under A$10 (U.S.$7). If your credit card is linked to your bank account, you can use it to withdraw cash from an ATM (just keep in mind that interest starts accruing immediately on credit-card cash advances.)

TRAVELER'S CHECKS   Traveler's checks are something of an anachronism from the days before ATMs made cash accessible at any time. The only sound alternative to traveling with dangerously large amounts of cash, traveler's checks were as reliable as currency, unlike personal checks, but could be replaced if lost or stolen, unlike cash. These days, traveler's checks seem less necessary because most cities have 24-hour ATMs and most establishments accept credit cards. Still, they are a safe means of carrying money.

You can get traveler's checks at almost any bank. Get the checks in **Australian dollars.** While U.S. dollar traveler's checks are widely accepted at banks, big hotels, and currency exchanges, many smaller hotels, restaurants, and businesses will have no idea what the current exchange rate is when you present a U.S. check. Another plus of Australian-dollar checks is that two of the largest Aussie banks, **ANZ** and **Westpac,** cash them for free. If you bring checks in U.S. dollars, pounds Sterling, or any other foreign currency, each transaction will cost you A$7 (U.S.$4.90) at Westpac, A$6.50 (U.S.$4.55) for amounts under A$3,000 (U.S.$2,100) at ANZ, A$7 (U.S.$4.90) at Commonwealth, and A$5 (U.S.$3.50) at National.

You can get **American Express traveler's checks** over the phone by calling ☎ **800/221-7282;** by using this number, Amex gold and platinum cardholders are exempt from the 1% fee charged by travel service outlets. Platinum cardholders are also exempt from the fee at travel service outlets. Banks may charge up to 4% in fees for

The Australian Dollar, the U.S. Dollar & the British Pound

For U.S. Readers   The rate of exchange used to calculate the dollar values given in this book was U.S.$1 = approximately A$1.43 (or A$1 = U.S.70¢).

For British Readers   The rate of exchange used to calculate the pound values in the accompanying table was 1 British pound = A$2.50 (or A$1 = 40p).

Note: International exchange rates can fluctuate markedly. Check the latest rate when you plan your trip. The table below should only be used as a guide.

A$	U.S.$	U.K.£	A$	U.S.$	U.K.£
0.25	0.17	0.10	30.00	21.00	12.00
0.50	0.35	0.20	35.00	24.50	14.00
1.00	0.70	0.40	40.00	28.00	16.00
2.00	1.40	0.80	45.00	31.50	18.00
3.00	2.10	1.20	50.00	35.00	20.00
4.00	2.80	1.60	55.00	38.50	22.00
5.00	3.50	2.00	60.00	42.00	24.00
6.00	4.20	2.40	65.00	45.50	26.00
7.00	4.90	2.80	70.00	49.00	28.00
8.00	5.60	3.20	75.00	52.50	30.00
9.00	6.30	3.60	80.00	56.00	32.00
10.00	7.00	4.00	85.00	59.50	34.00
15.00	10.50	6.00	90.00	63.00	36.00
20.00	14.00	8.00	95.00	66.50	38.00
25.00	17.50	10.00	100.00	70.00	40.00

American Express checks. AAA members can obtain checks without a fee at most AAA offices.

Visa offers traveler's checks at Citibank locations, as well as at several other banks. Call ☎ **800/227-6811** in the United States and Canada for the nearest location. The service charge varies, depending on where you buy them, so shop around; checks come in denominations of A$50, A$100, and A$200. **MasterCard** also offers traveler's checks. Call ☎ **800/223-7373** for a location near you.

What Things Cost in Sydney	U.S.$	U.K.£
Taxi from the airport to the city center	12.60	7.20
Bus from Central Station to downtown	85¢	48p
Local telephone call from a pay phone	28¢	16p
Double at the Wattle Private Hotel (inexpensive)	69.30	39.60
Double at the Park Regis (moderate)	112.00	64.00
Double at The Stafford (expensive)	171.50	98.00
Lunch for one at The Olive (inexpensive)	5.40	3.10
Lunch for one at Old Saigon (moderate)	15.15	8.65
Dinner for one, without wine, at No Names (inexpensive)	9.45	5.40
Dinner for one, without wine, at MCA Café (moderate)	17.15	9.80
Dinner for one, without wine, at Merrony's (very expensive)	31.50	18.00
Beer (285ml)	1.45	85p
Coca-Cola (375ml)	95¢	55p
Roll of Kodak ASA 100 film, 36 exposures	4.25	2.45
Adult admission to Taronga Zoo	11.20	6.40
Movie ticket	8.75	5.00

THEFT Almost every credit-card company has an emergency toll-free number that you can call if your wallet or purse is stolen. **MasterCard's** emergency number in Australia is ☎ **1800/12 113,** and **Visa's** number is ☎ **1800/125 440.** To report a lost **American Express** card, call ☎ **1800/230 100.**

If you opt to carry traveler's checks, be sure to keep a record of their serial numbers, separately from the checks of course, so you're ensured a refund in just such an emergency. To report lost or stolen **American Express traveler's checks,** call ☎ **1800/25 1902** anywhere in Australia, or 02/9271 8689 in Sydney).

Odds are that if your wallet is stolen, the police won't be able to recover it for you. However, after you realize that it's gone and you cancel your credit cards, it is still worth informing them. Your credit-card company or insurer may require a police report number.

3 When to Go

THE CLIMATE & HIGH/LOW TRAVEL SEASONS

There are a couple of things to keep in mind when deciding when to travel to Sydney. The first, of course, is the climate. Because seasons are created by the earth tilting on its axis, when countries in the Northern Hemisphere have winter, Australia and the Southern Hemisphere have summer, and vice versa. And, unlike in the Northern Hemisphere, the farther south you go in Australia, the colder it gets. Temperatures in Sydney are pleasant year-round. If you visit in the Australian summer (December, January, and February), you can take full advantage of the beaches. March, April, and May are the rainiest months.

Next, you will need to take into account the high and low travel seasons, which will determine when you're most likely to get the best deal on airfare. Surprisingly, the low season for flights to Australia from the United States corresponds to Australia's high season. Airfares on U.S. airlines are lowest from mid-April to late August, or, in other words, from the middle of Australia's autumn through the winter.

Sydney's Average Temperatures (°F) and Rainfall

	Jan	Feb	Mar	Apr	May	June	July	Aug	Sept	Oct	Nov	Dec
Max	78	78	76	71	66	61	60	63	67	71	74	77
Min	65	65	63	58	52	48	46	48	51	56	60	63
Days of Rain	8.3	9.1	12.3	12.5	12.3	11.0	11.0	8.4	7.9	7.7	7.9	7.2

Source: Australian Tourist Commission Australia Vacation Planner.

HOLIDAYS

Aussies love their public holidays. It's fair to say they care more about getting the day off than they do about celebrating the actual holiday. Whenever some well-meaning authority suggests Australians should actually celebrate the holiday on the day it falls, rather than on the Monday following the weekend closest to the holiday to make a long weekend, there is a national outcry.

Try to stay away from Australia from **Boxing Day** (Dec 26) to the end of January, which is when Aussies take their summer vacations. Hotel rooms and seats on planes get scarce and very expensive. The four days at **Easter** (from Good Friday through Easter Monday) and all **school holiday periods** are also very busy, so book ahead. Almost everything shuts down on Good Friday, and much is closed Easter Sunday and Monday. Most things are closed until 1pm, if not all day, on **Anzac Day,** a World War I commemorative day on April 25.

MAJOR NATIONAL HOLIDAYS

New Year's Day	January 1
Australia Day	January 26
Good Friday	Varies
Easter Sunday	Varies
Easter Monday	Varies
Anzac Day	April 25
Queen's Birthday	Second Monday in June
Labour Day	First Monday in October (NSW, SA)
Melbourne Cup Day	First Tuesday in November (Melbourne only)
Christmas Day	December 25
Boxing Day	December 26 (usually celebrated on the next Monday if 26th falls on a weekend)

SCHOOL HOLIDAYS

The school year in Australia is broken into four semesters, with two-week holidays falling around the last half of April, the last week of June and the first week of July, and the last week of September and the first week of October. There's a two-week summer/Christmas vacation from mid-December to the end of January.

SYDNEY CALENDAR OF EVENTS

January

✪ **New Year's Eve.** The big treat on this day is to watch the Sydney Harbour Bridge light up with fireworks. The main show is at 9pm, not midnight, so young kids don't miss out. Pack a picnic and snag a Harbour-side spot by 4pm, or even earlier at the best vantage points—Mrs. Macquarie's Point in the Royal Botanic Gardens, Cremorne Point on the North Shore (take the ferry), and the Sydney Opera House.

✪ **Sydney Festival.** Sydney pulls out all the stops for this summer-time visual and performing arts festival with visiting international acts, impromptu nightclubs, and more. Outdoor events, such as cinema under the stars by the Opera House, are a big item. Highlights are the free jazz, opera, and classical music concerts held outdoors Saturday nights in the Domain near the Botanic Gardens. Contact the **Sydney Festival,** 36-38 Young St., Sydney, NSW 2000 (☎ 02/8248 6500, fax 02/8248 6599, www.sydneyfestival.org.au). For three weeks in January.

- **Australia Day.** Australia's answer to the Fourth of July marks the landing of the First Fleet at Sydney Cove in 1788. Most Aussies celebrate by heading to the nearest beach, but every large town and city has some kind of celebration. In Sydney, there are ferry races and tall ships on the harbor, free performing arts at Darling Harbour, a vintage car festival, and fireworks in the evening. January 26.

February

✪ **Sydney Gay & Lesbian Mardi Gras.** A spectacular parade of floats, costumes, and dancers. Contact Sydney Gay & Lesbian Mardi Gras Ltd, 21–23 Erskineville Rd., Erskineville, NSW 2043 (☎ 02/9557 4332, fax 02/9516 4446, e-mail: mardigras@ mardigras.com.au). Usually the last Saturday night in February; occasionally the first Saturday in March.

June

- **Sydney Film Festival.** World and Australian premieres of leading Aussie and international flicks are shown in the ornate State Theatre and other venues. Tickets start at A$21 (U.S.$14.70) for any three films, or you can pay up to A$250 (U.S.$175) for a two-week subscription to the best seats in the house. Contact the Sydney Film Festival, PO Box 950, Glebe, NSW 2037 (☎ **02/ 9660 3844,** fax 02/9692 8793; www.sydfilm-fest.com.au). Runs for two weeks from first or second Friday in June.

August

- **Sun-Herald City to Surf,** Sydney. Fifty thousand Sydneysiders pound the pavement annually in this 14-kilometer (9-mile) "fun run" from the city to Bondi Beach. There are also walking and wheelchair categories. Entry is around A$20 (U.S.$14) for adults and A$15 (U.S.$10.50) for kids. For an entry form, write to the *Sun-Herald* City to Surf, 201 Sussex St., Sydney, NSW 2000 (☎ **02/9282 2822,** fax 02/9282 2360), or enter on the day of the race. Usually the second Sunday in August, but it may be a month earlier in 2000 to avoid clashing with the Olympic Games.

September

✪ **Sydney 2000 Olympic Games.** Australia will once again play host to the Olympic Games, this time in Sydney. The games will be held from September 15 to October 1, 2000. See chapter 3 for complete details.

December

• **Sydney-to-Hobart Yacht Race.** Find a cliff-top spot near the Heads to watch the glorious show of spinnakers as a hundred or so yachts leave Sydney Harbour for this grueling world-class event. Contact Tourism New South Wales (☎ **02/ 9931 1111,** fax 02/9931 1490, www.tourism.nsw.gov.au). Starts December 26.

4 Health & Insurance

You don't have a lot to worry about health-wise on a trip to Sydney. Hygiene standards are high, hospitals are modern, and doctors and dentists are all well educated. No vaccinations are needed to enter the country unless you have been in a yellow fever danger zone— that is, South America or Africa—in the past six days.

Ask your doctor to recommend treatments for common problems like travel sickness, insomnia, jet lag, constipation, and diarrhea. Drink plenty of water on the plane as the air-conditioning dehydrates you quickly.

WHAT TO DO IF YOU GET SICK AWAY FROM HOME

If you worry about getting sick away from home, you may want to consider medical travel insurance (see the section on travel insurance below). In most cases, however, your existing health plan will provide all the coverage you need. Be sure to carry your identification card in your wallet.

If you suffer from a chronic illness, consult your doctor before your departure. For conditions like epilepsy, diabetes, or heart problems, wear a **Medic Alert Identification Tag** (☎ **800/825-3785;** www.medicalert.org), which will immediately alert doctors to your condition and give them access to your records through Medic Alert's 24-hour hot line. Membership is U.S.$35, then U.S.$15 for annual renewal.

Pack prescription medications in your carry-on luggage. Carry written prescriptions in generic, not brand-name form, and dispense all prescription medications from their original labeled vials. Also bring along copies of your prescriptions in case you lose your pills or run out. Usually a three-month supply is the maximum quantity of prescription drugs you are permitted to carry in Australia, so if you are carrying large amounts of medication, contact the Australian embassy or consulate in your home country to check that your supply does not exceed the maximum. If you need more medication while you're in Australia, you will need to get an Australian doctor to write the prescription for you.

If you wear contact lenses, pack an extra pair in case you lose one.

Contact the **International Association for Medical Assistance to Travelers (IAMAT)** (☎ **716/754-4883** in the U.S. or 516/836-0102 in Canada; www.sentex.net/~iamat). This organization offers tips on travel and health concerns in the countries you'll be visiting, and lists many local English-speaking doctors. Membership is free. The **United States Centers for Disease Control and Prevention** (☎ **404/639-3311;** www.cdc.gov) provides up-to-date information on necessary vaccines and health hazards by region or country. By mail, their booklet is $20 (call ☎ **202/512-1800** to order it); on the Internet, it's free. When you're abroad, any local consulate can provide a list of area doctors who speak English, which just about all of them do in Australia. If you do get sick, you may want to ask the concierge at your hotel to recommend a local doctor—even his or her own. If you can't find a doctor who can help you right away, try the emergency room at the local hospital. Doctors are listed under "M" for Medical Practitioners in the Australian Yellow Pages.

WARNING: SUNSHINE MAY BE HAZARDOUS TO YOUR HEALTH

There's a reason Australians have the world's highest death rate from skin cancer—the country's intense sunlight. Limit your exposure to the sun, especially during the first few days of your trip and, thereafter, from 11am to 3pm in summer and 10am to 2pm in winter. Keep in mind that scattered UV rays that bounce off surfaces such city walls, water, and even the ground can burn you, too. Use a broad-spectrum sunscreen with a high protection factor (SPF 30+) and apply it liberally. It's also a good idea to wear a broad-brimmed hat that covers the back of your neck, ears, and face (not a baseball cap); and a long-sleeved shirt to cover your forearms. Remember that children need more protection than adults do.

Don't even think about coming to Oz without sunglasses, or you'll spend your entire vacation with your eyes shut against

A Word about Smoking

Smoking in many public areas, such as museums, cinemas, and theaters, is restricted if not banned. Smokers can take heart that few Oz restaurants totally ban smoking yet; they just have smoking and no-smoking sections. Pubs are a territorial victory for smokers; after a night in an Aussie pub nonsmokers go home smelling as if they smoked the whole pack (which they probably did, albeit passively). Most hotels have smoking and no-smoking rooms. Australian aircraft on all domestic and international routes are completely no-smoking, even on long-haul flights to the United States and Europe.

Australia's hard, bright "diamond light," that cuts your eyes like, well, a diamond.

INSURANCE

There are three kinds of travel insurance: **trip cancellation, medical,** and **lost luggage coverage.** Trip cancellation insurance is a good idea if you have paid a large portion of your vacation expenses up front. The other two types of insurance, however, don't make sense for most travelers. Rule number one: check your existing policies before you buy any additional coverage.

Your existing health insurance should cover you if you get sick while on vacation (though if you belong to an HMO, you should check to see whether you are fully covered when away from home). If you need hospital treatment, most health insurance plans and HMOs will cover out-of-country hospital visits and procedures, at least to some extent. However, most make you pay the bills up front at the time of care, and you'll get a refund after you've returned and filed all the paperwork. Members of **Blue Cross/Blue Shield** can now use their cards at select hospitals in most major cities worldwide (☎ **800/810-BLUE** or www.bluecares.com/bluecard/index.html for a list of hospitals). Check to see exactly what your existing health insurance covers, though. For example, your policy may not cover helicopter or Royal Flying Doctor Service airlift, which you might well need if you become sick or injured in the Outback. Your policy should also cover the cost to fly you back home in a stretcher, along with a nurse, should that be necessary. A stretcher takes up three coach class seats, plus you may need extra seats for a nurse and medical equipment. Medicare only covers U.S. citizens traveling in Mexico and Canada.

Australia has a reciprocal medical-care agreement with Great Britain and New Zealand and a limited agreement with Ireland, under which travelers are covered for most medical expenses for immediately necessary treatment (but not evacuation, ambulances, funerals, dental care, and other expenses) by Australia's national health system. It's still a good idea to buy insurance, though, as Australia's national health-care system typically only covers 85%, sometimes much less, of treatment. Foreign students of any nationality must take out the Australian government's Overseas Student Health Cover as a condition of entry.

For independent travel health-insurance providers, see below.

Your homeowner's insurance should cover stolen luggage. The airlines are responsible for $1,250 on domestic flights if they lose your luggage; if you plan to carry anything more valuable than that, keep it in your carry-on bag.

The differences between travel assistance and insurance are often blurred, but in general the former offers on-the-spot assistance and 24-hour hot lines (mostly oriented toward medical problems), while the latter reimburses you for travel problems (medical, travel, or otherwise) after you have filed the paperwork. The coverage you should consider will depend on how much protection is already contained in your existing health insurance or other policies. Some credit- and charge-card companies may insure you against travel accidents if you buy plane, train, or bus tickets with their cards. Before purchasing additional insurance, read your policies and agreements over carefully. Call your insurers or credit/charge-card companies if you have any questions.

Some credit cards (American Express and certain gold and platinum Visa and MasterCards, for example) offer automatic flight insurance against death or dismemberment in case of an airplane crash.

If you do require additional insurance, try one of the companies listed below. But don't pay for more than you need. For example, if you need only trip cancellation insurance, don't purchase coverage for lost or stolen property. Trip cancellation insurance costs approximately 6% to 8% of the total value of your vacation.

Among the reputable issuers of travel insurance are:

- **Access America,** 6600 W. Broad St., Richmond, VA 23230 (☎ 800/284-8300)
- **Travel Guard International,** 1145 Clark St., Stevens Point, WI 54481 (☎ 800/826-1300)

- **Travel Insured International,** Inc., P.O. Box 280568, East Hartford, CT 06128 (☎ 800/243-3174)
- **Columbus Travel Insurance,** 279 High St., Croydon CR0 1QH (☎ 0171/375 0011 in London; www2.columbusdirect. com/columbusdirect)
- **International SOS Assistance,** P.O. Box 11568, Philadelphia, PA 11916 (☎ 800/523-8930 or 215/244-1500), strictly an assistance company
- **Travelex Insurance Services,** P.O. Box 9408, Garden City, NY 11530-9408 (☎ 800/228-9792)

Companies specializing in accident and medical care include:

- **MEDEX International,** P.O. Box 5375, Timonium, MD 21094-5375 (☎ 888/MEDEX-00 or 410/453-6300; fax 410/453-6301; www.medexassist.com)
- **Travel Assistance International** (Worldwide Assistance Services, Inc.), 1133 15th St. NW, Suite 400, Washington, DC 20005 (☎ 800/821-2828 or 202/828-5894; fax 202/828-5896)
- **The Divers Alert Network (DAN)** (☎ 800/446-2671 or 919/684-2948) insures scuba divers.

5 Tips for Travelers with Special Needs

FOR TRAVELERS WITH DISABILITIES   Most public hotels, major stores, museums, attractions, and public restrooms have wheelchair access. Many smaller lodges and even B&Bs are starting to cater to guests with disabilities. National parks make a big effort to include wheelchair-friendly pathways through their more picturesque scenery.

An excellent source of information on all kinds of facilities and services in Australia for people with disabilities is the **National Information Communication Awareness Network (NICAN),** P.O. Box 407, Curtin ACT 2605 (☎ **1800/806 769** in Australia or 02/6285 3713; fax 02/6285 3714; e-mail nican@spirit.com.au). This free service can put you in touch with accessible accommodations and attractions throughout Australia, as well as with travel agents and tour operators who understand your needs. Taxi companies in bigger cities can usually supply a cab equipped for wheelchairs.

A World of Options, a 658-page book of resources for travelers with disabilities, covers everything from biking trips to scuba outfitters. It costs U.S.$35 (U.S.$30 for members) and is available from

Mobility International USA, P.O. Box 10767, Eugene, OR, 97440 (☎ **541/343-1284,** voice and TDD; www.miusa.org). Annual membership for Mobility International is U.S.$35, which includes their quarterly newsletter, *Over the Rainbow.* In addition, **Twin Peaks Press,** P.O. Box 129, Vancouver, WA 98666-0129 (☎ **360/694-2462**), publishes travel-related books for people with disabilities.

FOR GAY & LESBIAN TRAVELERS   Sydney is probably the biggest gay city in the world after San Francisco. The annual **Sydney Gay & Lesbian Mardi Gras,** culminating in a huge street parade and gay-only party on the last Saturday in February, is a high point on the city's calendar for people of all sexual persuasions, and attracts thousands of gay visitors from around the world.

The **International Gay & Lesbian Travel Association (IGLTA),** (☎ **800/448-8550** or 954/776-2626; fax 954/776-3303; www.iglta.org), links gay travelers up with gay-friendly hotels, travel agents, tour suppliers, and other travel organizations.

One of the biggest travel agencies specializing in gay travel in Australia is **Jornada,** 263 Liverpool St., Darlinghurst, NSW 2010 (☎ **1800/672 120 in Australia,** or 02/9360 9611; fax 02/9326 0199; www.jornada.com.au).

Australia has several **gay publications,** including the *Sydney Star Observer,* a free weekly newspaper available from newsagents, clubs, and cafes, and glossy mags *Outrage* and *Campaign* sold in newsagents.

Some services you may find useful are the **Gay & Lesbian Counselling Service of NSW** (☎ **02/9207 2888** for the administration office), which runs a hot line from 4pm to midnight daily (☎ 02/9207 2800). The **Albion Street Centre** (☎ **1800/451 600** in Australia or 02/9332 4000 for the information lines, which operate Mon–Fri 9am–8pm, Sat 10am–6pm, or 02/9332 1090 for administration) in Sydney is an AIDS clinic and information service.

FOR SENIORS   Seniors—often referred to as "pensioners" by Aussies—visiting Australia from other countries don't always qualify for the discounted entry prices to tours, attractions, and events that Australian seniors enjoy, but mostly they do. The best ID to bring is something that shows your date of birth, or something that marks you as an "official" senior, like a membership card from the **American Association of Retired Persons (AARP)** (☎ **800/424-3410** in the U.S.; www.aarp.org). Membership in AARP is open to working or retired people over 50 and costs U.S.$8 a year. AARP has a Purchases Privileges program that entitles members to discounts of 10% to 50% on a wide range of travel operators including airlines, many hotels, cruise lines, rental cars, and more.

Elderhostel (☎ 877/426-8056 toll-free in the U.S. and Canada; www.elderhostel.org), is a nonprofit organization that sells educational package tours, including ones to Australia, for travelers 55 years and over.

The **Australian College for Seniors** at the University of Wollongong, south of Sydney (☎ 02/4221 3531; fax 02/4226 2521; e-mail acfs@uow.edu.au), runs about 20 trips a year within Australia for people over 50 under the "Odyssey Travel" name. Many trips have heritage, eco-tourism, or soft adventure themes. The college is the Australian program coordinator for Elderhostel.

Senior Tours, Level 2, 32 York St., Sydney, NSW 2000 (☎ 02/9262 6140; fax 02/9262 2085), is a travel company specializing in vacations for seniors in Australia.

FOR FAMILIES   Sydney is a great destination for kids. Lots of the sorts of things kids like to do, like playing in the park and building sandcastles at the beach, are widely available and free. Australians travel widely with their own kids, so facilities for families, including family passes to attractions, are common.

Most hotels in Australia accommodate kids up to 12 and even older kids free in your room if they use existing beds; if a hotel does charge extra for a child, it's usually only A$10 (U.S.$7), A$20 (U.S.$14) at the most. Some motels have family rooms that sleep three, four, or even more, and these often have kitchenettes. Interconnecting rooms are often discounted as much as 50% for families. Many hotels will arrange baby-sitting given a day's notice.

Aussie families often stay in serviced apartments, because they often cost considerably less than a hotel room, yet have a living room, a kitchen, often two bathrooms, and the privacy of a separate bedroom for adults.

International airlines and domestic airlines within Australia charge 67% of the adult fare for kids under 12. Most charge 10% for infants under two not occupying a seat. Australian coach and rail companies often charge around half-price for kids, as do most attractions and tours throughout the country.

Rascals in Paradise (☎ 800/U RASCAL in the U.S. or 415/978 9800; www.RascalsInParadise.com), sells family vacation packages to Australia.

FOR SINGLES   Striking up a conversation with friendly Aussies is very easy when you're travelling solo, and single women will be glad to know the crime rate is low. When it comes to accommodations for singles, pricing policies vary widely. Many hotels charge singles the full room rate, a very few charge singles at half the room rate, but the majority charge a "single rate," which is about three-quarters of the full room rate. Pubs and hostels often charge a flat "per person" rate whether there is one, two, or more of you. B&Bs usually charge less for a single than a couple.

FOR STUDENTS   Australia is cheap, sporty, and laid back, and has stunning scenery, great weather, fun pubs, and beautiful beaches—in other words, it's paradise for students. The **Australian Tourist Commission** publishes a groovy vacation guide just for students called *Australia Unplugged* (see "Visitor Information," earlier in this chapter).

STA Travel (☎ 800/781 4040 in the U.S., 171/361 6262 in the U.K., and 1300/360 960 in Australia) is a good source of tips and advice for students traveling Down Under. It specializes in discounted airfares, bus and rail passes, and affordable accommodation and tours for students and young travelers, and, most important of all, issues **International Student Identification Cards (ISIC).** The ISIC is the most widely recognized proof in Australia that you really are a student, assuring you discounts to a huge range of travel, tours, and attractions; it also comes with a 24-hour emergency help line for medical, financial, legal, and all kinds of scenarios. Available to any full-time student over 12, in the United States it costs U.S.$20 and comes with sickness and accident insurance, including emergency evacuation of up to $25,000. Ask for the free ISIC 48-page *Student Travel Handbook,* which details some of the enormous range of discounts available to you on a country by country basis. The Card also entitles you to use ISIConnect, a global voice/fax/email messaging system that comes with discounted international telephone calls. Check out STA Travel's Web site at **www.statravel.com** in the U.S., or www.statravel.com.au in Australia. The company has loads of offices across Australia and the world.

You can also obtain an ISIC from **Council on International Educational Exchange,** or CIEE, another excellent source for students. Their travel branch, **Council Travel** (☎ **800/2-COUNCIL** in the U.S. or 0171/478 2000 in the U.K.; www.counciltravel.com), is the biggest student travel agency in the world. It can get you discounts on plane tickets, rail passes, and the like. Ask them for a list of CTS offices in major cities so you can keep the discounts flowing (and aid lines open) as you travel.

Connections (call Goway ☎ **800/387 8850** in Canada, 0181/742 8612 in the U.K., 1800/077 251 in Australia, or 07/3839 7877, fax 07/3839 7876; www.connections1835.com.au) and **Contiki** (☎ 800/CONTIKI in the U.S. and Canada, 22/929 9200 in the U.K., or 02/9511 2200 in Australia; www.contiki.com) specialize in package tours for 18 to 35 year olds. These trips attract a lot of Australians, too, so they are a good way to meet locals.

The **Australian Youth Hostels Association (YHA),** 422 Kent St., Sydney, NSW 2000 (☎ **02/9261 1111,** fax 02/9261 1969; www.yha.org.au) is the Australian arm of Hostelling International, and has more than 140 hostels in Australia. Despite the name, people of any age can stay at them. Quality and facilities vary, but all YHA hostels are clean, and have communal kitchens and 24-hour access. You don't have to join the association to stay at its hostels, but members receive discounted rates and are entitled to myriad other discounts—on car rental, bus travel, and tours, for example—that can repay the membership fee many times over.

It is best to join before you arrive in Australia. In the United States, contact **Hostelling International** (☎ **202/783-6161;** www.hiayh.org) or join at any of the approximately 150 hostels in the United States. The 12-month membership is free if you are 17 or under, U.S.$25 if you are 18 to 54, and U.S.$15 if you are 55 years or older. Hostelling International sells a directory of all Australian youth hostels for $5.50.

In Canada, contact **Hostelling Internationa–Canada** (☎ 613/237-7884). In England and Wales, contact **Youth Hostels Association (England and Wales)** (tel] 1727/855 215). In Scotland, contact the **Scottish Youth Hostels Association** (☎ 1786/891 400). All of these offices are accessible on the Web at www.iyhf.org.

In Ireland, contact **An Oige** (☎ 1/830 4555). In Northern Ireland, contact **Hostelling International–Northern Ireland** (☎ 1232/324 733; www.hini.org.uk).

It is possible to join once you arrive in Oz at some, but not all, Australian hostels, and at YHA Membership and Travel Centres in all state capital cities.

If you want to stay with an Aussie family and really get involved in their life, even down to sitting at their table, **Homestay Network,** 5 Locksley St. Killara, NSW 2071 (☎ **02/9498 4400,** fax 02/9498 8324; e-mail: thenetwork@bigpond.com; www. sydney.citysearch.com.au—you will find it under Staying in Sydney, then Where to Stay, then Guesthouses), specializes in placing students with Sydney families on a self-catered or three-meals-a-day basis. Student placements will cost around A$185 (U.S.$129.50) a week with all meals, plus a A$120 (U.S.$84) booking fee. This is ideal for long-term stays.

6 Booking a Package or Escorted Tour

It's possible to buy a package tour to Sydney that includes airfare and, say, five nights' accommodation in a decent hotel for less than the cost of the airfare alone. Because each element of a package—airfare, hotel, tour, car rental—costs the package company less than if you had booked the same components yourself, packages are a terrific value and well worth investigating.

There are two kinds of "package tours"—independent and escorted—and there are pros and cons of each. **Independent packages** usually include some combination of airfare, accommodations, and car rental, with an occasional tour or shopping discount voucher book thrown in. The main advantage is that you travel at your own pace and according to your own interests, rather than sticking to a group schedule. Your car and hotel arrangements are already booked, leaving you free to get on with your day instead of fussing about finding a hotel for the night.

Escorted tours have different advantages—you don't have to carry your own luggage, for starters. Nor do you need to constantly plan ahead, and if you have free time, there is someone to advise you on fun things to do and even to make your tour bookings for you. A significant argument for escorted tours is that you usually have a well-informed guide who can offer interesting tidbits about the country as you go along, so that you'll probably learn more than you would on your own. You also get to meet and travel with other people. Escorted tours tend to be more expensive because you're paying for the guide, but most meals are included.

And what are the cons of each? If you fancy an independent tour, think about whether you really want to book your own tours day after day, do all the driving yourself (on the wrong side of the road, don't forget!), and schlep up the stairs carrying your own luggage. If you're considering an escorted tour, do you really want your magical bushwalk in the Blue Mountains cut short because the schedule says at noon we all have to be back in Sydney for opal shopping? And can you stand the thought of traveling with the same strangers for days or weeks on end?

The airlines themselves are often a good source of package tours. Check newspaper ads, the Internet, or your travel agent. The following American companies also offer independent packages Down Under: **Austravel** (☎ **800/633-3404** in the U.S. and Canada, www.austravel.net), **Inta-Aussie South Pacific** (☎ **800/531-9222** in the U.S.; www.inta-aussie.com), **Sunmakers, Inc.** (☎ **800/ 841-4321** in the U.S. and Canada; www.sunmakers.com), and **United Vacations** (☎ **800/32-TOURS** in the U.S. and Canada; www.unitedvacations.com).

Escorted tours are available from **Collette Tours** (☎ **800/ 340-5158** in the U.S. and Canada; www.collettetours.com), **Maupintour** (☎ **800/255-4266** in the U.S. and Canada; www.maupintour. com), and **Sunbeam Tours** (☎ **800/955-1818** in the U.S. and Canada; www.sunbeamtours.com).

The following companies offer both independent and escorted tours: **ATS Tours** (☎ **800/423-2880** in the U.S. and Canada; www.atstours.com), **Goway** (☎ **800/387-8850** in the U.S. and Canada; www.goway.com), **Qantas Vacations** (☎ **800/ 348-8139** in the U.S. and 800/268-7525 in Canada; www.qantasvacations.com), and **Swain Australia Tours** (☎ **800/ 22-SWAIN;** www.swainaustralia.com). Swain Australia is owned and largely staffed by Aussies. **ANZA Travel** (☎ **888/269-2166** in the U.S. and Canada; www.anza-travel.com) specializes in special-interest vacations with an active bent, such as golfing, sailing and fishing.

7 Flying to Australia

There's no doubt about it—Australia is a looong flight from anywhere except New Zealand. Sydney is a 14-hour nonstop flight from Los Angeles, longer if your flight stops in Honolulu. From the East Coast, add 5½ hours. If you're coming from the states via Auckland, add transit time in New Zealand plus another 3 hours for the Auckland-Sydney leg. If you are coming from the United Kingdom, brace yourself for a flight of more or less 12 hours from London to Asia; then a long day in transit, as flights to Australia have a nasty habit of arriving in Asia early in the morning and departing around midnight; and finally the 8 to 9 hour flight to Sydney.

THE MAJOR CARRIERS

Here are toll-free reservations numbers and Web sites for the major international airlines serving Australia. The "13" prefix in

Australia means the number is charged at the cost of a local call from anywhere in the country.

MAJOR CARRIERS FLYING FROM NORTH AMERICA

- **Air New Zealand** (☎ 800/262-1234 in the U.S.; 800/663-5494 in English and 800/799-5494 in French, or 604/606-0150 in Vancouver in Canada; 0800/737 000 in New Zealand; or 13 24 76 in Australia; www.airnz.co.nz/)
- **Canada 3000** (☎ 888/CAN3000 in Canada, 416/259-1118 in the United States, or 02/9567 9631 in Australia; www.canada3000.com)
- **Canadian Airlines** (☎ 800/665-1177 in Canada, 800/363-7530 in French in Canada outside Quebec, 800/426-7000 in the U.S. or 1300/655 767 in Australia; www.cdnair.ca)
- **Qantas** (☎ 800/227-4500 in the U.S. and Canada , 0800/808 767 in New Zealand, or 13 13 13 in Australia; www.qantas.com.au)
- **United Airlines** (☎ 800/538 2929 in the U.S. and Canada, 09/379 3800 in New Zealand, or 13 17 77 in Australia; www.ual.com)

MAJOR CARRIERS FLYING FROM THE U.K.

- **British Airways** (☎ 0345/222 111 in the U.K., 1800/626 747 in Ireland, or 02/8904 8800 in Sydney, 07/3223 3123 in Brisbane, 1800/113 722 in Canberra, 03/9603 1133 in Melbourne, 08/8238 2138 in Adelaide, and 08/9425 7711 in Perth; www.british-airways.com)
- **Cathay Pacific** (☎ 0345/581 581 in the U.K. or 13 17 47 in Australia; www.cathaypacific.com).
- **Malaysia Airlines** (☎ 0171/341 2020 in the U.K., 1/676 2131 in Ireland, 13 26 27 in Australia; www.malaysiaairlines.com.my).
- **Qantas** (☎ 0345/747 767 in the U.K., or 13 13 13 in Australia; www.qantas.com.au).
- **Singapore Airlines** (☎ 0870/608 8886 in the U.K., or 13 10 11 in Australia; www.singaporeair.com).
- **Thai Airways International** (☎ 0171/499 9113 in London, 0161/831 7861 in Manchester, or 1300/651 960 in Australia; www.thaiair.com)

FINDING THE BEST AIRFARE

If you are flying from America, keep in mind that the airlines' low season is mid-April to the end of August—this is when you'll find the cheapest fares. High season is December through February, and shoulder season is September through November, and again from March to mid-April. Keep an eye out for special deals offered throughout the year. Unexpected lows in airline passenger loads often lead airlines to put cheap offers on the market. The catch is these usually have a short lead time, requiring you to travel in the next six weeks or so. Some deals involve taking a circuitous route, via Fiji or Japan for instance. Canada 3000 has good rates from Vancouver in low season and often has promotional specials. **Austravel** (☎ **800/ 633-3404** in the U.S. and Canada publishes a quarterly guide to airfares, carriers, stopovers, and flying times to Australia. Some travel agents specializing in cheap fares to Australia include **Austravel** (☎ **800/633-3404** in the U.S. and Canada; www.austravel.net); **DownUnder Direct,** which is a division of Swain Australia (☎ 800/22-SWAIN in the U.S.); **Goway** (☎ 800/387-8850 in the U.S. and Canada; www.goway.com); and **South Pacific Travel Shops** (☎ 800/894-7722 in the U.S. and Canada; via www. inta-aussie.com).

   Consolidators, also known as "bucket shops," are another good source for low fares. Consolidators buy seats in bulk from the airlines and then sell them back to the public at low prices, sometimes even below the airlines' discounted rates. Their small ads usually run in the Sunday travel section at the bottom of the page. Before you pay, however, ask for a confirmation number from the consolidator and then call the airline itself to confirm your seat. Be prepared to book your ticket with a different consolidator—there are many to choose from—if the airline can't confirm your reservation. Also be aware that consolidator tickets are usually nonrefundable or rigged with stiff cancellation penalties, often as high as 50% to 75% of the ticket price.

   Council Travel (☎ **800/2-COUNCIL;** www.counciltravel.com) and **STA Travel** (☎ **800/781-4040;** www.sta.travel.com) cater especially to young travelers, but their bargain basement prices are available to people of all ages. Other reliable consolidators include **1-800-FLY-CHEAP** (www.1800flycheap.com); **TFI Tours International** (☎ **800-745-8000** or 212/736-1140), which serves as a clearinghouse for unused seats; or "rebators" such as **Travel Avenue** (☎ **800/333-3335** in the U.S. or 312/876-1116; www. travelavenue. com) and the **Smart Traveller** (☎ **800/448-3338** in the U.S. or 305/448-3338), which rebate part of their commissions to you.

You can also search the Internet for cheap fares—though it's still best to compare your findings with the research of a dedicated travel agent, if you're lucky enough to have one, especially when you're booking more than just a flight. A few of the better-respected virtual travel agents are **Travelocity** (www.travelocity.com) and **Microsoft Expedia** (www.expedia.com). Just enter the dates you want to fly and the cities you want to visit, and the computer roots out the lowest fares. Expedia's site will e-mail you the best airfare deal once a week if you so choose; Travelocity will email you whenever fares change. Travelocity uses the SABRE computer reservations system that most travel agents use, and has a "Special Deals" database that advertises really cheap fares for those who can get away at a moment's notice.

IN-FLIGHT COMFORT

To relieve the discomfort on this long-distance flight, wear loose clothing and a roomy pair of shoes, because your feet will swell en route. Drink plenty of water and go easy on the free alcohol. To while away the hours, consider traveling with an airline that offers in-seat videos. Requesting a bulkhead or exit door seat will give you more legroom. Some airlines allow you to request seats when you book, but others allocate seats only at check-in—in that case be early to beat savvy Aussies queuing for the same thing!

Jet lag is a foregone conclusion on such a long trip, so don't plan to hit all the museums the first morning you arrive, or book opera tickets for your first evening. There is no "cure" for jet lag, but you will help fight it if you get as much sleep as possible on the flight and don't overeat. Try to acclimatize yourself to the local time as quickly as possible. Stay up as long as you can the first day, then try to wake up at a normal hour the next morning.

On such a long journey, it makes sense to break the trip with a one-night stopover if you have time. If you're coming from America, this will probably be Honolulu; if you're coming from Europe, you have any number of Asian cities—Bangkok, Singapore, Hong Kong—in which to spend a night or two. If you're coming from Europe and you have a long layover in Asia, it's a very good idea to book a day room at a hotel with a 6pm checkout. Wandering around a humid, crowded city at 2pm when your body thinks it's 3am is not fun.

2

Getting to Know Sydney

*I*t would take you more time than you probably have to learn all the ins and outs of the Emerald City, with its numerous beaches, neighborhoods, and sprawling suburbs. Luckily, this book has done the legwork for you. What follows is a crash course to get you oriented and on your way.

1 Orientation

ARRIVING

BY PLANE **Sydney International Airport** is 8 kilometers (about 5 miles) from the city center. The international and domestic terminals are separate, but are linked by regular free shuttle buses. In both terminals, you'll find free luggage carts, wheelchairs, a post office (open Monday through Friday from 9am to 5pm), mailboxes, duty-free shops (including one before you go through customs on arrival), restaurants, bars, stores, showers, luggage lockers, and tourist information desks. There is also a State Transit Kiosk selling bus, train, and ferry tickets; a New South Wales Travel Centre desk offering cheap deals on hotels; and a Thomas Cook currency exchange. The airport is completely no-smoking.

Getting into Town Fast and comfortable green-and-yellow **Airport Express buses** travel between the city center and both the international and domestic terminals from 5am to 11pm. The number 300 bus runs to and from Circular Quay, The Rocks, Wynyard, and Town Hall every 15 minutes Monday to Friday and approximately every 30 minutes early mornings, nights, weekends, and public holidays. The trip to Circular Quay takes about 45 minutes. Bus 350 runs to and from Kings Cross, Potts Point, and Elizabeth Bay every 20 minutes and takes around 30 minutes to reach Kings Cross. Both buses travel via Central Station (around 20 minutes from the International Terminal).

Bus 351 leaves for Coogee, Bronte and Bondi beaches every 30 minutes. It takes around 55 minutes to reach Bondi Beach from the International Terminal. Bus 352 travels between Central,

Chinatown, Darling Harbour, the Star City casino, the Sydney Fish Markets, and Glebe, approximately every 30 minutes. The trip time is about 30 minutes to Darling Harbour and 50 minutes to Glebe.

One-way tickets for all buses cost A$6 (U.S. $4.20) for adults, A$4 (U.S. $2.80) for kids under 16, and A$15 (U.S. $10.50) for families (any number of children). A round-trip ticket costs A$10 (U.S. $7) for adults, A$5 (U.S. $3.50) for kids, and A$25 (U.S. $17.50) for families. You must use the return portion within two months. Buy your tickets from the Airport Express booth outside the airport terminal, or on the bus. The Airport Express buses also travel between the international and domestic terminals; an interterminal ticket costs A$2.50 (U.S.$1.75) for adults, A$1.50 (U.S.$1.05) for children, and A$6.50 (U.S.$4.55) for families.

The **Kingsford Smith Airport Coach** also operates to the city center from bus stops outside the terminals. This service will drop you off (and pick you up) at your hotel (pick-ups require at least one hour's advance notice; call ☎ **02/9667 3221**). Tickets cost A$6 (U.S. $4.20) one-way and A$11 round-trip (the return portion can be used at any time in the future).

Privately operated shuttle buses also connect the airport with city center, Kings Cross, Darling Harbour, and Glebe hotels; you'll have no trouble spotting them when you leave the terminal. These buses depart when they're full and run from the city to the airport between 5am and 8pm and from the airport to the city between the first and last flights each day. Each company requires advance reservations for pickups from your hotel to the airport. One company to try is **Silks Sydney Airport-Hotel Transfers** (☎ **02/9371 4466;** e-mail: Silksydtransfer@seltek.com.au). The one-way fare is A$6 (U.S. $4.20) for adults and A$4.50 (U.S.$3.15) for children 5 to 11. These buses are less comfortable than the government buses and can take much longer since they stop at numerous hotels.

The **Bondi Jetbus** (☎ 0500 886008 mobile phone; fax 02/9487 3554) will deliver you anywhere on the eastern beaches, including Bondi and Bronte. Tickets are A$8 (U.S. $5.60) for adults and A$4 (U.S.$2.80) for children. Call when you arrive at the airport, and they'll come pick you up within 15 minutes or less. The **Pittwater Airport Shuttle** (☎ and fax **02/9973 1877**) will take you to any of the northern beaches. A trip to Manly, for example, costs A$20 (U.S. $14) for the first person, A$10 (U.S. $7) for the second, and A$5 (U.S. $3.50) for each subsequent passenger. Shuttles depart the airport around six times a day; it may not be worth your

Sydney & Environs

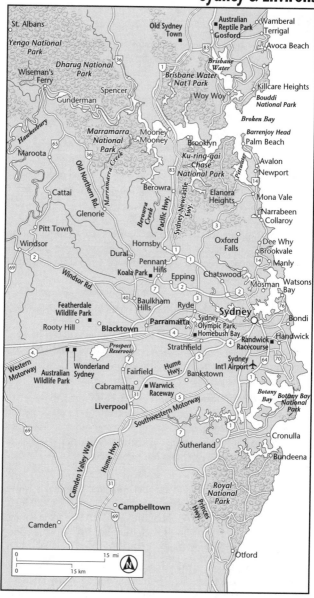

Taxi Tip

Especially in busy periods, taxi queues can be long and cab drivers may try to cash in by insisting you share a cab with other passengers waiting in line at the airport. Here's the scam: After dropping off the other passengers, the cab driver will then attempt to charge you the full price of the journey, despite the fact that the other passengers paid for their sections. You certainly won't save any money sharing a cab if this happens, and your journey will be a long one. I find it's often better to wait until you can get your own cab, or catch an airport bus to the city center (and then take a taxi from there to your hotel, if necessary). If you are first in line in the taxi rank, the law states that you can refuse to share the cab with anyone else.

while waiting around for the next shuttle when a taxi for two to Manly will cost around A$40 (U.S.$28) anyway. Reservations are essential and must be made a day in advance; travel agents can make reservations for you.

A **taxi** from the airport to the city center costs between A$16 (U.S.$ 11.20) and A$20 (U.S. $14). To Kings Cross expect to pay around A$28 (U.S.$19.60).

A rail link from the airport to Central Station is due to be completed in time for the Olympics. It is expected to cost A$10 (U.S.$7) one-way. From Central Station, it's just a short taxi, CityRail train, or bus ride to other areas of the city center.

BY TRAIN   Central Station (☎ **13 15 00** for CityRail, and ☎ **13 22 32** for Countrylink interstate trains) is the main city and interstate train station. It's at the top of George Street in downtown Sydney. All interstate trains depart from here, and it's a major CityRail hub. Many city buses leave from here for Town Hall and Circular Quay.

BY BUS   The Greyhound-Pioneer Australia terminal is on the corner of Oxford and Riley streets in Darlinghurst (☎ **13 20 30** in Australia or 02/9283 5977). **McCafferty's** (☎ **13 14 99** in Australia) operates from the **Sydney Coach Terminal** (☎ **02/9281 9366**) on the corner of Eddy Avenue and Pitt Street, near Central Station.

BY CRUISE SHIP   Cruise ships dock at the **Overseas Passenger Terminal in The Rocks, just opposite the Sydney Opera House, or in Darling Harbour if The Rocks facility is already occupied by another vessel.

BY CAR Drivers coming into Sydney from the north enter the city on the Pacific Highway, drivers approaching from the south enter the city via the Hume and Princes highways, and those coming from the west enter the city via the Great Western Highway.

VISITOR INFORMATION

The **Sydney Visitor Center,** 106, George St., The Rocks (☎ 02/9255 1788), is a good place for maps, brochures, and general tourist information; it also has two floors of excellent displays on The Rocks. The office is open daily from 6am to 6pm. Also in The Rocks is the **National Parks & Wildlife Center** (☎ 02/9247 8861), in Cadmans Cottage, 110 George St. If you are in Circular Quay, the **CityRail Host Center** (no phone), opposite No. 5 jetty, has a wide range of brochures and a staff member on hand to help with general inquiries. It's open daily 9am to 5pm. Elsewhere, the **Sydney Convention and Visitors Bureau** (☎ 02/9235 2424) operates an information kiosk in Martin Place, near Castlereagh Street, Monday through Friday from 9am to 5pm. The **Manly Visitors Information Bureau** (☎ 02/9977 1088), right opposite Manly beach near the Corso, offers general information, but specializes in Manly and the northern beaches. If you want to inquire about destinations and holidays within Sydney or the rest of New South Wales, call **Tourism New South Wales'** helpline at ☎ 13 20 77 in Australia.

Electronic information on cinema, theater, exhibitions, and other events can be accessed through **Talking Guides** (☎ 13 16 20 in Australia). You'll need a code number for each topic, which you can find on page 3 of the A-K section of the *Sydney Yellow Pages* phone directory. The service costs the same as a local call.

Good **Web sites** include **CitySearch Sydney** (www.sydney.citysearch.com.au), for events, entertainment, dining, and shopping; and **City of Sydney** (www.cityofsydney.nsw.gov.au), the official information site, which includes updates on the Olympics.

CITY LAYOUT

Sydney is one of the largest cities in the world by area, covering more than 1,730 square kilometers (668 square miles) from the sea to the foothills of the Blue Mountains. The jewel in Sydney's crown is its harbor, which empties into the South Pacific Ocean through head lands known simply as North Head and South Head. On the southern side of the harbor are the high rises of the city center; the Sydney Opera House; a string of beaches, including Bondi; and the inner-city suburbs. The Sydney Harbour Bridge and a tunnel connect the city center to the high rises of the North Sydney business district and the affluent northern suburbs and beautiful ocean beaches beyond.

MAIN ARTERIES & STREETS   The city's main thoroughfare, **George Street,** runs up from **Circular Quay** (pronounced "key"), past Town Hall and on past Central Station. A whole host of streets bisect the city parallel to George, including Pitt, Elizabeth, and Macquarie streets. **Macquarie Street** runs up from the Sydney Opera House, past the Royal Botanic Gardens, colonial architecture, and Hyde Park. **Martin Place** is a pedestrian thoroughfare that stretches from Macquarie to George streets. It's about halfway between Circular Quay and Town Hall—in the heart of the city center. The easy-to-spot **AMP Centerpoint Tower,** facing onto the pedestrian-only **Pitt Street Mall,** is the main city-center landmark. Next to Circular Quay and across from the Opera House is **The Rocks,** a cluster of small streets that was once city slums but is now a tourist attraction. From Town Hall, roads converge at Kings Cross in one direction and Darling Harbour in the other.

NEIGHBORHOODS IN BRIEF

SOUTH OF THE HARBOUR

Circular Quay   This transport hub for ferries, buses, and CityRail trains is tucked between the Harbour Bridge and the Sydney Opera House. The Quay, as it's known to the locals, is a good spot for a stroll, and its outdoor restaurants and buskers (street musicians/performers) are very popular. The Rocks, the Royal Botanic Gardens, the Contemporary Art Museum, and the start of the main shopping area (centered on Pitt and George streets) are all just a short walk away. To reach the area via public transportation, take a CityRail train, ferry, or city-bound bus to Circular Quay.

The Rocks   This small historic area, just a short stroll west of Circular Quay, is closely packed with colonial stone buildings, intriguing back streets, boutiques, popular pubs, tourist stores, and top-notch restaurants and hotels. It's the most exclusive place to stay in the city because of its beauty and its proximity to the Opera House and the harbour. Shops here are geared mostly toward Sydney's yuppies and wealthy Asian tourists—don't expect many bargains. On weekends, a portion of George Street is blocked off for The Rocks Market, with its many street stalls selling tourist-oriented souvenirs and crafts. To reach the area via

Sydney Harbour

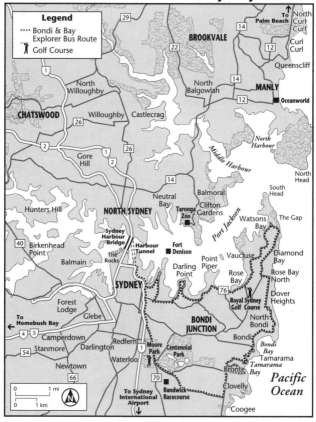

public transportation, take any bus bound for Circular Quay or The Rocks (via George Street) or a CityRail train or ferry to Circular Quay

Town Hall   Right in the heart of the city, this area is home to all the main department stores and to two Sydney landmarks, the Town Hall and the Queen Victoria Building (QVB). In this area are also the AMP Centerpoint Tower and the boutique-style chain stores of Pitt Street Mall. Farther up George Street (on the same side of the street as the Town Hall) are major cinema complexes, the entrance to Sydney's Spanish district (around Liverpool Street), and the city's small Chinatown. To reach the area via public transportation, take any bus from Circular Quay via George Street, or take a CityRail train to the Town Hall stop.

Sydney at a Glance

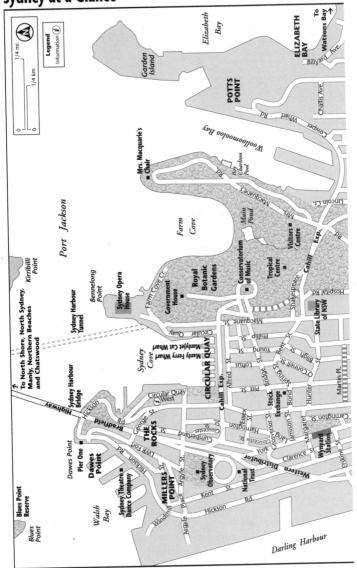

Legend
ⓘ Information

0 ¼ mi
0 ¼ km

Port Jackson

Blues Point

Blues Point Reserve

Walsh Bay

Kirribilli Point

Bennelong Point

Farm Cove

Garden Island

Elizabeth Bay

Darling Harbour

Woolloomooloo Bay

ELIZABETH BAY

POTTS POINT

Highway
Bradfield
Dawes Point
Pier One
Dawes Point
Sydney Theatre & Dance Company
MILLERS POINT
Sydney Observatory
National Trust
Hickson Rd.
Windmill St.
Argyle Pl.
Kent St.
Lower Fort St.
Argyle St.
Cumberland St.
Gloucester St.
Harrington St.
George St.
THE ROCKS
Essex St.
Jamison St.
Grosvenor St.
York St.
Clarence St.
Margaret St.
Erskine St.
Western Distributor
Wynyard Station
Sydney Harbour Bridge
Sydney Harbour Tunnel
Sydney Cove
Circular Quay West
Manly Ferry Wharf & JetCat Wharf
Circular Quay
CIRCULAR QUAY
Cahill Exp.
Alfred St.
Pitt St.
Loftus St.
Bridge St.
Spring St.
Bond St.
Hunter St.
O'Connell St.
Bligh St.
Young St.
Phillip St.
Macquarie St.
Stock Exchange
Martin Pl.
Sydney Opera House
Government House
Royal Botanic Gardens
Farm Cove Cr.
Conservatorium of Music
Main Pond
Tropical Centre
Visitors Centre
Mrs. Macquarie's Chair
Mrs. Macquarie's Rd.
Boy Charlton Pool
Shakespeare Pl.
State Library of NSW
Hospital Rd.
Cahill Exp.
Lincoln Cr.
Cowper Wharf Rd.
Challis Ave.
Billyard Ave.
To Watsons Bay

To North Shore, North Sydney, Manly, Northern Beaches and Chatswood

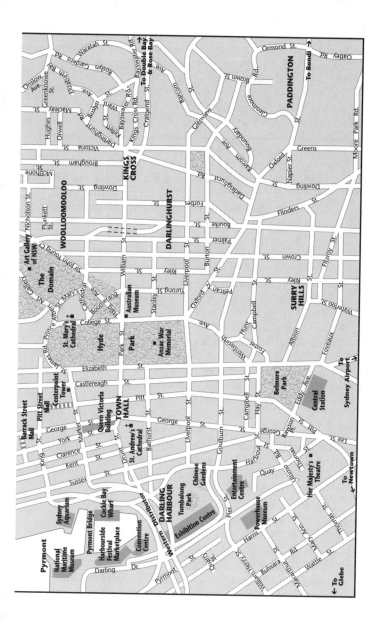

National Maritime Museum
Sydney Aquarium
Pyrmont Bridge
Cockle Bay Wharf
Convention Centre
Harbourside Festival Marketplace
Darling Dr.
Pyrmont
PYRMONT
Western Distributor
DARLING HARBOUR
Exhibition Centre
Tumbalong Park
Chinese Gardens
Entertainment Centre
Powerhouse Museum
Pier St.
Quay St.
Harris St.
William Henry St.
Bulwara Rd.
Macarthur St.
Wattle St.
Mary Ann St.
Thomas St.
To Glebe
To Newtown
Her Majesty's Theatre
Goulburn St.
Liverpool St.
George St.
Bathurst St.
St. Andrew's Cathedral
Queen Victoria Building
TOWN HALL
Centrepoint Tower
Pitt Street Mall
Barrack Street
King St.
York St.
Clarence St.
Kent St.
Sussex St.
Druitt St.
Market St.
George St.
Pitt St.
Castlereagh St.
Elizabeth St.
Hyde Park
St. Mary's Cathedral
The Domain
Art Gallery of NSW
Art Gallery Rd.
Mrs. Macquarie's Rd.
Prince Albert Rd.
College St.
Cathedral St.
Park St.
Australian Museum
Anzac War Memorial
William St.
Riley St.
Stanley St.
Yurong St.
Palmer St.
Bourke St.
Forbes St.
Dowling St.
Plunkett St.
Nicholson St.
Sir John Young Cr.
WOOLLOOMOOLOO
KINGS CROSS
Brougham St.
McElhone St.
Victoria St.
Orwell St.
Hughes St.
Mackay St.
Greenknowe Ave.
Onslow Ave.
Elizabeth Bay Rd.
Roslyn Gardens Rd.
Waratah St.
Bayswater Rd.
Kings Cross Rd.
Ward Ave.
Kellett St.
Darlinghurst Rd.
Craigend St.
To Double Bay & Rose Bay
Ormond St.
To Bondi
Oatley Rd.
Brown St.
Glenmore Rd.
Glenview St.
Barcom Ave.
PADDINGTON
Moore Park Rd.
Greens Rd.
Napier St.
Dowling St.
Oxford St.
Flinders St.
Boundary St.
DARLINGHURST
Darlinghurst Rd.
Liverpool St.
Oxford St.
Burton St.
Crown St.
Pelican St.
Riley St.
Fitzroy St.
SURRY HILLS
Campbell St.
Foveaux St.
Waterloo St.
Albion St.
Hunt St.
Wentworth Ave.
Campbell St.
Hay St.
Belmore Park
Central Station
Eddy Ave.
To Sydney Airport
Lee St.
Pitt St.
Rawson Pl.
George St.
Regent St.
Thomas St.

37

Darling Harbour   Designed from scratch as a tourist precinct, Darling Harbour now features Sydney's main convention, exhibition, and entertainment centers; a huge waterfront promenade; the Sydney Aquarium; the giant screen Panasonic IMAX Theatre; the Sega World theme park; the Australian Maritime Museum; the Powerhouse Museum; a major food court; and plenty of shops. Star City, Sydney's casino and theater complex, opened in Darling Harbour in late 1997. Until Cockle Bay Wharf opened in early 1999 (near the Sydney Aquarium on the city side of Darling Harbour) and brought with it a few good bars and restaurants, few Sydneysiders ever visited the place. To reach the area via public transportation, take a ferry from Circular Quay (wharf 5), the monorail from Town Hall, or the light rail (tram) from Central Station. Or, you can simply walk down the side road to the right of the Queen Victoria Building as you are facing it, and across the pedestrian bridge which spans the water.

Kings Cross & the Suburbs Beyond   "The Cross," as it's known, is famous as the city's red-light district—though it's also home to some of the city's best-known nightclubs and restaurants. It also houses plenty of backpacker hostels, as well as some upscale hotels. The main drag, Darlinghurst Road, is crammed with strip joints, prostitutes, drug addicts, drunks, and street kids. Fortunately, there's a heavy police presence. Beyond the strip clubs and glitter, the attractive suburbs of Elizabeth Bay, Double Bay, and Rose Bay hug the waterfront. To reach the area via public transportation, take bus 324, 325, or 327 from Circular Quay; bus 311 from Railway Square, Central Station; or a CityRail train to Kings Cross station.

Paddington/Oxford Street   This inner-city suburb, centered on trendy Oxford Street, is known for its expensive terrace houses, off-the-wall boutiques and bookshops, and popular restaurants, pubs, and nightclubs. It's also the heart of Sydney's very large gay community (the world's largest after San Francisco) and has a liberal scattering of gay bars and dance spots. To reach the area via public transportation, take bus 380 or 382 from Circular Quay (via Elizabeth Street); 378 from Railway Square, Central Station; or 380 and 382 from Bondi Junction.

Darlinghurst   Wedged between grungy Kings Cross and upscale Oxford Street, this extroverted and grimy terraced suburb is home to some of Sydney's finest cafes. It's probably wise not to walk around here at night. Take the CityRail train to Kings Cross and head right from the exit.

Central   The congested and badly polluted crossroads around Central Station, the city's main train station, has little to recommend it. The Sydney Central YHA is located here.

Newtown   This popular student area is centered around car-clogged King Street, which is lined with many alternative shops, bookstores, and cheap ethnic restaurants. People-watching is an interesting sport here—see how many belly button rings, violently colored hair-dos, and Celtic arm tattoos you can spot. To reach the area via public transportation, take bus 422, 423, 426, or 428 from Circular Quay (via Castlereagh Street and City Road), or take the CityRail train to Newtown Station.

Glebe   A mecca for young professionals and students, this inner-city suburb is known for its cafes, restaurants, pubs, and shops spread out along the main thoroughfare, Glebe Point Road. All this, plus its location just 15 minutes from the city and 30 minutes from Circular Quay, makes it a good place to stay for budget-conscious travelers. To reach Glebe via public transportation, take bus 431, 433, or 434 from Millers Point, The Rocks (via George St.), or bus 459 from behind Town Hall.

Bondi & the Southern Beaches   Some of Sydney's most glamorous surf beaches—Bondi, Bronte, and Coogee—can be found basking along the South Pacific Ocean coastline southeast of the city center. Bondi is a disappointment to many tourists who are expecting more than this former working-class suburb has to offer. It does have a wide sweep of beach (which is crowded in summer), some interesting eateries and drinking holes, and plenty of attitude. On weekends, it's a favorite with macho suburbanites, who stand next to their souped-up cars and attempt to look cool. To reach the beaches via public transportation, take bus 380 or 382 to Bondi Beach from Circular Quay or a CityRail train to Bondi Junction to connect with same buses; bus 378 to Bronte from Railway Square, Central Station (via Oxford Street); or bus 373 or 374 to Coogee from Circular Quay.

Watsons Bay   Watsons Bay is known for The Gap—a section of dramatic sea cliffs—as well as several good restaurants, such as Doyles on the Beach, and the popular Watsons Bay Hotel beer garden. It's a terrific spot to spend a sunny afternoon. To reach the area via public transportation, take bus 324 or 325 from Circular Quay, or a ferry from Circular Quay (wharf 2) on Saturdays and Sundays.

NORTH OF THE HARBOUR

North Sydney   Just across the Harbour Bridge, the high rises of North Sydney attest to its prominence as a major business area. That said, there's little on offer for tourists here, except the possibility of being knocked down on some extremely busy thoroughfare. Take a CityRail train to the North Sydney stop. Chatswood (take a CityRail train from Central or Wynyard stations) has some pretty good suburban-type shopping, and Milsons Point, just across the bridge, has a fairly decent pub called the Kirribilli Hotel and a couple of restaurants and cafes worth checking out if you've walked across the Harbour Bridge.

The North Shore   Ferries and buses provide good access to these wealthy neighborhoods across the Harbour Bridge. The gorgeous Balmoral Beach, the Taronga Zoo, and upscale boutiques are the main attractions in Mosman. Take bus 250 from North Sydney to Taronga Zoo, or a ferry from Circular Quay (wharf 2) to Taronga Zoo and a bus from there to Balmoral Beach.

Manly & The Northern Beaches   Half an hour away by ferry, or just 15 minutes by the faster JetCat, Manly is famous for its beautiful ocean beach and scores of cheap food outlets. Farther north are more magnificent beaches popular with surfers. Unfortunately there is no CityRail train line to the northern beaches. The farthest beach from the city, Palm Beach, has magnificent surf and lagoon beaches, nice walking paths, and a scenic golf course. To reach the area via public transportation, take the ferry or JetCat from Circular Quay (wharves 2 and 3) to Manly. Change at Manly interchange for various buses to the northern beaches, numbers 148 and 154 through 159. You can also take bus L90 from Wynyard Station.

WEST OF THE CITY CENTER

Balmain   Located west of the city center, a short ferry ride from Circular Quay, Balmain was once Sydney's main ship-building area. In the last few decades the area has become trendy and expensive. The suburb has a village feel about it and is filled with restaurants and pubs and hosts a popular Saturday market in the grounds of the local church. Take bus 441, 442, or 432 from Town Hall or George Street, or a ferry from Circular Quay (wharf 5), and then a short bus ride up the hill to the main shopping area.

Homebush Bay   This is the main site of the Sydney 2000 Olympic Games. Here you'll find the Olympic Stadium, the Aquatic Center, and the Homebush Bay Information Center, as well as parklands and a water-bird reserve. To reach the area via public transportation, take a CityRail train from Circular Quay to the new Olympic Park station.

2   Getting Around

BY PUBLIC TRANSPORTION

State Transit operates the city's buses and the ferry network, CityRail runs the urban and suburban trains, and Sydney Ferries runs the public passenger ferries. Some private bus lines operate buses in the outer suburbs. In addition, a monorail connects the city center to Darling Harbour and a light rail line (tram) runs between Central Station and Wentworth Park in Pyrmont.

MONEY-SAVING TRANSIT PASSES   Several passes are available for visitors who will be using public transportation frequently—all work out to be much cheaper than buying individual tickets. The SydneyPass is a good buy if you plan to do *a lot* of sightseeing, but in my opinion you're better off with the flexibility offered by some of the other passes listed below.

The **SydneyPass** allows 3, 5, or 7 days of unlimited travel on buses and ferries, including the high-speed JetCat to Manly, the Red Sydney Explorer Bus (see below), the Blue Bondi and Bay Explorer Bus, the Airport Express Bus, and all harbor cruises operated by State Transit. A three-day pass costs A$70 (U.S.$49) for adults, A$60 (U.S.$42) for children under 16, and A$200 (U.S.$140) for families; a five-day pass is A$95 (U.S.$66.50) for adults, A$80 (U.S.$56) for children, and A$270 (U.S.$189) for families; a seven-day pass is A$110 (U.S.$77) for adults, A$95 (U.S.$66.50) for children, and A$315 (U.S.$220.50) for families. (State Transit defines a "family" as two adults and any number of children from the same family.) Buy the SydneyPass at the airport, Countrylink offices, Public Transport ticket offices, Circular Quay ferry ticket offices, and anywhere else the SydneyPass logo is displayed; proof of overseas residence is required.

A **Weekly Travel Pass** allows unlimited travel on buses, trains, and ferries. There are six different passes (denoted by color)

Transit Information

For timetable information on buses, ferries, and trains, call the **Infoline** at ☎ **13 15 00** daily from 6am to 10pm. Pick up a **Sydney Transport Map** (a guide to train, bus, and ferry services) at any rail, bus, or ferry information office.

Sydney Transportation Systems

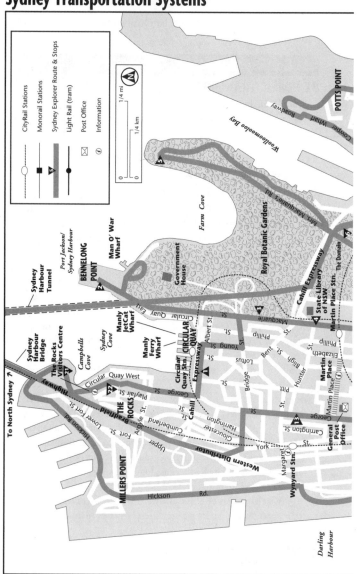

Legend:
- CityRail Stations
- Monorail Stations
- Sydney Explorer Route & Stops
- Light Rail (tram)
- Post Office
- Information

1/4 mi
1/4 km

Sydney Harbour Tunnel
Sydney Harbour Bridge
The Rocks Visitors Centre
To North Side
Bradfield Highway
Campbells Cove
Circular Quay West
THE ROCKS
MILLERS POINT
Hickson Rd.
Western Distributor
Wynyard Stn.
General Post Office
Martin Place
Martin Place Stn.
State Library of NSW
Cahill Expressway
Royal Botanic Gardens
Government House
Farm Cove
Man O' War Wharf
BENNELONG POINT
Manly JetCat Wharf
Manly Ferry Wharf
CIRCULAR QUAY
Circular Quay Stn.
Sydney Cove
Port Jackson/Sydney Harbour
Woolloomooloo Bay
POTTS POINT
Cowper Wharf Roadway
Mrs. Macquaries Rd.
The Domain
Darling Harbour

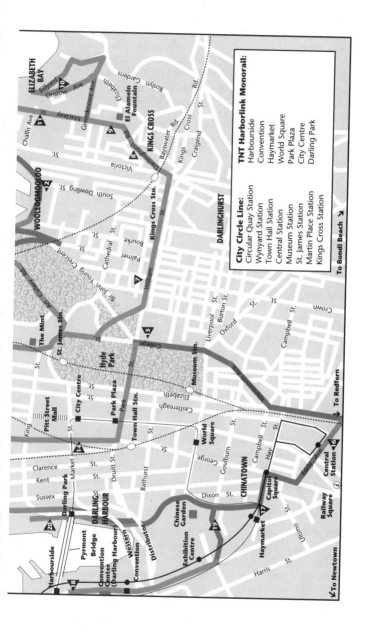

City Circle Line:
Circular Quay Station
Wynyard Station
Town Hall Station
Central Station
Museum Station
St. James Station
Martin Place Station
Kings Cross Station

TNT Harborlink Monorail:
Harbourside
Convention
Haymarket
World Square
Park Plaza
City Centre
Darling Park

ELIZABETH BAY

KINGS CROSS

WOOLLOOMOOLOO

DARLINGHURST

CHINATOWN

DARLING HARBOUR

The Mint

St. James Stn.

Hyde Park

Museum Stn.

City Centre

Park Plaza

Town Hall Stn.

Pitt Street Mall

World Square

Capitol Square

Haymarket

Railway Square

Central Station

Chinese Garden

Exhibition Centre

Convention Center (Darling Harbour)

Pyrmont Bridge

Harbourside

Darling Park

Western Convention

Distributor

El Alamein Fountain

Kings Cross Stn.

To Bondi Beach ↗

To Redfern →

To Newtown ↙

43

depending on the distance you need to travel. The passes most commonly used by visitors are the Red Pass and the Green Pass. The **Red Pass** costs A\$26 (U.S.\$18.20) and covers all transportation within the city center and near surrounds. This pass will get you aboard inner harbor ferries, for example, but not the ferry to Manly. The **Green Pass,** which costs A\$33 (U.S.\$23.10), will take you to more far-flung destinations, including Manly (aboard the ferry but not the JetCat). You can buy either pass at newsagents or bus, train, and ferry ticket outlets.

The **Day Rover** gives you unlimited bus, train, and ferry travel for one day. Tickets cost A\$20 (U.S.\$14) for adults and A\$10 (U.S.\$7) for children for travel in peak hours (before 9am), and A\$16 (U.S.\$11.20) for adults and A\$8 (U.S.\$5.60) for children for travel in off-peak hours (after 9am). The pass is available at all bus, train, and ferry ticket outlets.

A **Travelten** ticket offers 10 bus or ferry rides for a discounted price. A blue Travelten covers two sections on the bus route and costs A\$9.50 (U.S.\$6.65) for adults and A\$4.40 (U.S.\$3.10) for children; a red Travelten covers up to nine sections and costs A\$17.60 (U.S.\$12.30) for adults and A\$8.80 (U.S.\$6.15) for children. The Travelten ferry ticket costs A\$17 (U.S.\$11.90) for ten trips within the inner harbor (this excludes Manly). Buy Travelten tickets at newsagents, bus depots, or at the Circular Quay ferry terminal. If you will be traveling short distances by bus mostly purchase a blue Travelten. These tickets are transferable, so if two or more people are traveling together, you can all use the same ticket.

For a full day's unlimited travel by bus, you can't go wrong with the **Bus Tripper.** It costs A\$8.30 (U.S.\$5.80) for adults and A\$3.90 (U.S.\$2.75) for children 4 to 15, and can be bought from newsagents and at bus depots. An unlimited one-day bus/ferry tripper costs A\$12 (U.S. \$8.40) for adults and A\$6 (U.S. \$4.20) for children.

BY PUBLIC BUS   Buses are frequent and fairly reliable and cover a wide area of metropolitan Sydney—though you might find the system a little difficult to navigate if you're visiting some of the outer suburbs. The minimum fare (which covers most short hops within the city) is A\$1.30 (U.S. 90¢) for a 4-kilometer (2.5-mile) "section." The farther you go, the cheaper each section is. For example, the 44-kilometer (27-mile) trip to beautiful Palm Beach, way past Manly, costs just A\$4.40 (U.S.\$3). Sections are marked on bus-stand signs (though most Sydneysiders are as confused about the system as you are sure to be). Basically, short city hops, such as Circular Quay to Town Hall, cost A$1.30 (U.S. 90¢), and slightly longer ones, say Circular Quay to Central Station, cost A$2.50 (U.S.$1.75).

Most buses bound for the northern suburbs, including night buses to Manly and the bus to Taronga Zoo, leave from Wynyard Park on Carrington Street, behind the main Wynyard CityRail station on George Street. Buses headed to the southern beaches, such as Bondi and Bronte, and the western and eastern suburbs leave from Circular Quay. Buses to Balmain leave from behind the Queen Victoria Building.

Call ☎ **13 15 00** for timetable and fare information, or ask the staff at the bus information kiosk on the corner of Alfred and Loftus streets, just behind Circular Quay CityRail station (☎ **02/9219 1680**). The kiosk is open Monday through Saturday from 8am to 8pm and Sunday from 8am to 6pm. Buses run from 4am to around midnight during the week, less frequently on weekends and public holidays. Some night buses to outer suburbs run after midnight and throughout the night. You can purchase single tickets onboard from the driver; exact change is not required.

BY RED SYDNEY EXPLORER BUS These bright red buses travel a 35-kilometer (22-mile) circuit making 22 stops at top sightseeing attractions around the city. Passengers can get on and off anytime they like. Buses run every 20 minutes between 9am and 3pm. One-day tickets cost A$25 (U.S.$17.50) for adults, A$18 (U.S.$12.60) for children under 16, and A$60 (U.S.$42) for a family of two adults with two or more children. Tickets are sold onboard and are only valid on the day of purchase—so start early. Bus stops are marked with red-and-green Sydney Explorer signs. The same ticket gives free travel on any State Transit bus within the boundaries of the Explorer circuit until midnight on the day of purchase.

BY BLUE BONDI & BAY EXPLORER BUS This bus operates on the same principle as the Red Sydney Explorer Bus, but visits Sydney's famous Bondi Beach and the scenic harbor suburbs of Double Bay, Rose Bay, and Watsons Bay. The bus covers a 45-kilometer (28-mile) route and stops at 20 locations, including Circular Quay, the oceanfront suburbs of Bronte and Clovelly, the Royal Randwick Racecourse, and the Sydney Cricket Ground. Buses run every 30 minutes between 9am and 6pm. The one-day fare is A$25 (U.S.$17.50) for adults, A$18 (U.S.$12.60) for children under 16, and A$68 (U.S.$47.60) for families.

BY FERRY & JETCAT   The best way to get a taste of a city that revolves around its harbor is to jump aboard a ferry. The main ferry terminal is at Circular Quay. Tickets can be bought at machines at each wharf (there are also change machines) or at the main Circular Quay ticket offices just opposite wharf 4. For ferry information, call ☎ **13 15 00,** or visit the ferry information office opposite wharf 4. Timetables are available for all routes.

One-way journeys within the inner harbor (virtually everywhere except Manly and Parramatta) cost A$3.70 (U.S.$2.60) for adults and A$1.60 (U.S.$1.10) for children. The ferry to Manly takes 30 minutes and costs A$4.60 (U.S.$3.25) for adults and A$2.40 (U.S.$1.70) for children. It leaves from wharf 3. The rapid JetCat service to Manly takes 15 minutes and costs A$5.80 (U.S.$4.05) for adults and children alike. After 7pm, all trips to and from Manly are by JetCat at ferry prices. Ferries run from 6am to midnight.

Sydney Ferries also operates a special **Summer Harbour Beaches** service between Manly, Watsons Bay, and Balmoral on weekends only. This loop service allows you to get on and off when you want and rejoin a later ferry. Tickets, valid for one day, cost A$10 (U.S.$7) for adults and A$5 (U.S.$3.50) for children and include the return fare to Circular Quay. Timetables are available from the ferry information office opposite wharf 4.

BY HARBOUR EXPRESS   Matilda Cruises (☎ **02/9264 7377**) operates the high-speed **Matilda Rocket** that runs between Darling Harbour and Circular Quay daily from 9:30am to 4:30pm. The Rocket leaves Darling Harbour Aquarium Wharf on the half-hour and Circular Quay Commissioner Steps (a small wharf opposite the Museum of Contemporary Art) at a quarter to the hour. The boat stops off at the Opera House and the Harbourside Festival Marketplace at Darling Harbour and includes commentary along the way.

Tour the Olympic Venues

Guided tours by ferry to **Homebush Bay,** the site of the new Olympic Park, depart Circular Quay Monday through Friday at 10am, 11am, noon, 1pm, and 1:30pm, and Saturday and Sunday at 10:35am and 12:25pm. Weekday tours cost A$15 (U.S.$10.50) per person; weekend tours cost A$22 (U.S.$15.40) per person and include an extra tour of the Aquatic Center, built specifically for the Sydney Olympic Games. Buy tickets at wharf 5. Contact **State Transit** at ☎ **02/9207 3170** for more details.

Sydney Ferries

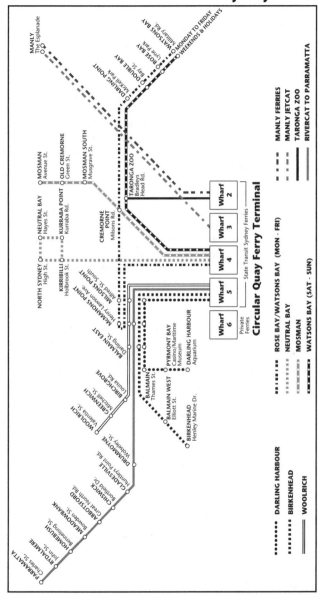

Circular Quay Ferry Terminal

State Transit Sydney Ferries

Private Ferries

Wharf 2
Wharf 3
Wharf 4
Wharf 5
Wharf 6

Legend

- **MANLY FERRIES**
- **MANLY JETCAT**
- **TARONGA ZOO**
- **RIVERCAT TO PARRAMATTA**

- **ROSE BAY/WATSONS BAY (MON - FRI)**
- **NEUTRAL BAY**
- **MOSMAN**
- **WATSONS BAY (SAT - SUN)**

- **DARLING HARBOUR**
- **BIRKENHEAD**
- **WOOLRICH**

Stations

MANLY — The Esplanade
WATSONS BAY — Military Rd.
MONDAY TO FRIDAY
ROSE BAY — Lyne Park
WEEKENDS & HOLIDAYS
DOUBLE BAY — Bay St.
DARLING POINT — McKell Park

MOSMAN — Avenue St.
OLD CREMORNE — Green St.
MOSMAN SOUTH — Musgrave St.
TARONGA ZOO — Bradleys Head Rd.

NEUTRAL BAY — Hayes St.
KURRABA POINT — Kurraba Rd.
CREMORNE POINT — Milsons Rd.

NORTH SYDNEY — High St.
KIRRIBILLI — Holbrook St.
MILSONS POINT — Alfred St. South
McMAHONS POINT — Henry Lawson Ave.
BALMAIN EAST — Darling St.

PYRMONT BAY — Casino/Maritime Museum
DARLING HARBOUR — Aquarium

BALMAIN — Thames St.
BALMAIN WEST — Elliott St.
BIRKENHEAD — Henley Marine Dr.

WOOLRICH — Valentia St.
GREENWICH — Mitchell St.
BIRCHGROVE — Louisa Rd.

DRUMMOYNE — Wolseley St.
GLADESVILLE — Barnfield Dr.
CHISWICK — Great North Rd.
ABBOTSFORD — Humphris Point Rd.
MEADOWBANK — Bowden St.
HOMEBUSH — Hornberg St.
RYDALMERE — John St.
PARRAMATTA — Charles St.

47

You get on and off when you want. The fare is A$18 (U.S.$12.60) for adults and A$9 (U.S.$6.30) for children 5 to 12; children under 5 are free. Buy tickets on the boat.

BY CITYRAIL   Sydney's publicly owned train system is a cheap and relatively efficient way to see the city. The system is limited, though, with many tourist areas—including Manly, Bondi Beach, and Darling Harbour—not connected to the railway network. The CityRail system is somewhat antiquated, signage is generally poor (especially—and remarkably—at the main intersections of Circular Quay and Town Hall), and trains have a reputation of running late and out of timetable order. All train stations have automatic ticket machines, and most have ticket offices.

The off-peak (after 9am) round-trip fare within the city center is A$2 (U.S.$1.40). Before 9am the same journey will cost you A$3.20 (U.S.$2.25). Information is available from **InfoLine** (☎ **13 15 00**) and at the **CityRail Host Centers** located opposite Wharf 4 at Circular Quay (☎ **02/9224 2649**) and at Central Station (☎ **02/9219 1977**); both centers are open daily from 9am to 5pm.

Comfortable and efficient **Countrylink** trains operating out of Central Station link the city with the far suburbs and beyond. For reservations, call ☎ **13 22 32** between 6:30am and 10pm, or visit the **Countrylink Travel Center,** 11–31 York St., Wynyard (☎ **02/9224 4744**), open Monday through Friday from 8:30am to 5pm, or the Countrylink Travel Center at Circular Quay (☎ **02/9224 3400**), open Monday through Friday from 10am to 5:30pm and Saturday from 10am to 2pm.

BY METRO MONORAIL   The metro monorail, with its single overhead line, is seen by many as a blight on the city and by others as a futuristic addition. The monorail connects the central business district to Darling Harbour. The system operates Monday through Wednesday from 7am to 10pm, Thursday and Friday from 7am to midnight, Saturday from 7am to midnight, and Sunday from 8am to 10pm. Tickets are A$3 (U.S.$1.75); children under 5 ride free. An all-day monorail pass costs A$6 (U.S.$4.20). The trip from the city center to Darling Harbour takes around 12 minutes. Look out for the gray overhead line and the plastic tube-like structures that are the stations. Call **Metro Monorail** at ☎ **02/9552 2288** for more information.

BY METRO LIGHT RAIL   A new system of "trams" opened in late 1997 with a route that traverses a 3.6-kilometer (2.2-mile) track between Central Station and Wentworth Park in Pyrmont. The system provides good access to Chinatown, Paddy's Markets, Darling Harbour, the Star City casino, and the Sydney Fish Markets. The trams run every 10 minutes. The one-way fare is A$2 or A$3 (U.S.$1.40 or $2.10) for adults (depending on distance—check at the station) and A$1 or A$2 (U.S.70¢ or $1.40) for children 4 to 15. The round-trip fare is A$3 or A$4 (U.S.$2.10 or $2.80) for adults and A$2 or A$3 (U.S.$1.40 or $2.10) for children. Call **Metro Light Rail** at ☎ **02/9552 2288** for details.

BY TAXI

Taxis are a relatively economical way to get around Sydney. Several taxi companies service the city center and suburbs. All journeys are metered and cost A$3 (U.S.$2.10) when you get in and A$1.07 (U.S.75¢) per kilometer thereafter. It costs an extra A$1 (U.S.70¢) if you call for a cab. You must also pay extra for waiting time, luggage weighing over 25 kilograms (55 lb.), and if you cross either way on the Harbour Bridge or through the Harbour Tunnel (A$2/ U.S.$1.40). An extra 10% will be added to your fare if you pay by credit card.

Taxis line up at ranks in the city, such as those found opposite Circular Quay and Central Station. They are also frequently found in front hotels. A small yellow light on top of the cab means it's vacant. Cabs can be particularly hard to get on Friday and Saturday nights and between 2 and 3pm everyday, when tired cabbies are changing shift after 12 hours on the road. Tipping is not necessary, but appreciated. Some people prefer to sit up front with the driver, but it's certainly not considered rude if you don't. It is compulsory for all passengers to wear seat belts in Australia. The **Taxi Complaints Hotline** (☎ **1800/648 478** in Australia) deals with problem taxi drivers. Taxis are licensed to carry four people.

The main cab companies are **Taxis Combined Services** (☎ **02/ 9332 8888**); **RSL Taxis** (☎ **02/9581 1111**); **Legion Cabs** (☎ **13 14 51**); and Premier (☎ **13 10 17**).

BY WATER TAXI

Harbour Taxis, as they are called, operate 24-hours a day and are a quick and convenient way to get to waterfront restaurants, harbor attractions, and some suburbs. They can also be hired for private cruises of the harbor. A journey from Circular Quay to Watsons Bay, for example, costs about A$45 ($31.50) for two. Extra passenger costs just A$5 (U.S.$3.50); some taxis can hold up to 28 people. An hour's sightseeing excursion around the harbor costs A$150 (U.S. $105) for two. The two main operators are **Taxis Afloat**

(☎ **02/9955 3222**) and **Water Taxis Combined** (☎ **02/9810 5010**).

BY CAR

Traffic restrictions, parking problems, and congestion can make getting around the city center by car a frustrating experience, but if you plan to visit some of the outer suburbs or take excursions elsewhere in New South Wales, then renting a car will give you more flexibility. The **NRMA's** (National Roads and Motorists' Association—the New South Wales auto club) **emergency breakdown service** can be contacted at ☎ **13 11 11.**

RENTALS   The "big four" car-rental companies all have extensive networks across Australia:

- **Avis** (☎ **1800/22 5533** in Australia or 02/9353 9000 in Sydney; 800/230-4898 in the U.S.; 800/272-5871 in Canada; 01344/70 7070 or 0990/900 500 in the United Kingdom; 21/28 1111 in Ireland; www.avis.com). Sydney office: 214 William St., Kings Cross (☎ **02/9357 2000**).

- **Budget** (☎ **1300/36 2848** in Australia, or 13 27 27 which puts you through to the nearest Budget office; 800/472-3325 in the U.S.; 800/268-8900 in Canada; 0800/626 063 in the U.K.; 09/375 2222 in New Zealand; www.drivebudget.com). Sydney office: 93 William St., Kings Cross (☎ **13 28 48** or 02/9339 8888).

- **Hertz** (☎ **13 30 39** in Australia; 800/654-3001 in the U.S.; 800/263-0600 in English, 800/263-0678 in French in Canada, or 416/620-9620 if calling from Toronto; 0181/679 1799 in the U.K.; 1/676 7476 in Ireland; 0800/655 955 in New Zealand; www.hertz.com). Sydney office: corner of William and Riley streets, Kings Cross (☎ **02/9360 6621**).

- **Thrifty** (☎ **1300/367 2277** in Australia; 800/FOR-CARS in the U.S. and Canada; 1494/44 2110 in the U.K.; www.thrifty. com). Sydney office: 75 William St., Kings Cross (☎ **02/9380 5399**).

All four also have desks at the airport. Rates average about A\$40 (U.S.\$28) per day for weekly rentals and around A\$70 (U.S.\$49) for single-day rentals.

You can rent a campervan from **Campervan Rentals** (☎ **1800/ 246 869** in Australia or 02/9797 8027; fax 02/9716 5087) or **Brits Campervans,** 182 O'Riordan St., Mascot, NSW 2020 (☎ **1800/ 331 454** in Australia or 02/9667 0402). Both companies allow you to drop off your van at most state capitals, and Cairns, though Brits charges an extra A\$150 (U.S.\$105) for the convenience.

Money-Saving Tip

One nifty way to cut an average of 30% off your car rental rate is to join the Australian Youth Hostels Association (YHA) or Hostelling International (see "For Students" under "Tips for Travelers with Special Needs," in chapter 1). Along with a host of other discounts, membership entitles you discounts from Avis, Budget, and Hertz.

Insurance for theft, loss, or damage to the car and third party insurance are usually included in the rate, but always have the rental company spell out exactly what kinds of insurance are and are not covered in the quoted rate. For example, damage to the car body may be covered, but not damage to the windscreen or tires, or damage caused by water.

The **deductible,** known as "excess" in Australia, on insurance may be as high as A$2,000 (U.S.$1,400) for regular cars and considerably more for 4WDs. You can reduce or avoid the deductible by paying a premium of around A$6 to $15 (U.S.$4.20 to $10.50) per day. Again, check the conditions; some reduction payments do not reduce excesses on single-vehicle accidents, for example.

GAS The price of petrol (gasoline) will elicit a cry of dismay from Americans and a whoop of delight from Brits. Prices go up and down a lot, but expect to pay about A79¢ a liter (or U.S.$2.12 per U.S. gallon) for unleaded petrol in New South Wales. One liter equals .26 U.S. gallons.

DRIVING RULES Australians drive on the left, which means you give way to the right. Left turns on a red light are *not* permitted unless a sign says so. Roundabouts are common at intersections; approach these slow enough so you can stop if you have to, and give way to all traffic on the roundabout. It is illegal not to flash your indicator light as you leave the roundabout, even if you're going straight ahead, although most Aussies never do.

The maximum permitted blood alcohol level when driving is 0.05, which equals approximately two 200 milliliter (6.6 fl. oz.) drinks in the first hour for men, one for women, and one drink per hour for both sexes after that. The police set up random breath-testing units (RBTs) in cunningly disguised and unlikely places all the time, so it is easy to get caught. You will face a court appearance if you do.

The **speed limit** is 60 kilometers per hour (37.5 m.p.h.) in urban areas and 100 kilometers per hour (63 m.p.h.) or 110 kilometers per hour (69 m.p.h.) in most country areas. Speed limit signs are black numbers circled in red on a white background.

Drivers and passengers must wear a **seatbelt** at all times when the vehicle is moving forwards. Young children are required to sit in a child-safety seat or wear a safety harness; car-rental companies will rent these to you when you rent your car.

FAST FACTS: Sydney

American Express   For all travel-related inquiries regarding any American Express Service, including reporting a lost card, call ☎ 1800/230-100. To report lost or stolen traveler's checks, call ☎ 1800/251-902. The main AMEX office is at 92 Pitt St., near Martin Place (☎ **02/9239 0666**). It's open Monday through Friday from 8:30am to 5:30pm and Saturday from 9am to noon. If you've lost your traveler's checks, then you need to head to the office at 175 Liverpool St. (☎ **02/ 9271 1111**). It's a locked security building so you'll need to call ahead first.

Baby-Sitters   Dial an Angel (☎ **02/9416 7511** or 02/ 9362 4225) offers a well-regarded baby-sitting service.

Business Hours   General office and banking hours are Monday through Friday from 9am to 5pm. Many banks, especially in the city center, are also open from around 9.30am to 12:30pm on Saturdays. Shopping hours are usually 8:30am to 5:30pm daily (9am to 5pm on Saturdays), and most stores stay open until 9pm on Thursdays. Most city-center stores are open from around 10am to 4pm on Sundays.

Camera Repair   The Camera Service Centre, 1st Floor, 203 Castlereagh St. (☎ **02/9264 7091**), is a tiny place up a flight of stairs not far from the Town Hall CityRail station. It repairs all kinds of cameras on the spot, or within a couple of days if parts are needed.

Car Rentals   See "Getting Around," earlier in this chapter.

Currency Exchange   Most major bank branches offer currency exchange services. Small foreign currency exchange offices are clustered at the airport and around Circular Quay and Kings Cross. **Thomas Cook** can be found at the airport; at 175 Pitt St.

(☎ **02/9231 2877**), open Monday to Friday from 6:45am to 5:15pm and Saturday from 10am to 2pm; in the Kingsgate Shopping Center, Kings Cross (☎ **02/9356 2211**), open Monday to Friday from 9am to 5pm; and on the lower ground floor of the Queen Victoria Building (☎ **02/9264 1133**), open Monday to Friday from 9am to 6pm (until 9pm Friday), Saturday from 9am to 6pm, and Sunday from 11am to 5pm.

Dentist   A well-respected dentist office in the city is **City Dental Practice,** Level 2, 229 Macquarie St. (near Martin Place) (☎ **02/9221 3300**). For dental problems after hours, call Dental Emergency Information (☎ **02/9369 7050**).

Doctor   The **Park Medical Centre,** Shop 4, 27 Park St. (☎ **02/ 9264 4488**), in the city center near Town Hall, is open Monday through Friday from 8am to 6pm; consultations cost $A35 (U.S. $24.50) for 15 minutes. *Note:* If you plan to take a dive course while in Australia, get your medical exam done here. It costs A$45/ U.S.$31.50, which is about the cheapest in Australia). **The Kings Cross Travelers' Clinic,** Suite 1, 13 Springfield Ave., Kings Cross, just off Darlinghurst Road (☎ **1300/369 359** in Australia or ☎ 02/9358 3066), is a great place for travel medicines and emergency contraception pills among other things. Hotel visits in the Kings Cross area cost A$60 to $80 (U.S.$42 to 56); consultations cost A$35 (U.S.$24.50). **The Travelers' Medical & Vaccination Centre,** Level 7, 428 George St., in the city center (☎ **02/ 9221 7133**), stocks and administers all travel-related vaccinations and medications.

Drugstores   See "Pharmacies," below.

Electricity   The current is 240 volts AC, 50 Hertz. Sockets take two or three flat, not rounded, prongs. North Americans and Europeans will need to buy a converter before they leave home (don't wait until you get to Australia, because Australian stores only sell converters for Aussie appliances to fit American and European outlets). Some hotels have 110V outlets for electric shavers or dual-voltage, and some will lend converters, but don't count on it. Power does not start automatically when you plug in an appliance; you need to flick the switch located beside the socket to the "on" position.

Embassies/Consulates   All foreign embassies are based in Canberra: **British High Commission,** Commonwealth Avenue, Canberra, ACT 2600 (☎ 02/6270 6666); **High Commission**

of Canada, Commonwealth Avenue, Yarralumla, ACT 2600
(☎ 02/6273 3844); **New Zealand High Commission,** Commonwealth Avenue, Canberra ACT 2600 (☎ 02/6270 4211); and
the **United States Embassy,** 21 Moonah Place, Yarralumla,
ACT 2600 (☎ 02/6214 5600). You'll find the following consulates in Sydney: **United Kingdom,** Level 16, Gateway Building, 1 Macquarie Place, Circular Quay (☎ 02/9247 7521); **New
Zealand,** 1 Alfred St., Circular Quay (☎ 02/9247 1344); **United
States,** 19–29 Martin Place (☎ 02/9373 9200); and **Canada,**
Level 5, 111 Harrington St., The Rocks (☎ 02/9364 3000).
For Australian embassies abroad, see "Entry Requirements," in
chapter 1.

Emergencies   Dial ☎ **000** to call police, the fire service, or an
ambulance. Call the Emergency Prescription Service (☎ **02/9235
0333**) for emergency drug prescriptions, and the NRMA for car
breakdowns (☎ **13 11 11**).

Etiquette   Australia's laid-back disposition means it's first names
from the start, handshakes all round, and no standing on ceremony,
mate. Always return a "shout" (round) at the pub, and don't butt
in if there's a queue (line). Avoid using a mobile telephone in a
restaurant if you can and turn it off in the theater.

Eyeglass Repair   **Perfect Vision,** Shop C22A, in the Centerpoint
Tower, 100 Market St. (☎ **02/9221 1010**), is open Monday
through Friday from 9am to 6pm (until 9pm Thursday) and Saturday from 9am to 5pm.

Holidays   See "When to Go," in chapter 1. New South Wales
also observes Labour Day on the first Monday in October.

Hospitals   Make your way to **Sydney Hospital,** on Macquarie
Street, at the top end of Martin Place (☎ **02/9382 7111** for
emergencies). **St. Vincents Hospital** is on Victoria and Burton
streets in Darlinghurst (near Kings Cross) (☎ **02/9339 1111**).

Hotlines   Contact the **Poisons Information Center** at ☎ 13
11 26; the **Gay and Lesbian Counseling Line** (4pm to midnight)
at ☎ 02/9207 2800; the Rape Crisis Center at ☎ 02/9819 6565;
and the **Crisis Center** at ☎ 02/9358 6577.

Information   See "Visitor Information," earlier in this chapter
and in chapter 1.

Internet Access   **Global Gossip,** at 770 George St., near Central Station (☎ **02/9212 1466**), and 111 Darlinghurst Rd., Kings

Cross (☎ **02/9326 9777**), offers Internet, e-mail, and computer access for A\$2 (U.S.\$1.40) for 10 minutes or A\$10 (U.S.\$7) per hour. It's open daily from 8am to midnight. Elsewhere in the city, the **Surfnet Café** (☎ **02/9976 0808**), next to the public library in Manly, is open Monday through Saturday from 9am to 9pm and Sunday from 9am to 7pm; the **Internet Café,** Level 3, Hotel Sweeney, 236 Clarence St. (☎ **02/9261 5666**), is open Monday through Friday from 10am to 9pm and Saturday from noon to 6pm; and the **Well Connected Café,** 35 Glebe Point Rd., Glebe (☎ **02/9566 2655**), is open Monday through Thursday from 10am to 11pm, Friday and Saturday from 10am to 6pm, and Sunday from noon to 10pm.

Liquor Laws Pub (bar) hours vary from pub to pub, but most are open Monday through Saturday from around 10am to 10pm or midnight. The minimum drinking age is 18. Random breath tests to catch drunk drivers are common, and drink-driving laws are strictly enforced. The maximum permitted blood alcohol level is 0.05. Alcohol is only sold in liquor stores, or "bottle shops" attached to a pub, and rarely in supermarkets.

Lost Property There is no general lost property bureau in Sydney. Contact the nearest police station if you think you've lost something. For items lost on trains, contact the **Lost Property Office,** 494 Pitt St., near Central Railway Station (☎ **02/9379 3000**). The office is open Monday through Friday from 8:30am to 4:30pm. For items left behind on planes or lost at the airport, go to the Federal Airport Corporation's administration office on the top floor of the international terminal at Sydney International Airport (☎ **02/9667 9583**). For stuff left behind on buses or fer-ries, call ☎ **02/9245 5777.** Each taxi company has its own lost property office.

Luggage Storage You can leave your bags at the International Terminal at the airport. A locker here costs A\$4 (U.S.\$2.80) per day, or you can put them in the storage room for A\$6 (U.S.\$4.20) per day per piece. The storage room is open from 4:30am to the last flight of the day. Call ☎ **02/9667 9848** for information. Otherwise, leave luggage at the cloakroom at Central Station, near the front of the main building off George Street (☎ 02/9219 4395). Storage at the rail station costs A\$1.50 (U.S.\$1.05) per article until 10:30pm the following evening and A\$4.50 (U.S.\$3.15) per article every day thereafter. Travelers Contact

Point, 7th floor, 428 George St. (☎ **02/9221 8744**), stores luggage for A$10 (U.S.$7) per piece per month.

Newspapers   The *Sydney Morning Herald* is considered one of the world's best newspapers and is available throughout metropolitan Sydney. The equally prestigious *Australian* is available nationwide. The metropolitan *Telegraph Mirror* is a more casual read. The *International Herald Tribune, USA Today,* the *British Guardian Weekly* and other U.K. newspapers can be found at Circular Quay newspaper stands and most newsagents.

Pets   Leave 'em at home. You will be back home planning your next vacation before Fluffy clears quarantine in Oz.

Pharmacies   Most suburbs have pharmacies that are open late. For after-hours referral, contact the **Emergency Prescription Service** (☎ **02/9235 0333**).

Police   In an emergency dial ☎ **000.** Make nonemergency police inquiries through the Sydney Police Centre (☎ **02/9281 0000**).

Post Office   Australia's single postal service, Australia Post (☎ **13 13 17** in Australia) has a post office in every suburb. Every state capital has a central General Post Office (GPO) offering a complete range of services. Sydney's GPO is at 130 Pitt St. (☎ **13 13 17** in Australia). It's open Monday through Friday from 8:30am to 5:30pm and Saturday from 8am to noon. Letters can be sent c/o Poste Restante, GPO, Sydney, NSW 2000, Australia (☎ **02/9244 3733**), and collected at 310 George St., on the 3rd floor of the Hunter Connection shopping center. It's open Monday to Friday from 8:15am to 5:30pm. For directions to the post office nearest you, call ☎ **1800/043 300.** Some newsagents sell stamps. A postcard costs A95¢ (U.S.67¢) to the United States or Canada, A$1 to the United Kingdom, and A70¢ to New Zealand. American Express cardholders can have mail sent to any American Express office in Australia for collection.

Rest Rooms   These can be found in the Queen Victoria Building (second floor), most department stores, at Central Station and Circular Quay, near the escalators by the Sydney Aquarium, at Darling Harbour, and in the Harbourside Festival Marketplace in Darling Harbour.

Safety   Sydney is an extremely safe city overall, but as anywhere else, it's good to keep your wits about you and your wallet hidden. If you wear a moneybelt, keep it underneath your shirt. Be wary in Kings Cross and Redfern at all hours, and around the cinema strip on George Street near Town Hall station in the evening—it's a hangout for local gangs. Other places of concern are the back lanes of Darlinghurst and along the Bondi restaurant strip when the drunks spill out after midnight. Several people have reported thieves operating at the airport on odd occasions. If traveling by train at night, travel in the carriages next to the guard's van, marked with a blue light on the outside.

Taxes   Beginning July 1, 2000, Australia will have a 10% Goods and Services Tax (GST) on most goods sold in Australia. By law, the tax has to be included in the advertised price of the product. A 10% state government "Bed Tax" was introduced for all hotels in New South Wales, except backpacker accommodations, in September 1998; this tax will be abolished as soon as the GST takes effect.

Taxis   See "Getting Around," earlier in this chapter.

Telephone   **To call Australia from North America:** Dial the international access code ☎ **011;** then Australia's country code (☎ **61**); then the area code (02 for Sydney and all of New South Wales); then the local number. The area codes found throughout this book all begin with "0"; you drop the "0" if you're calling from outside Australia, but you need to dial it along with the area code if you're calling long distance within Australia. For example, to ring the Sydney Opera House (☎ **02/9250 7111**) from the United States, dial 011-61-2-9250-7111.

   To call Australia from the United Kingdom: Dial the international access code ☎ 00, and then follow the instructions above.

   To make an international call from Australia: Dial the international access code ☎ 0011 (note it has two zeros, not one like the international access code from North America); then the country code, then the area code, and finally the local number. Dial 0012 instead of 0011, and the operator will ring back within

Caller, Beware

Some hotels routinely add outrageous surcharges onto phone calls made from your room. Inquire before you call! It'll be a lot cheaper to use your own calling card (although some hotels will charge you for this, too) or find a pay phone.

minutes of the call to tell you what the call will cost. To find out a country code, call ☎ 1222 or look in the back of the Australian White Pages. Common country codes are USA and Canada, 1; United Kingdom, 44; New Zealand, 64; and South Africa, 27.

To make an international credit card or collect call from Australia, dial one of the following access codes to your country:

- **United States:** AT&T Direct ☎ 1800/881 011, Sprint ☎ 1800/881 877, MCI ☎ 1800/881 100, Worldcom ☎ 1800/881 212, or Bell Atlantic ☎ 1800/881 152;
- **United Kingdom:** BT ☎ 1800/881 441 or Mercury ☎ 1800/881 417;
- **New Zealand:** ☎ 1800/881 640.

To use a calling card from some pay phones, you will need to deposit 40¢ to put the call through, but this is usually refunded when you hang up.

Global Gossip, at 770 George St., near Central Station (☎ 02/9212 1466), and 111 Darlinghurst Rd., Kings Cross (☎ 02/9326 9777), offers cheap international telephone calls.

Australia's Toll-Free Numbers: Australian phone numbers starting with 1800 are toll-free; numbers starting with 13 or 1300 are charged at the local fee of 25¢ from anywhere in Australia. These numbers can only be dialed within Australia. Numbers beginning with 1900 (or 1901, 1902, etc) are pay-for-service lines (like 900 numbers in the United States); expect to be charged as much as A$5 (U.S.$3.50) a minute

Local Calls: Local calls in Australia are untimed and cost a flat A40¢ from a public telephone, or A25¢ from a private phone in a home or office.

Newsagents and some tourist information booths sell Smart Phonecards (which you swipe in the pay-phone) and PhoneAway cards (which you use by dialing access codes printed on the card) containing a prepaid allotment of call time; not all public telephones take these cards yet.

Cellular or "mobile" telephones are hugely popular in Australia and are available for daily rental in major cities.

Operator Assistance: To reach the operator for help making a call, dial ☎ **1234.** To make a collect or "reverse charges" call, dial the operator at ☎ **12550.**

To find out a telephone number, call Directory Assistance at ☎ **1223** for numbers within Australia, or ☎ **1225** for overseas numbers.

Time   Australia crosses three time zones. When it is noon in New South Wales, the A.C.T., Victoria, Queensland, and Tasmania, it is 11:30am in South Australia and the Northern Territory and 10am in Western Australia. All states except Queensland, the Northern Territory, and Western Australia observe daylight savings time from around the last Sunday in October (the first Sunday in October in Tasmania's case) to around the first Sunday in March. To confuse things, not all states switch over to daylight savings on the same day or even in the same week.

The east coast of Australia is GMT (Greenwich Mean Time) plus 10 hours. When it is noon (Eastern Standard Time or EST) on the east coast, it is 2am in London that morning, and 6pm in Los Angeles and 9pm in New York the previous night. These times are based on standard time, so allow for daylight savings in the Australian summer, or in the country you are calling. New Zealand is two hours ahead of the east coast of Australia.

For the exact local time in Australia, call ☎ **1194,** or ☎ **1222** for the exact local time overseas. For national and international time zones, ring ☎ **1900/937 106.**

Travelers Assistance   Travelers Contact Point, at Level 7, 428 George St. (☎ **02/9221 8744;** fax 02/9221 3746), offers an in-house employment agency for working holidays, an Australia-wide mail forwarding service, Internet access, and short-term mobile phones.

Useful Telephone Numbers   For news, dial ☎ **1199;** for the time, ☎ **1194;** for Sydney entertainment, ☎ **11 688;** for phone directory/assistance, ☎ **013** (local numbers), ☎ **0175** (interstate numbers) or ☎ **0103** (international numbers); and for Travelers Aid Society, ☎ **02/9211 2469.**

Weather   For the local forecast, call ☎ **1196.**

3

About the Sydney 2000 Olympic Games

*S*ince the announcement that the Games of the XXVIIth Olympiad will be held in Sydney from September 15 to October 1, 2000, the city has been busily preparing for an influx of more than two million guests. Most of the city center streets have been repaved, the area around Circular Quay has been upgraded, developers have rushed to complete new hotels in time, stadiums have been constructed, and almost all of the city's sightseeing attractions have been planning special events and exhibits.

The Sydney Olympic Games, which start on September 15 with the Opening Ceremony and finish with the spectacular Closing Ceremony on October 1, will have some 1,700 separate competitions with 300 medal events in 28 separate sports. Approximately 10,000 athletes from some 200 countries will vie for gold, silver, and bronze.

1 Sources of Information

The official site of the **Sydney Organising Committee for the Olympic Games (SOCOG)** is the best place to go for general information: www.sydney.olympic.org/.

Another Web site, **www.sydney.auscape.net.au**, bills itself as offering supplementary information to the official site. It also includes information on private homeowners offering accommodations during the Games.

The **Sydney Visitor Center,** 106 George St., The Rocks (☎ **02/ 9255 1788**), is a good place for maps, brochures, and general tourist and Olympic information. The office is open daily from 6am to 6pm (though it could be open for longer hours during the Games).

When in town, check out the *Sydney Morning Herald* for up-to-date information on possible session and location changes for some events.

2   The Venues & Events

The events will be primarily held in two major Olympic "zones"—
the **Sydney Olympic Park** and the **Sydney Harbour Zone.**

SYDNEY OLYMPIC PARK (HOMEBUSH BAY)   The Sydney
Olympic Park, at Homebush Bay, a 30-minute drive from downtown Sydney, is the site of the new 110,000-seat **Olympic Stadium,**
where the opening and closing ceremonies and soccer and track
and field events will be held, and the **Athletes' Village.** Next door
to the Olympic Stadium is the SuperDome, intended to hold
18,000 spectators during the Games, and which will house artistic
gymnastics and trampoline competitions as well as the basketball
finals.

Also at Homebush Bay is the **Sydney Showground** (where
baseball, rhythmic gymnastics, and basketball preliminaries will be
held, among other events), and the 17,500-seat **Sydney International Aquatic Centre,** which will host swimming, synchronized
swimming, and diving events as well as the semifinals and finals
of water polo. (Public tours of this facility—except during the
Games period—are offered from Sydney; see "Getting Around," in
chapter 2).

SYDNEY HARBOUR ZONE   Events to be held in the Sydney
Harbour Zone include portions of the marathon, which will begin
in North Sydney and head across the Harbour Bridge and through
The Rocks, the Botanic Garden, and Darling Harbour before finishing at the Olympic Stadium; basketball, boxing, and weightlifting
at Darling Harbour; and yachting in Sydney Harbour. Sydney's
famous Bondi Beach will be the venue for beach volleyball, which
was first introduced in Olympic competition in 1996 at the Atlanta
Olympic Games.

Olly, Millie & Syd

What's a major sporting event without a mascot? The Sydney 2000
Olympic Games will have three such critters designed to embody the
spirit of the Games. All are cuddly versions of native Aussie animals:
Olly, an "honest, enthusiastic, and open-hearted" kookaburra; Millie,
a sharp echidna (it's like a spiny-coated anteater) who's a "techno-
whiz and information guru"; and Syd, a "focused, dynamic, and
enthusiastic" platypus.

The Sydney Olympics Outside Sydney

The 2000 Olympic Games are truly an Australian event, with other state capitals getting involved with the action, too. So, if you are traveling around Australia during the Games period you might want to get a taste of the Olympic spirit in some place other than Sydney.

Canberra's **Bruce Stadium** will play host to first round matches of men's and women's football (soccer) as well as a women's soccer semi-final. You can contact Canberra Tourism at www.canberatourism.com.au, get additional Olympic Games information by ringing ☎ **13 63 63** in Australia, or visit the Canberra Olympic site at www.project2000.act.gov.au. The **Melbourne Cricket Ground** in Melbourne, the **Hindmarsh Stadium** in Adelaide, and the **Brisbane Cricket Ground** in Brisbane will also host preliminary soccer games.

3 Getting Tickets

Tickets are divided into four categories, with Category A seats offering the best views and category C and D seats being quite far back from the action. Each day's events will be split up into two sessions, with the finals taking place mostly in the afternoon sessions.

GETTING TICKETS IN ADVANCE

Tickets went on sale in Australia in July 1999, when a vast mail-order program was initiated. Eighty percent of the approximately 5.5 million tickets will be sold in Australia; check the SOCOG Web site (see above) for details. Residents of other countries should check with their country's National Olympic Committee for details on obtaining tickets. For a list of National Olympic Committees and links to their Web sites, go to www.olympic.org/family/noc/noc_list.html.

In the **United States,** the Official Ticket Agent responsible for the exclusive sale of tickets to the general public is **Cartan Tours, Inc.,** 1334 Parkview Ave., Suite 210, Manhattan Beach, CA 90266 (☎ **800/818-1998,** or 310/546-9662; fax 310/546-8433). To request information or receive Cartan's Olympic Brochure, call or visit the agency's Web site at **www.cartan.com** or contact them via e-mail at sales@cartan.com. Cartan will also offer a variety of exclusive travel packages.

Sydney Olympic Park, Homebush Bay

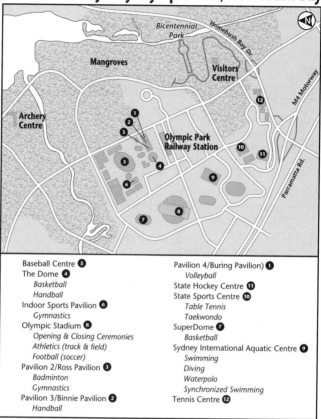

Baseball Centre **5**

The Dome **4**
Basketball
Handball

Indoor Sports Pavilion **6**
Gymnastics

Olympic Stadium **8**
Opening & Closing Ceremonies
Athletics (track & field)
Football (soccer)

Pavilion 2/Ross Pavilion **3**
Badminton
Gymnastics

Pavilion 3/Binnie Pavilion **2**
Handball

Pavilion 4/Buring Pavilion) **1**
Volleyball

State Hockey Centre **11**

State Sports Centre **10**
Table Tennis
Taekwondo

SuperDome **7**
Basketball

Sydney International Aquatic Centre **9**
Swimming
Diving
Waterpolo
Synchronized Swimming

Tennis Centre **12**

In the **United Kingdom,** contact the official British Ticket and Tour Agent: **Sportsworld Travel,** New Abbey Court, Stert Street, Abingdon, OX14 3JZ (☎ **01235/554 844;** fax 01235/554 841).

In **Canada,** contact the **Canadian Olympic Association,** Olympic House, 2380 Ave. Pierre Dupuy, Montréal, PQ H3C 3R4 (☎ **514/861-3371;** fax 514/861-2896; www.coa.ca/).

In the **Republic of Ireland,** contact the **Olympic Council of Ireland,** 27 Mespil Road, Dublin 4 (**01/668-0444;** fax 01/668-0650).

People wishing to buy tickets from outside Australia will most likely have to buy a package that includes tickets and accommodations. Though these packages may be good deals, if you have your

OLYMPIC PROGRAM	Schedule is subject to change
Major Event/Sport	**Venue**
OPENING CEREMONY	Sydney Olympic Park, Olympic Stadium
AQUATICS	
Diving	Sydney Olympic Park, Sydney Intnl. Aquatic Centre
Swimming	Sydney Olympic Park, Sydney Intnl. Aquatic Centre
Synchronized Swimming	Sydney Olympic Park, Sydney Intnl. Aquatic Centre
Water Polo—Men's	Sydney Olympic Park, Sydney Intnl. Aquatic Centre
	Sydney West, Ryde Aquatic Leisure Center
Water Polo—Women's	Sydney Olympic Park, Sydney Intnl. Aquatic Centre
	Sydney West, Ryde Aquatic Leisure Center
ARCHERY	Sydney Olympic Park, Archery Centre
ATHLETICS	
Track and Field	Sydney Olympic Park, Olympic Stadium
Marathon	Sydney East, Marathon Course
Race Walk	Sydney Olympic Park, Race Walks Course
BADMINTON	Sydney Olympic Park Showground, Pavilion 2
BASEBALL	Sydney Olympic Park, Baseball Stadium
	Sydney West, Baseball Centre, Blacktown
BASKETBALL—Men's	Sydney Olympic Park, The Dome
	Sydney Olympic Park, Sydney SuperDome
BASKETBALL—Women's	Sydney Olympic Park, The Dome
	Sydney Olympic Park, Sydney SuperDome
BOXING	Darling Harbour, Exhibition Halls 3 and 4
CANOE/KAYAK	
Sprint	Sydney West, Sydney Intnl. Regatta Centre, Penrith Lakes
Slalom	Sydney West, Slalom Course, Penrith Whitewater Stadium
CYCLING	
Mountain Bike	Sydney West, Mountain Bike Course, Fairfield City Farm
Road Race	Sydney East, Cycling Road Course, Centennial Pklds.
Track	Sydney West, Dunc Gray Velodrome, Bankstown
EQUESTRIAN	Sydney West, Equestrian Centre, Horsley Park
FENCING	Darling Harbour, Exhibition Halls 4 and 5
FOOTBALL—Men's (Soccer)	Sydney Olympic Park, Olympic Stadium
	Sydney East, Sydney Football Stadium
	Melbourne Cricket Grounds, Melbourne
	Bruce Stadium, Canberra
	Hindmarsh Stadium, Adelaide
	Brisbane Cricket Ground, Brisbane

Key: ✪ =*Gala Event* T = *Training* TT = *Ticketed Training* • = *Dates of Events*

	September																		Oct.
Date	13	14	15	16	17	18	19	20	21	22	23	24	25	26	27	28	29	30	1
Day	W	Th	F	S	Su	M	T	W	Th	F	S	Su	M	T	W	Th	F	S	Su
			✪																
										•		•	•	•	•	•	•	•	
				•	•	•	•	•	•	•	•								
											•	•	•		•	•			•
											•								
										•						•	•	•	•
												•							•
										•						•	•		
				•	•	•	•	•	•	•	•								
					•	•	•	•		•	•	•		•	•				
					•	•	•	•		•	•	•							
					•		•		•		•		•	•					
																•	•	•	•
				•		•		•		•		•		•					
																•	•	•	
				•	•	•	•	•	•	•	•	•		•	•	•	•	•	•
													•	•	•	•	•	•	•
				•	•	•	•												
										•	•							•	
												TT	•	•			•		
				•	•	•	•	•	•										
				•	•	•	•	•	•	•	•	T		•	•	•	•	•	•
				•	•	•	•	•	•	•	•								
																		•	
				•			•				•			•			•		
	•	•		•	•		•	•			•			•					
	•	•		•	•			•											
	•	•		•	•		•	•			•								
	•	•		•	•		•	•			•								

Major Event/Sport	Venue
OLYMPIC PROGRAM	
FOOTBALL—Women's (Soccer)	Sydney East, Sydney Football Stadium
	Melbourne Cricket Grounds, Melbourne
	Bruce Stadium, Canberra
GYMNASTICS	
Artistic	Sydney Olympic Park, Sydney SuperDome
Trampolining	Sydney Olympic Park, Sydney SuperDome
Rhythmic	Sydney Olympic Park, Pavilion 2
HANDBALL—Men's	Sydney Olympic Park, Pavilion 3
	Sydney Olympic Park, The Dome
HANDBALL—Women's	Sydney Olympic Park, Pavilion 3
	Sydney Olympic Park, The Dome
HOCKEY—Men's	Sydney Olympic Park, State Hockey Centre
HOCKEY—Women's	Sydney Olympic Park, State Hockey Centre
JUDO	Darling Harbour, Exhibition Halls 1 and 2
MODERN PENTATHLON	
Shooting and Fencing	Sydney Olympic Park, Pavilion 3
Swimming	Sydney Olympic Park, Sydney Intnl. Aquatic Centre
Riding and Running	Sydney Olympic Park, Baseball Centre
ROWING	Sydney West, Sydney Intnl. Regatta Centre, Penrith Lakes
SAILING	Sydney East, Sailing Marina, Rushcutters Bay
SHOOTING	Sydney West, Sydney Intnl. Shooting Centre, Cecil Park, Liverpool
SOFTBALL	Sydney West, Softball Centre, Blacktown
TABLE TENNIS	Sydney Olympic Park, State Sports Centre
TAEKWONDO	Sydney Olympic Park, State Sports Centre
TENNIS	Sydney Olympic Park, Tennis Centre
TRIATHLON	Sydney East, Triathlon Course, Sydney Opera House
VOLLEYBALL	
Beach	Sydney East, Beach Volleyball Centre, Bondi
Indoor—Men's	Darling Harbour, Sydney Entertainment Centre
	Sydney Olympic Park, Pavilion 4
Indoor—Women's	Darling Harbour, Sydney Entertainment Centre
	Sydney Olympic Park, Pavilion 4
WEIGHTLIFTING	Darling Harbour, Sydney Convention Centre
WRESTLING	
Freestyle	Darling Harbour, Exhibition Halls 1 and 2
Greco-Roman	Darling Harbour, Exhibition Halls 1 and 2
CLOSING CEREMONY	Sydney Olympic Park, Olympic Stadium

	__ September __																		Oct.
Date	13	14	15	16	17	18	19	20	21	22	23	24	25	26	27	28	29	30	1
Day	W	Th	F	S	Su	M	T	W	Th	F	S	Su	M	T	W	Th	F	S	Su
				•			•					•				•			
	•	•		•			•	•											
	•	•		•	•			•				•							
		TT	TT	•	•	•	•	•	•			•	•	✪					
										•	•								
														TT	TT	•	•	•	•
				•		•		•		•		•		•					
																•	•	
					•		•		•		•		•						
																•	•	•	•
				•	•	•	•	•	•	•	•	•	•	•	•	•	•	•	
				•	•	•	•	•	•	•		•	•		•		•		
				•	•	•	•	•	•	•	•								
																	•	•	•
																	•	•	•
																	•	•	•
					•	•	•	•	•	•	•	•							
					•	•	•	•	•	•	•	•	•	•	•	•	•	•	•
				•	•	•	•	•	•	•	•								
					•	•	•	•	•	•			•	•					
				•	•	•	•	•	•	•	•	•	•						
															•	•	•	•	
						•	•	•	•	•	•	•	•	•	•	•			
				•	•														
				•	•	•	•			•	•	•	•	•	•				
					•		•		•		•		•		•		•		•
					•		•		•		•		•		•		•		
				•		•		•		•		•		•		•		•	
				•		•		•		•		•		•					
				•	•	•	•	•		•	•	•	•	•	•				
																•	•	•	•
												•	•	•	•				
																			✪

The Toughest Tickets

The hardest tickets to come by will be for the opening and closing ceremonies and the finals in swimming, athletics (track and field), and basketball.

heart set on seeing certain events, you'll want to know just what tickets the packages include. You might decide to buy your tickets and book your accommodations separately, if possible. See section 4 below, "Accommodations during the Games," for tips on finding lodging. If you make accommodations on your own, be sure to get written confirmation of your reservation and quoted room rates.

TICKET PRICES

Seventy percent of all tickets for the Games will cost A$60 (U.S.$42) or less, with some, such as the equestrian events, costing as little as A$17 (U.S.$11.90) per session. For A$19 (U.S.$13.30), you can see qualification rounds of the such sports as soccer, volleyball, baseball, and softball. Tickets for the qualification rounds of the athletics (track and field) or swimming go for as little as A$35 (U.S.$24.50) per session (if you don't mind sitting in the back row).

Prices rise dramatically from here on up, with ringside seats for the finals of the athletics (track and field) going for a cool A$455 (U.S.$318.50). For a ticket to the opening ceremony expect to pay from A$105 (U.S.$73.50) for a spot in the nosebleed section to A$1,382 (U.S.$967.40) for something nearer the action.

GETTING TICKETS AT THE LAST MINUTE

While SOCOG says it cannot guarantee that tickets will be available just before or during the Games, there's no need to panic if you don't get yours before the Games start, because Olympic Games simply do not sell out. For every session, it's very likely that many tickets will be on sale at the door or from scalpers, especially for low-demand events, such as soccer, baseball, handball, wrestling, judo, taekwondo, rowing, and kayaking. Keep in mind that some five million tickets were set aside for Australians—a record. At the 1996 Games in Barcelona, in a country with more than double the population of Australia, only 1.76 million tickets were made available to the locals, and they weren't even close to selling out. As well, hundreds of thousands of tickets are sold in advance to sponsors and to the national Olympic committees of the 200 countries sending athletes to the Games. These groups are forced to buy packages that include the big events as well as less-popular ones. This means that sponsors and committees will come to Sydney with suitcases stuffed full of tickets they couldn't hope to sell beforehand. They will most likely sell them to ticket brokers for a lot less than the going rate, and these entrepreneurs will sell them for the best price they can get. Even tickets to premium events can sell for a lot less than the face value. Closing ceremony tickets for the Atlanta Games, for example, were changing hands outside the stadium for U.S.$50 less than the U.S.$350 face value.

4 Accommodations During the Games

Virtually all four- and five-star hotels in Sydney are already completely booked for the period of the Games—and have been for years. Most of the rooms were gobbled up by SOCOG for visiting dignitaries and officials and by corporate sponsors of the Games.

In addition to exploring the options listed below, international visitors should contact their country's National Olympic Committee for the name of the officially appointed tour operator responsible for ticket sales and package tours to the Games (see section 3, "Getting Tickets," earlier in this chapter).

Just about everyone you meet in Sydney at the moment is weighing the pros and cons of renting out his or her home during the Games. Staying in a private home or apartment can be a good option, as many of the venues will be located centrally, though it is well worth finding out precisely how long it will take to get to the various venues by public transportation.

Ray White Real Estate is the official agency for finding rooms for visitors during the Games via its **Residential Accommodation Program** (☎ **02/9262 3700;** fax 02/9262 3737; e-mail: accomm@ raywhite.net). The program offers two categories of accommodation:

The Olympics for Free

From Day 2 to Day 13, Sydney Harbour, especially The Heads (the sea cliffs at the entrance to the harbor) and around the harbor foreshore, is the place to head to watch the sailing competitions for free. Other free events are the women's triathlon on Day 1, the men's triathlon on Day 2, the men's road cycling race on Day 12, the women's road cycling race on Day 11, the women's marathon on Day 9, and the men's marathon on Day 16.

Helpful Hints for Enjoying the Games

A city holding an Olympic Games is a very different animal than what you might imagine. The Games transform a city for two weeks or more, and getting around can be difficult and confusing. Here are some tips to make life a little easier.

1. Keep game times and geographic proximity in mind when making your ticket selections. This will both prevent exhaustion and increase the number of sessions you'll have time to see.

2. Allow plenty of time to get to venues. Remember that walking in large crowds is always slow going. You should be in your seat at least 30 minutes before the event starts.

3. Treat your tickets like gold. Lost tickets cannot be replaced and you won't be allowed into venues if your tickets are in bad condition.

4. Check the local newspaper to ensure that events have not been rescheduled. Refunds will not be available if the schedules have changed.

5. Come prepared. Although it will be winter in Australia when the Games are held, there will still be days when you'll need a hat and sunscreen. Other days are likely to be quite chilly and rainy.

Homestay, in which guests stay in vacant, furnished homes; and **Homehost,** in which guests stay with an Australian family (breakfast is provided). Accommodations are expected to range from A$90 (U.S.$63) to A$500+ (U.S.$350+) per bedroom per night. Prices vary according to the quality of the accommodation and the distance from events. The minimum booking period is one week for Homehost accommodations and three weeks for Homestay accommodations. Contact the agency's Web site at www.raywhite.com.au for complete details.

Another option is to check the Web site **www. sydneybudget. com.au**, which specializes in budget accommodations in cabins or bunks. Don't expect any bargains, though, as even "budget" accommodations will cost around A$1,000 (U.S.$700) per person per week.

Another Web site, **http://sydney.auscape.net.au/**, includes listings for private homes available for rent during the Games, though

I would be very wary of doing any business over the Internet (apart from the official agency—see above).

5   Transportation

Forget about driving anywhere in Sydney during the Games—the traffic is bad enough during normal times. The best way to get around is by bus, train, and ferry. See chapter 2, "Getting to Know Sydney," for complete details on getting around Sydney via public transportation.

Public transportation to Homebush Bay during the games will be free, with regular CityRail trains running between Circular Quay and the new Olympic Park station and a procession of buses running from various points in the city, such as outside Central Station and from Circular Quay and Wynyard. Parking will be impossible at the main Olympic sites.

6   The Cultural Olympiad/Olympic Arts Festival

If you're more of a culture vulture than a sports buff, then you'll want to know about the **Sydney 2000 Olympic Arts Festival, Harbour of Life,** which starts a month before the Opening Ceremony of the Games. The athletic competitions of the Sydney 2000 Olympic Games will be complemented by a Cultural Olympiad featuring concerts, dance performances, theater, opera, art exhibitions, and other special events designed to showcase Australian and international talent. The key venue for festival events will be the world-renowned Sydney Opera House, but events will be held throughout the city. The Olympic Arts Festivals provide an opportunity for each host city to present a cultural program that demonstrates the cultural life of that city and nation.

Tickets for the Sydney 2000 Olympic Arts Festival went on sale in Australia in October 1999. See the SOCOG Web site (see "Sources of Information," in section 1) for details. Below is a small sampling of events. *Note:* All schedules are subject to change.

- **Toobowgulie—Opening Ceremony**
  An Aboriginal ceremony will officially open the Sydney 2000 Olympic Arts Festival. The event will be held in front of the Sydney Opera House and is free to the public. August 18.
- **Film Festival**
  The new Fox Studios Australia will be the site of this festival presenting the best of Australian film from the early 1900s

Dining During the Games

Hotels aren't the only places that will be completely booked during the Games. Many restaurants, particularly those in the city center, will be sold out to corporate clients far in advance, while the massive influx of people from overseas and elsewhere in Sydney will mean that finding a table anywhere in the city could be tricky. Your best bet is to make restaurant reservations as far in advance as possible. Eating meals outside regular lunch and dinner times could make things a little easier, too. Hotel restaurants will make it a priority to serve their guests; after you've booked your hotel room, see about making reservations in the hotel dining room.

---

to contemporary favorites. August 25–27 and September 1–3 and 8–10.

- **World Music Festival**

  Renowned contemporary artists from across the globe will be featured at this weekend-long celebration at Centennial Park. The large-scale event, designed to complement the international nature of the Olympic Games, will also feature cuisine from around the world. September 8–10.

- **Opera Australia**

  The Opera Theatre at the world-renowned Sydney Opera House will be the site of several major productions during the Olympic Arts Festival, including *Capriccio* (Aug 19, 22. 25, and 29; Sept 1, 7, and 9), *Don Giovanni* (Aug 23, 26, 31; Sept 2 and 8), *La Traviata* (Sept 22, 27, 30); *Simon Boccanegra* (Aug 30; Sept 2, 5, 9, 12, 17, 23, 26, and 28), and *Tosca* (Sept 16, 18, 20 and 24).

- **Sydney Dance Company—Fragments**

  A highlight of the Olympic Arts Festival will be this exciting new work choreographed by Graeme Murphy with a musical score by leading contemporary Australian composer Carl Vine, performed by Australia's leading contemporary dance company.

- **Australian Icons**

  The Art Gallery of New South Wales will be the site of this exhibition featuring the works of major Australian and Aboriginal artists. August–October.

- **Art and Sport**
  This major exhibition at the Museum of Contemporary Art will trace the development of sport in the 20th century, through art and film. August–October.

In addition to the above events, the Sydney Symphony Orchestra will present a series of popular concerts in the Sydney Opera House. From August through October, art galleries throughout Sydney will host solo exhibitions by major Australian contemporary artists.

7   The Paralympic Games

The Paralympic movement celebrates its 40th anniversary at the 2000 Games in Sydney. The first Paralympic Games were held in Rome in 1960. Some 4,000 athletes from 125 countries are expected to compete at the Games of the XI Paralympiad, to be held in Sydney from October 18 to 29, making them the largest Paralympic Games ever.

Athletes will compete in 18 sports at the Sydney 2000 Paralympic Games, 14 of which are also on the Sydney 2000 Olympic Games program. Two new sports, sailing and wheelchair rugby, will be introduced at the Sydney Games. The full-medal sports for the Paralympics are archery, athletics (track, throwing and jumping, pentathlon, and marathon), basketball, boccia (an Italian game played by athletes with cerebral palsy; the object is to place balls closest to a white target ball on a long alley-like field), cycling, equestrian, fencing, goalball (a game played by blind competitors who try to throw balls equipped with bells into their opponents' goal), judo, lawn bowls, powerlifting, football (soccer), rugby, sailing, shooting, swimming, table tennis, wheelchair tennis, and volleyball. The Paralympic Games will include more than 700 events—more than twice the number of Olympic events—because Paralympic athletes compete according to degree of disability and functional level, creating additional categories. Events will utilize most of the Olympic Games venues as well as other Sydney locations.

4

Accommodations

*H*otels are generally clustered around the main tourist spots, with the more expensive ones generally occupying the prime positions. Those in The Rocks and around Circular Quay are just a short stroll from the Sydney Opera House, the Harbour Bridge, the Royal Botanic Gardens, the ferry terminals, and the train station, and are close to the main shopping areas.

Hotels around Darling Harbour offer good access to the local facilities, including museums, the Sydney Aquarium, the Star City Casino, the IMAX Theatre, and Sega World. Most Darling Harbour hotels are a 10-minute walk, or a short monorail or light rail ride, from Town Hall and the central shopping district in and around the AMP Centerpoint Tower and the Pitt Street Mall.

More hotels are grouped around Kings Cross, Sydney's red-light district. While some of the hotels found here are among the city's best, in this area you'll also find a range of cheaper lodgings, including several backpacker hostels. Kings Cross can be unnerving at any time, but especially so on Friday and Saturday nights when the area's strip joints and nightclubs are doing their best business. Staying here does have its advantages, though: you get a real inner-city feel and it's close to some excellent restaurants and cafes located around the Kings Cross/Darlinghurst and Oxford Street areas.

Glebe, with its many ethnic restaurants, is another inner-city suburb popular with tourists. It's well served by local buses, as well as Airport Express Bus route 352.

If you want to stay near the beach, check out the options in Manly and Bondi, though you should consider their distance from the city center and the lack of CityRail trains to these areas. A taxi to Manly from the city will cost around A$30 (U.S.$21), and to Bondi around A$20 (U.S.$14).

The prices given below for very expensive and expensive hotels are the **"rack rates,"** the official published rates, which almost nobody pays. Always ask about discounts rates, package deals, and any other special offerings when booking a hotel, especially if you are traveling in winter when hotels are less likely to be full. Ask about

Rooms During the Olympic Games

For details on finding a place to stay during the Sydney Olympic Games, see chapter 3.

---

weekend discounts, corporate rates, and family plans. **Serviced apartments** are also well worth considering, because you can save a bundle by cooking your own meals; many also have free laundry facilities.

Almost all hotels offer no-smoking rooms; inquire when you make a reservation if it's important to you. Most moderately priced to very expensive rooms will have a hair dryer, tea- and coffee-making facilities, and access to an iron and ironing board. In moderate to expensive hotels, there's an increasing trend to rip off guests with pay-per-view movie channels (around A$13/U.S.$9 per movie), rather than to provide full access to a range of free cable TV channels.

1 Near Circular Quay

All Seasons Premier Menzies. 14 Carrington St., Sydney, NSW 2000. ☎ **1300/363 600** in Australia or 02/9299 1000. 446 units. A/C MINIBAR TV TEL. A$300–$325 (U.S.$210–$227.50) double; A$480 (U.S.$336) suite. Extra person A$40 (U.S.$28). Children under 12 stay free in parents' room. Ask about special packages. AE, BC, DC, JCB, MC, V. Parking A$22 (U.S.$15.40). CityRail: Wynyard.

The 14-story Menzies was built in 1963 as Sydney's first premier hotel. It's positioned right in the center of town and sports one of the city's few public clocks on top of its impressive facade. Rooms are spacious and newly refurbished, decorated with colonial furniture and outfitted with a fax machine and all the mod cons (modern conveniences). Deluxe rooms, as you'd expect, are slightly larger and a touch more upscale. Though it took A$14 million (U.S.$9.8 million) to modernize it in 1997, this hotel has retained its grand dame appeal.

Dining: The Carrington Restaurant serves high-class à la carte meals and fabulous lunch and dinner buffets. A brasserie offers snacks, lunch, and afternoon tea in a very elegant atmosphere.

Amenities: Indoor pool, sauna, spa, massage, gym, concierge, 24-hour room service, free daily newspapers, nightly turndown, shoe shine, laundry, valet, business services, gift shop, newsstand, currency exchange.

Central Sydney Accommodations

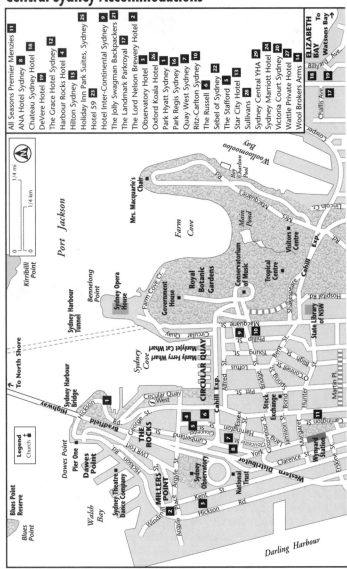

All Seasons Premier Menzies 11
ANA Hotel Sydney 8
Chateau Sydney Hotel 18
DeVere Hotel 19
The Grace Hotel Sydney 12
Harbour Rocks Hotel 4
Hilton Sydney 15
Holiday Inn Park Suites, Sydney 25
Hotel 59 23
Hotel Inter-Continental Sydney 9
The Jolly Swagman Backpackers 21
The Landmark Parkroyal 17
The Lord Nelson Brewery Hotel 2
Observatory Hotel 3
Oxford Koala Hotel 26
Park Hyatt Sydney 1
Park Regis Sydney 16
Quay West Sydney 7
Ritz-Carlton Sydney 10
The Russell 6
Sebel of Sydney 22
The Stafford 5
Star City Hotel 13
Sullivans 28
Sydney Central YHA 29
Sydney Marriott Hotel 24
Victoria Court Sydney 20
Wattle Private Hotel 27
Wool Brokers Arms 14

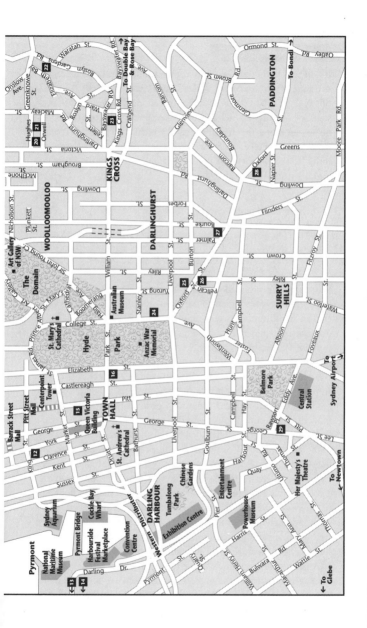

Last-Minute Room Deals

If you turn up in town without a reservation, you should definitely make use of the **New South Wales Travel Centre desk** (☎ **02/9667 6050**) on the Arrivals Level of the International Terminal. It represents every Sydney hotel and offers exceptional discounts—up to 50%—on rooms that haven't been filled that day. The desk is open from 6am to the last flight of the day and also offers discounts on tours (to the Blue Mountains, for example), and cheap tickets for flights within Australia.

✪ **Hotel Inter-Continental Sydney.** 117 Macquarie St., Sydney, NSW 2000. ☎ **1800/221 828** in Australia (outside New South Wales) or 02/9230 9000. Fax 02/9240 1240. 498 units. A/C MINIBAR TV TEL. A$375–$495 (U.S.$262.50–$346.50) double; from A$765 (U.S.$535.50) suite. Extra person A$60 (U.S.$42). Children under 15 stay free in parents' room. AE, BC, DC, JCB, MC, V. Parking A$20 (U.S.$14). CityRail, bus, or ferry: Circular Quay.

Wonderfully positioned opposite the Royal Botanic Gardens and just a stroll away from many other main attractions, the hotel is situated in the former Treasury building (later the VD clinic), built between 1849 and 1917. All rooms have been elegantly refurbished to unite 19th-century classicism with the best of the 20th century. Half of the rooms have a harbor view and all come complete with everything you'd expect, and some features, like a toaster, that might surprise you. Special rooms for business travelers are slightly larger (and more expensive) and come with dedicated business facilities: modem lines, printer, scanner, and fax machine.

Dining/Diversions: Afternoon tea, lunch, and cocktails are taken in the white marbled Cortile, the building's architectural focal point. The Cortile features live classical music Wednesday through Sunday. One One Seven, the hotel's fine-dining venue, is picking up quite a good reputation. The 30-Something Lounge on the 31st floor has panoramic views over Sydney Harbour and the Royal Botanic Gardens and serves good pizzas and pasta. Sketches Bar & Bistro serves freshly made pasta (see chapter 5, "Dining"). Café Opera is an informal buffet specializing in sushi and wok-prepared foods.

Amenities: Indoor pool, sauna, spa, gym, power-walking classes, massage therapists, concierge, 24-hour room service, free daily newspapers, nightly turndown, shoe shine, laundry, valet, babysitting, business center, secretarial services, hair/beauty salon, gift shop, newsstand, early-arrivals/late-departures lounge, currency exchange.

✪ Ritz-Carlton, Sydney. 93 Macquarie St., Sydney, NSW 2000. ☎ **1800/ 145 004** in Australia or 02/9252 4600. Fax 02/9252 4286. 106 units. A/C MINIBAR TV TEL. A$419 (U.S.$293) double, A$449 (U.S.$314) deluxe harborview double; A$569–$2,000 (U.S.$398–$1,400) suite. AE, BC, DC, MC, V. Parking A$25 (U.S.$17.50). CityRail, bus, or ferry: Circular Quay.

Talk about plush! This is Sydney's most deluxe hotel—from the moment the doorman doffs his top hat to you, you enter the world of the aristocracy. The lobby is cozy and elegant, with plenty of antiques scattered around and the slight scent of cigar smoke and aged brandy in the air. It has a prime location, just a short walk from Circular Quay and the Opera House, and just across the road from the Royal Botanic Gardens. Rooms are exceptionally large and luxurious with good-size marble bathrooms. Most rooms have a small balcony. The rooms on the east side of the hotel have the best views across the gardens.

Dining: The Dining Room serves up fine cuisine in a well-heeled atmosphere. The Bar serves a buffet meal at lunchtime and has promotional evenings, such as Oyster night.

Amenities: Indoor pool, sauna, gym, massage, concierge, 24-hour room service, free daily newspapers, nightly turndown, shoe shine, laundry, valet, baby-sitting, business center, secretarial services, hair/ beauty salon, gift shop, newsstand, currency exchange.

2   In The Rocks

VERY EXPENSIVE

✪ ANA Hotel Sydney. 176 Cumberland St., The Rocks, Sydney, NSW 2000. ☎ **1800/801 088** in Australia or 02/9250 6000. Fax 02/9250 6250. 563 units. MINIBAR TV TEL. A$370–$460 (U.S.$259–$322) double depending on view; from A$620 (U.S.$434) and way up for suites. Extra person $40 (U.S.$28). Children stay free in parents' room. AE, BC, DC, JCB, MC, V. Parking A$17 (U.S.$11.90). CityRail or ferry: Circular Quay.

For a room with a view, you're not going to do better than this ultramodern landmark hotel. All rooms look out onto either Darling Harbour, or across the Opera House and Harbour Bridge. Try to book a room on the 20th floor or above, because from here Sydney is laid out at your feet, with the ferries buzzing around below you like wind-up bathtub toys. If you really want to splurge, book a corner suite for an extraordinary vista. Rooms are comfortably furnished and decorated to blend with sky, city, and sea. The hotel is popular with tour groups, particularly from Japan.

Dining/Diversions: The Lilyvale restaurant serves delicious Modern Australian dishes, The Rocks Teppanyaki is the hotel's popular Japanese food outlet, and the Lobby Lounge serves up cock-tails and a view of the landscaped gardens, though it can get noisy when tour groups arrive.

Amenities: Indoor pool, spa and sauna, fitness center, massage, concierge, 24-hour room service, free daily newspapers, nightly turn-down, shoe shine, laundry, valet, baby-sitting, business center, meet-ing facilities, hair/beauty salon, sundry/gift shop, currency exchange, early arrivals/late departures lounge.

✪ **Observatory Hotel.** 89–113 Kent St., Sydney, NSW 2000. ☎ **1800/806 245** in Australia or 02/9256 2222. Fax 02/9256 2233. www.observatoryhotel.com.au. E-mail: observatory@mail.co. 100 units. A/C MINIBAR TV TEL. A$350–$425 (U.S.$245–$297.50) double; from A$595 (U.S.$416.50) suite. Extra person A$60 (U.S.$42) extra. Children under 14 stay free in parents' room. AE, BC, DC, JCB, MC, V. Parking A$22 (U.S.$15.40). Bus: 339, 431, or 433 to Millers Point.

This exclusive hotel, a 10-minute walk uphill from The Rocks and George Street, is a turn-of-the-century beauty competing for top-hotel-in-Sydney honors. Up there with the Ritz-Carlton Sydney (see above) for unadulterated style, it's outfitted with antiques, objets d'art, and the finest carpets, wallpapers, and draperies, and is renowned for its personalized service. Rooms are plush, quiet, and come with all the modern amenities, including a CD player and a VCR. The huge bath is a great place for a glass of champagne and some takeaway sushi. Some rooms have city views while others look out over the harbor. If you don't fancy the 15-minute walk into town, then take advantage of the hotel's free BMW limo service, which delivers guests to the central business district on weekdays. The pool here is one of the best in Sydney: Note the Southern Hemisphere constellations on the roof. The health club offers everything from massage and beauty therapies to a free float in the flotation tank for early arrivals coming in from overseas.

Dining/Diversions: The Galileo Restaurant offers very good food in an elegant candlelit atmosphere with silk wallpaper, polished walnut furniture, and original Venetian etchings and Australian Impressionist works of art. The Globe Bar feels like an old-world colonial English club.

Amenities: Chemical-free indoor pool, sauna, steam room, flotation tank, health club, tennis courts, concierge, 24-hour room service, newspaper delivery, nightly turndown, twice-daily maid service, dry cleaning/laundry, business center.

✪ **Park Hyatt Sydney.** 7 Hickson Rd., The Rocks, Sydney, NSW 2000. ☎ **13 12 34** in Australia, 800/835-7742 in the U.S. and Canada, or 02/9241 1234. Fax 02/9256 1555. http://sydney.hyatt.com/ or www.hyatt.com. 158 units. A/C MINIBAR TV TEL. A$650–$800 (U.S.$455–$560) double depending on view; A$800–$1,000 (U.S.$560–$700) executive studio; from A$1,000 (U.S.$700) suite. Extra person A$50 (U.S.$21). Children under 18 stay free in parents' room. Ask about lower weekend rates and packages. AE, BC, DC, JCB, MC, V. Parking A$20 (U.S.$14). CityRail, bus, or ferry: Circular Quay.

This artistically curving property on The Rocks foreshore is without a doubt the best-positioned hotel in Sydney. It's literally right on the water, with some rooms having fantastic views directly across the harbor to the Sydney Opera House. Its location and general appeal mean it's usually full and frequently has to turn guests away. The room rates have rocketed here in the last year or so; unless you are really looking for a splurge, there are plenty of places around that are far cheaper and just as good, if not better overall.

The building itself is a pleasure to look at, and from a ferry on the harbor it looks like a wonderful addition to the toy-town feel of The Rocks. The marble lobby is elegant, and every possible luxury has been incorporated into the rooms. Room rates here really depend on views; the least expensive units have only glimpses of the harbor. Each of the 33 executive suites has two balconies with a telescope.

Dining/Diversions: Verandah on the Park offers good buffet food either indoors or in a fabulous location on the edge of the harbor. No. 7 at the Park is more formal and has excellent harbor views. The bar has a fireplace and resembles an English club.

Amenities: Outdoor pool, health club, gym, steam room, sauna, spa, massage, concierge, butler, 24-hour room service, nightly turndown, free newspaper, laundry, shoe shine, valet, baby-sitting, business center, lobby shop.

Quay West Sydney. 98 Gloucester St. (corner of Essex St.), The Rocks, Sydney, NSW 2000. ☎ **1800/805 031** in Australia, 0800/444 300 in New Zealand, or 02/9240 6000. Fax 02/9240 6060. 132 units. A/C MINIBAR TV TEL. A$320–$415 (U.S.$224–$290.50) 1-bedroom apt depending on view; A$530 (U.S.$371) 2-bedroom apt. Extra person A$30 (U.S.$21). Ask about weekend packages and rates for long-term stays. AE, BC, DC, JCB, MC, V. Parking A$15 (U.S.$10.50). CityRail, bus, or ferry: Circular Quay or Wynyard.

The very best serviced-apartment complexes, like this one, can even beat superior five-star hotels. Quay West is a hard-hitting competitor to its rivals in and around The Rocks area—it's got everything they have and more. The lobby is plush and hotel-like. The apartments are very spacious, each with, among other things, a fully equipped kitchen, a laundry, a CD player, a fold-out sofa in the living room as well as a queen-size bed in a separate bedroom, a dining table seating six, and a balcony. Bathrooms are large and feature a separate tub and shower. Some rooms have fantastic views over the Harbour Bridge and the harbor—but you pay through the nose for them. The 28-story apartment building has a spa, sauna, gym, beautiful indoor Roman-style swimming pool with great views, and the high-quality Carrington Restaurant.

EXPENSIVE

Harbour Rocks Hotel. 34–52 Harrington St., The Rocks, Sydney, NSW 2000. ☎ **1800/251 210** in Australia or 02/9251 8944. Fax 02/9251 8900. 55 units. MINIBAR TV TEL. A$210–$240 (U.S.$147–$168) double. Penthouse suite A$400 (U.S.$280). Extra person A$30 (U.S.$21). Children under 16 stay free in parents' room. AE, DC, JCB, MC, V. Parking A$16 (U.S.$11.20) across the road. CityRail or ferry: Circular Quay.

This four-story, heritage-listed boutique hotel is right in the heart of Sydney's historical Rocks district. Rooms are clean and well appointed with free videos thrown in, but there is no elevator, so guests have to climb the stairs. Rooms vary in size, with some being quite large and others much smaller; bathrooms also vary in size, and none (except the penthouse suite) has a tub. There's one room equipped for travelers with disabilities on the ground floor. In my experience, service here can be offhand.

Dining/Diversions: The beautiful Harbor Rocks Café overlooks a leafy balcony perfect for those sultry summer evenings. Live local jazz bands play in the bar area on Friday nights and Sunday afternoons.

Amenities: Limited room service, laundry service, secretarial services, coin-operated laundry, baby-sitting.

The Stafford. 75 Harrington St., The Rocks, Sydney, NSW 2000. ☎ **02/9251 6711.** Fax 02/9251 3458. www.citysearch.com.au/syd/thestafford. E-mail: staffordsydney@bigpond.com. 61 units. A/C TV TEL. A$210–$245 (U.S. $147–$171.50) studio double; A$250 (U.S. $175) 1-bedroom apt; A$280 (U.S. $196) executive 1-bedroom apt; A$265 (U.S.$185.50) terrace house; A$335 (U.S. $234.50) 1-bedroom penthouse. Extra person A$15 (U.S.$10.50). Children under 12 stay free in parents' room. Ask about lower weekly rates. AE, BC, DC, JCB, MC, V. Parking A$15 (U.S.$10.50). CityRail or ferry: Circular Quay.

Along with Quay West Sydney (see above), the Stafford offers the best-positioned serviced apartments in Sydney, right in the heart of The Rocks, very close to the harbor and Circular Quay, and a short stroll from the central business district. The property consists of modern apartments in a six-story building (the best units, for their harbor and Opera House views, are on the top three floors) and 7 two-story terrace houses dating from 1870 to 1895. While Stafford isn't as exclusive as Quay West, it's still highly recommended for its location, spacious rooms, and fully equipped kitchen. There's an outdoor pool, gym, spa and sauna, and complimentary self-service laundry.

MODERATE

The Lord Nelson Brewery Hotel. At the corner of Kent and Argyle Sts., The Rocks, Sydney, NSW 2000. ☎ **02/9251 4044.** Fax 02/9251 1532. E-mail: lordnelson.co.au. 10 units, 8 with bathroom. TV TEL. A$160 (U.S.$112) double without bathroom, A$180 (U.S.$126) double with bathroom. Extra person A$15 (U.S. $10.50). Rates include continental breakfast. AE, BC, DC, MC, V. Parking not available. CityRail or ferry: Circular Quay.

Sydney's oldest pub was established in 1841 after serving as a private residence since its construction in 1836. It's an attractive, three-story sandstone building with a busy pub on the ground floor, a good brasserie on the second, and hotel accommodations on the third. The "small" rooms are true to their name, with room for not much more than a bed and a small TV. For an extra A$30 (U.S.$21) you get lots more space. All rooms were totally upgraded and refurbished in late 1998. From its creaky floorboards and bedroom walls made from convict-hewn sandstone blocks, to the narrow corridors and the wood fire and homemade beer down in the bar, the Lord Nelson positively wallows in atmosphere.

✪ **The Russell.** 143A George St., The Rocks, Sydney, NSW 2000. ☎ **02/9241 3543.** Fax 02/9252 1652. 29 units, 19 with bathroom. TV TEL. A$110–$150 (U.S.$77–$105) double without bathroom; A$180–$229 (U.S.$126–$160.30) double with bathroom; A$230 (U.S.$161) suite. Extra person A$15 (U.S.$10.50). Rates include continental breakfast. AE, BC, DC, MC, V. Parking not available. CityRail or ferry: Circular Quay.

This is the coziest place to stay in The Rocks, and perhaps in all of Sydney. It's more than 100 years old, and it shows its age wonderfully in the creak of the floorboards and the ramshackle feel of its brightly painted corridors. Every room is totally different in style, size, and shape; all come with a queen size bed and half have cable TV (others can have a TV moved in if requested). All rooms have immense character, including a series of rooms added on in 1990 above the Fortune of War Hotel next door. There are no harbor views, but from some rooms you can see the tops of the ferry terminals at Circular Quay. Guests have the use of a comfortable sitting room, a living room scattered with magazines and books, and a rooftop garden. Boulders Restaurant serves good food on the ground floor.

3 Near Town Hall

VERY EXPENSIVE

The Grace Hotel Sydney. 77 York St., Sydney, NSW 2000. ☎ **1800/ 682 692** in Australia or 02/9299 8777. Fax 02/9299 8189. 382 units. A/C MINIBAR TV TEL. A$300–$350 (U.S.$210–$245) double; A$500 (U.S.$350) suite. Extra person A$40 (U.S.$28). Children under 17 stay free in parents' room. AE, BC, DC, MC, V. Parking A$25 (U.S.$17.50). CityRail: Wynyard.

Situated within the historic Grace Building, a replica of the Chicago Tribune Building in the United States and one of Australia's finest examples of commercial Gothic architecture, The Grace is one of the city's newest centrally located hotels. The 11-story building's L-shaped lobby has marble flagstones, stained-glass windows, a lace ironwork balcony, art-deco furniture and light fittings, and high ceilings supported by marble columns. Guest rooms vary in size, with either king-size beds or a pair of doubles, and are fronted by almost surreally wide corridors. Each room has three telephones, computer connections, and an in-room safe.

Dining: A cafe on the lobby level serves snacks and beverages in a relaxed, informal atmosphere. Breakfast, lunch, and à la carte evening meals are served in the second-floor brasserie.

Amenities: Heated outdoor swimming pool, sauna, gym, massage, concierge, 24-hour room service, free daily newspaper, nightly turndown on request, shoe shine, laundry, valet, baby-sitting, postal and business services, express checkout, currency exchange.

Hilton Sydney. 259 Pitt St., Sydney, NSW 2000. ☎ **1800/222 255** in Australia or 02/9266 2000. Fax 02/9265 6065. 585 units. A/C MINIBAR TV TEL. A$380 (U.S.$266) double; A$550–$1,500 (U.S.$385–U.S.$1,050) suite. Extra person A$40 (U.S.$28). Children under 18 stay free in parents' room. AE, BC, DC, JCB, MC, V. Parking $24 (U.S.$16.80). CityRail: Town Hall.

Right in the middle of town and close to all major shops, the Hilton is a 1970s conglomerate with a decidedly ugly facade rearing onto both Pitt and George streets. The lackluster gold lobby—if you can find it (the main entrance is hidden away in a warren of concrete)—is dimly lit and houses a popular cafe and boutique shops. The rooms were refurbished in 1999, and are the first in Australia to have a fully electronic minibar system (aimed at preventing disputes with guests). Many rooms, especially from the 32nd floor up, have panoramic views of the AMP Centerpoint Tower, the Harbour Bridge, and neighboring skyscrapers.

Dining/Diversions: Some of Sydney's best bars are in the Hilton, including the stunning Marble Bar, with its extravagant central-European feel, and the popular English-style Henry the Ninth Bar. The hotel has two restaurants.

Amenities: Outdoor pool, sauna, spa, gym, massage, concierge, 24-hour room service, free daily newspaper, nightly turndown, shoe shine, laundry, valet, baby-sitting, business center, tour desk, gift shop, newsstand, currency exchange.

Sydney Marriott Hotel. 36 College St., Sydney, NSW 2010. ☎ **1800/ 025 419** in Australia or 02/9361 8400. Fax 02/9361 8599. 241 units. A/C MINIBAR TV TEL. A$360 (U.S.$252) double; A$595 (U.S.$416.50) junior suite; A$735 (U.S.$514.50) premier suite. Extra person A$25 (U.S.$17.50). Children under 12 stay free in parents' room. Ask about lower weekend rates and discount packages. AE, BC, DC, JCB, MC, V. Free parking. CityRail: Museum.

The Marriott is finely positioned right opposite Hyde Park in the city center. It's a short walk from the major shopping areas around Town Hall, and a hop, skip, and a jump from the beginning of fashionable Oxford Street, with its nightlife and burgeoning restaurant scene. The rooms are typical four-star variety, but include such extras as plates, cutlery, toasters, and microwaves; one-third of the rooms also have hot plates. The views from the park-facing rooms are fabulous. All rooms have impressive triangular bathtubs. Many Frommer's readers have recommended the Marriott.

Dining/Diversions: Windows on the Park offers à la carte meals with nice views over Hyde Park. There's also a coffee shop and a cocktail bar.

Amenities: Heated outdoor pool and sundeck with nice views, health club, small gym, steam room, sauna, spa, concierge, arrivals lounge, 24-hour room service.

EXPENSIVE

Holiday Inn Park Suites, Sydney. 16–32 Oxford St., Sydney, NSW 2010. ☎ **1800/221 2599** in Australia, 800/HOLIDAY in the U.S. and Canada, or 02/ 8268 2599. Fax 02/8268 2599. E-mail: sydney@shg.com.au. 135 units. A/C MINIBAR TV TEL. A$230 (U.S.$161) 1-bedroom apt; A$255 (U.S.$178.50) 2-bedroom apt. Extra person A$25 (U.S.$17.50). Children under 15 stay free in parents' room. Ask about special rates. AE, BC, DC, JCB, MC, V. Parking A$5 (U.S.$3.50). CityRail: Museum.

A total refurbishment in 1998 resulted in higher room rates here. Although the serviced apartments are pleasant and nicely furnished and the complex is very well situated right at the start of Oxford Street and just a short walk across Hyde Park from the Pitt Street Mall shopping area, I feel it's overpriced. You may be able to

Where to Stay During the Gay & Lesbian Mardi Gras

The **Holiday Inn Park Suites** (see above) is a fabulous place from which to watch Sydney's annual Gay and Lesbian Mardi Gras, held every February (the parade is usually on the last Saturday in February or the first Saturday in March). Make your plans early, though, as most rooms are booked a year in advance. Four-night Mardi Gras packages range from around A$1,538–$1,992 (U.S.$1,076–$1,394). Sullivans (see below) on Oxford Street is also another popular place to stay during Mardi Gras.

---

negotiate a cheaper rate with the management, though; it never hurts to ask. All rooms have a sofa and a couple of armchairs, a separate kitchen, a balcony, and a bathroom with a smallish tub and separate shower. All come with a laundry and an iron and board. You can ask for a microwave. There's a small-but-functional outdoor pool, a sauna, and a spa; guests get free membership at a gym just down the road. The restaurant, called Zipp, looks fun and is open for lunch and dinner daily except Monday.

MODERATE

Park Regis Sydney. 27 Park St. (at Castlereagh St.), Sydney, NSW 2000. ☎ **1800/221 138** in Australia or 02/9267 6511. Fax 02/9264 2252. www.parkregis.com.au. E-mail: parksyd@maxi.net.au. 120 units. A/C TV TEL. A$160 (U.S.$112) double; A$190 (U.S.$133) suite. Extra person A$15 (U.S.$10.50). Children under 14 stay free in parents' room. Ask about lower rates available through Aussie auto clubs. AE, BC, DC, JCB, MC, V. Free parking. CityRail: Town Hall. Monorail: Park Plaza.

This hotel occupies the top 15 floors of a 45-story building and is well placed in the central business district, just two blocks from Hyde Park and Town Hall. There's nothing spectacular about the place; the lobby is plain and functional and the rooms light, modern, and equally practical. The bathrooms have a shower and no tub. Many of the guests are business travelers, which gives the hotel a corporate feel. Nevertheless, it's a relatively good value considering the location. Rooms at the front have views over the city and park. There's a rooftop pool.

INEXPENSIVE

Sydney Central YHA. 11 Rawson Place, Sydney, NSW 2000. ☎ **02/ 9281 9111.** Fax 02/9281 9199. E-mail: sydcentral@yhansw.org.au. 151 units (54 twin units). A$20–$23 (U.S.$14–$16) dorm bed; A$58 (U.S.$60.60) twin without bathroom; A$66 (U.S.$46.20) twin with bathroom. Non-YHA members pay A$3 (U.S. $2.10) extra. BC, JCB, MC, V. It's located on the corner of

Pitt St., right outside Central Station. On-street parking and limited parking for A$7 (U.S.$4.90). CityRail: Central.

This youth hostel is one of the biggest and busiest in the world. With a 98% year-round occupancy rate, you'll have to book early to secure a place. Opened in 1987 in a historic 9-story building, it offers far more than standard basic accommodation. In the basement is the Scu Bar, a very popular drinking hole with pool tables and occasional entertainment. There's also a bistro selling cheap meals, a convenience store, two fully equipped kitchens, and an entertainment room with more pool tables and e-mail facilities, TV rooms on every floor, and an audiovisual room showing movies. If you want more, try the heated swimming pool and the sauna! Rooms are clean and basic. The YHA is completely accessible to travelers with disabilities.

4 At Darling Harbour

Star City Hotel. 80 Pyrmont St., Pyrmont, Sydney, NSW 2009. ☎ **1800/ 700 700** in Australia or 02/9777 9000. Fax 02/9657 8344. 352 units. A/C MINIBAR TV TEL. A$340–$360 (U.S.$238–$252) double, depending on view; from A$450 (U.S.$315) and way up for suites. Extra person A$40 (U.S.$28). Ask about special packages. AE, BC, DC, JCB, MC, V. Parking A$15 (U.S.$10.50). Ferry: Pyrmont Bay. Monorail: Harbourside. Light rail: Star City. Free shuttle buses run from the central business district.

Opened at the end of 1997, this A$900 million (U.S.$630 million) gambling and entertainment complex includes Sydney's newest five-star hotel, with rooms overlooking both Darling Harbour and Pyrmont Bridge. Although the four split-level Royal Suites (A$1,500/U.S.$1,050) are quite spectacular, each with three TVs, a giant spa, a full kitchen, two bathrooms, its own sauna, and the services of the former butler to the governor of Queensland, the standard rooms, on the other hand, are somewhat sterile. If you aren't attracted to the glamour of this place, or the gambling, you can find nicer rooms for the price elsewhere. If you do stay here, pay the extra money for a room with truly spectacular views over Darling Harbour.

Dining/Diversions: The Astral restaurant is the top-flight dining choice here. It's reached by an external glass elevator and offers top-rated cuisine and the best service I've come across in Sydney. Other major restaurants are Al Porto, serving Italian, and the Lotus Pond, serving Chinese; there are also a couple of bistro-style places. The gaming rooms are sectioned into four areas; there are also two theaters, the 2,000-seat Lyric Theatre (the largest in Sydney) and the 900-seat Showroom, which presents Las Vegas–style productions.

Amenities: Heated outdoor pool, sauna, spa, massage, concierge, 24-hour room service, free daily newspaper, nightly turndown, shoe shine, laundry, valet, business center, shopping arcade, newsstand, beauty salon, currency exchange.

Wool Brokers Arms. 22 Allen St., Pyrmont, NSW 2009. ☎ **02/9552 4773.** Fax 02/9552 4771. E-mail: woolbrokers@ozemail.com.au. 26 units, none with bathroom. TV. A$79 (U.S.$55.30) double; A$90(U.S.$63) triple; A$105 (U.S.$73.50) family room for four. These discounted prices are for Frommer's readers only. Rates include continental breakfast. Extra person A$20 (U.S.$14). AE, BC, MC, V. Parking A$9 (U.S.$6.30) nearby. Bus: 501 from central business district or Central Station. Light Rail: Convention Centre.

You'll find this friendly 1886 heritage building on the far side of Darling Harbour, next to the prominent four-star Novotel hotel and hidden behind a monstrous above-ground parking garage. It's set on a noisy road, so unless you're used to traffic avoid the rooms at the front. Rooms are simply furnished with a double bed, a refrigerator, tea and coffee-making facilities, and a sink. Room 3 is one of the nicer ones. Family rooms have a king-size bed, a set of bunks, and two singles through an open doorway. There are 19 shared bathrooms, a coin-operated laundry, and a self-service breakfast room. It's a good place for a few nights. Stay anywhere else around here and you'll be forking out at least three times as much.

5 In Kings Cross & the Suburbs Beyond

VERY EXPENSIVE

The Landmark Parkroyal. 81 Macleay St., Potts Point, NSW 2011. ☎ **02/9368 3000.** Fax 02/9357 7600. 463 units. A/C MINIBAR TV TEL. A$300–$330 (U.S.$210–$231) double; A$750 (U.S.$525) suite. Extra bed A$25 (U.S.$17.50). Children under 14 stay free in parents' room. Ask about weekend and excellent money-saving packages. AE, BC, DC, JCB, MC, V. Parking A$9 (U.S.$6.30). CityRail: Kings Cross, then about a 1km (^{1}/2-mile) walk. Bus: 311 from Circular Quay.

This top-flight, four-star hotel is where airline pilots stay when they're stopping off in Sydney. Though not slap bang in the city center, it's just a five-minute walk from Kings Cross station and very close to some of the city's best restaurants. The lobby is big and grand and leads to the restaurant. The recently refurbished guest rooms are good sized and have large windows that open. Some rooms have spectacular views over the inner harbor, the Heads, and parts of the city; others have good skyline views; while still others look over the Sydney Opera House and the Harbour Bridge. Depending on the room, it will have either one or two queen-size beds, or a single king-size bed. Bathrooms are small, but come with a tub/shower combination. Guests on the two club floors (the 16th and 17th) receive complimentary breakfast and drinks every evening.

Dining: The hotel's restaurant serves an interesting seafood buffet and Asian gourmet foods.

Amenities: Small outdoor pool, free access to nearby gym, concierge, 24-hour room service, free daily newspaper, nightly turndown, shoe shine, laundry, valet, baby-sitting, gift shop, jogging track, courtesy limo.

Ritz-Carlton Double Bay. 33 Cross St., Double Bay, NSW 2028. ☎ **1300/ 361 180** in Australia, 800/241-3333 in the U.S. and Canada, 0800/443 030 in New Zealand, 0800/234 000 in the U.K., or 02/9362 4455. Fax 02/9362 4744. 140 units. A/C MINIBAR TV TEL. A$349–A$409 (U.S.$244.30–$286.30) double; from A$499 (U.S.$349.30) and up for suites. A$399–$449 (U.S.$279.30– $314.30) Club floor. AE, BC, DC, JCB, MC, V. Parking A$15 (U.S.$10.50). CityRail: Edgecliff, then about a 1km (1/2-mile) walk. Bus: 325 or 324 from Circular Quay. Ferry: Double Bay.

Madonna, the late Princess Diana, Tom Jones, George Bush, Neil Diamond—they've all stayed in this five-star darling of the establishment, situated about 4 kilometers (2.5 miles) from the city center in Sydney's poshest harborside suburb. The grand lobby is decked out in a maritime theme, the corridors are somberly lit, and antiques and Persian rugs are scattered tastefully here and there. The large guest rooms are done in Regency style and are almost unnervingly quiet. Everything you would expect at the best in town is here, from the enormous TV and the fluffy bathrobes down to designer bathtub salts and a perfect, single rose. Most rooms have balconies with water views.

Dining/Diversions: The Grill serves good continental cuisine in an intimate, elegant environment; the plush Bar is popular for cigars and brandy; and The Lobby Lounge is wonderfully civilized for breakfast and a favorite lunch and afternoon tea spot for the local social set.

Amenities: Heated rooftop pool, fitness center, concierge, 24-hour room service, nightly turndown, twice-daily maid service, valet, baby-sitting, separate kosher kitchen, business center, meeting facilities, sundry/gift shop, currency exchange.

EXPENSIVE

Chateau Sydney Hotel. 14 Macleay St., Potts Point, NSW 2011. ☎ **1800/ 221 412** in Australia, 800/624-3524 in the U.S. and Canada, or 02/9358 2500. Fax 02/9358 1959. 96 units. A/C MINIBAR TV TEL. A$200–$220 (U.S.$140– $154) double, depending on view; A$350 (U.S.$245) suite. Extra person A$20

(U.S.$14). Children under 12 stay free in parents' room. Ask about lower week-end rates and special packages. AE, BC, DC, JCB, MC, V. Free parking. CityRail: Kings Cross, then about a 1km (¹/₂-mile) walk. Bus: 311 from Circular Quay.

This boutique hotel is a sister to the Sebel of Sydney (see below) and in direct competition with the Rex and the Landmark Parkroyal (see below and above, respectively), all three of which I prefer to this older-style property. Rooms here are light and look out either across the city or onto the sailboats in Elizabeth Bay. There's a lot of 1970s wood grain around, and rooms have queen-size beds, pay-per-view movies, irons and ironing boards, and the like. Along with the views, the one thing this place does have in its favor is the superb service.

Dining: The Terrace is a comfortable restaurant serving pastas, steaks, and seafood.

Amenities: Outdoor heated pool, concierge, 24-hour room ser-vice, free daily newspapers, laundry, valet, and baby-sitting.

Sebel of Sydney. 23 Elizabeth Bay Rd., Elizabeth Bay, NSW 2011. ☎ 1800/ 222 266 in Australia or 02/9358 3244. Fax 02/9357 1926. 165 units. A/C MINIBAR TV TEL. A$225–$235 (U.S.$157.50–$164.50) standard double, depending on view; A$285–$295 (U.S.$199.50–$206.50) superior double, depending on view; from A$500 (U.S.$350) and up for suites. Extra person A$25 (U.S.$17.50). Children under 12 stay free in parents' room. Ask about dis-counted weekend and off-season rates. AE, BC, DC, JCB, MC, V. Free parking. CityRail: Kings Cross.

Just a block from the bright lights and sleazy sights of Kings Cross, the Sebel is an upscale boutique hotel known for its personal service and "theatrical" theme. It's long been hotel of choice for such inter-national celebs as Elton John, Richard Harris, Cliff Richard, Phil Collins, Rex Harrison, Lauren Bacall, and Rod Stewart, and it remains a place to see and be seen. Rooms are a great value for the price and come with either queen- or king-size beds and traditional furniture. Half of the rooms look out over the picturesque marina at Rushcutters Bay. Suites have VCRs and CD players, as well as kitchenettes.

Dining/Diversions: The Encore Restaurant offers semifine din-ing, serving up everything from steaks to stir-fries. The cocktail bar is a favorite with local actors and performers.

Amenities: Rooftop outdoor pool, gym, sauna, concierge, 24-hour room service, free daily newspaper, nightly turndown, shoe shine, laundry, valet, baby-sitting, business center, gift shop.

MODERATE

DeVere Hotel. 44-46 Macleay St., Potts Point, NSW 2011. ☎ 1800/818 790 in Australia, 0800/441 779 in New Zealand, or 02/9358 1211. Fax 02/9358

4685. www.devere.com.au. E-mail: info@devere.com.au. 98 units. A/C TV TEL. A$99 (U.S.$69.30) double; A$179 (U.S.$125.30) suite. Extra person A$30 (U.S.$21). Children under 12 stay free in parents' room. AE, BC, DC, MC, V. A$11 (U.S.$7.70) per exit parking across the road at the Landmark Hotel. CityRail: Kings Cross. Bus: 311 from Circular Quay.

The DeVere has been recommended by several readers who comment on the friendly staff and the bargain-basement price of A$65 (U.S.$45.50) a room when booked at the Tourism New South Wales Travel Centre at the Sydney airport. Although the rooms are very modern, they are a little too standard gray corporate for my liking. However, they are certainly a bargain compared to similar, but far more expensive, rooms elsewhere in Sydney. The suites have views of Elizabeth Bay, a spa bath, and a king-size bed rather than a queen. Some suites have a pretty useless kitchenette with no cooking facilities. Some standard rooms have an extra single bed. Breakfast is available from A$8 (U.S.$5.60).

✪ Hotel 59. 59 Bayswater Rd., Kings Cross, NSW 2011. ☎ **02/9360 5900.** Fax 02/9360 1828. E-mail: hotel59@enternet.com.au. 8 units. A/C TV TEL. A$100 (U.S.$70) standard double, A$110 (U.S.$77) deluxe double, A$125 (U.S.$87.50) superior room. Extra person A$15 (U.S.$10.50), extra children 2–12 A$10 (U.S.$7). Rates include cooked breakfast. BC, MC, V. Limited parking A$5 (U.S.$3.50). CityRail: Kings Cross.

This popular and friendly B&B is well worth considering if you want to be within walking distance of the Kings Cross action, but just far enough away to get a decent night's sleep. Deluxe rooms have either a queen- or king-size bed and a combined shower and tub, while the smaller standard rooms come with a double bed and a shower (no tub). If you decide to bring your kids here—or to any other Kings Cross area hotel—keep in mind that they'll get an eyeful of prostitutes and sex bars on the way to and from the CityRail station. The two large superior rooms come with two single beds and two more that can be locked together to form a king, and a separate living room. One comes with a small kitchen with a microwave and hot plates. All rooms are very clean and comfortable and have private bathrooms. There is also a small guest lounge with a TV. A fully cooked breakfast is served up in the cafe below. Guests also receive 10% off meals at the adjoining Thai and Japanese steak house restaurants. Smoking is allowed in all rooms except the lounge. Flights of stairs and no elevator (lift) might make this a bad choice for older travelers or those with disabilities.

Victoria Court Sydney. 122 Victoria St., Potts Point, NSW 2011. ☎ **1800/ 630 505** in Australia or 02/9357 3200. Fax 02/9357 7606. www.victoriacourt.

com.au. E-mail: info@victoriacourt.com.au. 22 units. A/C TV TEL. A$99–$115 (U.S.$69.30–$80.50) double, depending on the season; A$165 (U.S.$115.50) deluxe double with sundeck; A$250 (U.S.$175) honeymoon suite with balcony. Rates include buffet breakfast. Extra person A$20 (U.S.$14). AE, BC, DC, MC, V. Free parking in secured lot. CityRail: Kings Cross.

This cute little place is made up of two 1881 terrace houses joined together; it's situated near a string of backpacker hostels and popular cafes in a leafy street running parallel to sleazy Darlinghurst Road. The glass-roofed breakfast room on the ground floor is a work of art decked out with hanging ferns, giant bamboo, wrought-iron tables and chairs, and a trickling fountain. Just off this is a peaceful guest lounge stacked with books and newspapers. The very plush rooms come with either king- or queen-size beds, but lack a tub in the bathroom. There's a coin-op laundry just down the road.

INEXPENSIVE

The Jolly Swagman Backpackers. 27 Orwell St., Kings Cross NSW 2011. ☎ **1800/805 870** in Australia or 02/9358 6400. Fax 02/9331 0125. www.jollyswagman.com.au. E-mail: stay@jollyswagman.com.au. 53 units A$14 (U.S.$9.80) dorm bed; A$20 (U.S.$14) per person in double. Ask about 3-day, 5-day, and weekly deals. MC, V. On-street metered parking. CityRail: Kings Cross.

This is one of the best backpacker hostels that dot the area between Darlinghurst Road and Victoria Street in Kings Cross. The good thing about this place is that it has two sister properties right nearby, so you are almost certain to get a room. The 18 dorm rooms in this property have only two sets of bunk beds in each, which means things don't get too crowded—and couples traveling together will often find they get the room to themselves. There are also plenty of twin and double rooms to go around, as well as two female-only dorms. The atmosphere is young and typical backpacker, with cheap meals (all under A$5/U.S.$3.50) served in the ground floor cafe. There's a guest kitchen, two TV rooms, a laundry, an ironing room, bag storage, free Foxtel movies, 24-hour Internet access, and a 24-hour travel agency. Each room is spotless and comes with a security locker.

6 In Paddington/Oxford Street

Oxford Koala Hotel. Corner of Oxford & Pelican sts., Darlinghurst (P.O. Box 535, Darlinghurst, NSW 2010). ☎ **1800/222 144** in Australia (outside Sydney) or 02/9269 0645. Fax 02/9283 2741. www.oxfordkoala. com.au. 330 units (including 78 apts.). A/C TV TEL. A$120–$140 (U.S. $84–$98) double; A$160 (U.S. $112) 1-bedroom apt. Extra person A$25

(U.S.$17.50). Children under 12 stay free in parents' room. AE, BC, DC, JCB, MC, V. Parking A$15 (U.S.$10.50). Bus: 380 or any bus traveling via Taylor Square.

You won't find many three-star hotels that offer as much value for your dollar as the Oxford Koala. A very popular tourist hotel, it is well placed just off trendy Oxford Street, a 5- to 10-minute bus trip from the city center and Circular Quay. There are 13 floors of rooms in this tower block; rooms on the top floor have reasonable views over the city. Superior rooms (A$140/U.S.$98) are very comfortable and more spacious than standard rooms and have better furniture. All come with a shower/tub combination or just a shower. Apartments are good-size, come with a full kitchen, and are serviced daily. On the premises are a swimming pool, a restaurant, and a cocktail bar.

Sullivans. 21 Oxford St., Paddington, NSW 2021. ☎ **02/9361 0211.** Fax 02/9360 3735. 64 units. A/C TV TEL. A$118 (U.S.$82.60) double. AE, BC, DC, MC, V. Limited free parking. Bus: 378, or 380 from Circular Quay.

About half of this boutique hotel's guests come from overseas, mainly from the United Kingdom and Europe, and the United States. There's also a small corporate following. Sullivans is right in the heart of the action in one of Sydney's most popular shopping, entertainment, restaurant, and gay pub and club areas. The hotel is particularly popular with Americans during the Gay and Lesbian Mardi Gras, held over the month of February. Rooms are cozy, with queen-size beds and a refrigerator; all have an en suite bathroom with a shower (no tub). There's free bicycle hire, a small swimming pool, and a garden courtyard.

Wattle Private Hotel. 108 Oxford St. (at corner of Palmer St.), Darlinghurst, NSW 2010. ☎ **02/9332 4118.** Fax 02/9331 2074. 12 units. A/C MINIBAR TV TEL. A$99 (U.S.$69.30) double. Extra person A$11 (U.S.$7.70). Rates include continental breakfast. BC, MC, V. No parking. Bus: Any to Taylor Square from Circular Quay.

This attractive Edwardian-style house built between 1900 and 1910 offers homey accommodations in the increasingly fashionable inner-city suburb of Darlinghurst, known for its great cafes, nightlife, and restaurants. Rooms are found on four stories, but there's no elevator (lift), so if you don't fancy too many stairs try to get a room on the lower floor. Rooms are smallish, but are opened up by large windows. Twin rooms have a better bathroom, with a tub. The decor is a jumble of Chinese vases, ceiling fans, and contemporary bedspreads. Laundry facilities are on the premises.

7 In Glebe

Alishan International Guest House. 100 Glebe Point Rd., Glebe, NSW 2037. ☎ **02/9566 4048**. Fax 02/9525 4686. 19 units. www.alishan.com.au. E-mail: kevin@alishan.com.au. TV. A$30 (U.S.$21) dorm bed; A$90 (U.S.$63) double; A$95 (U.S.$66.50) family room. Extra person A$15 (U.S.$10.50). AE, BC, MC, V. Secured parking available for 6 cars, otherwise free on-street parking. Bus: 431 or 433 from George Street, or Airport Express route 352 from airport.

The Alishan is another quiet place with a real Aussie feel. It's at the city end of Glebe Point Road, just 10 minutes by bus from the shops around Town Hall. Standard dorm rooms are spotless, light and bright, and come with two sets of bunks. Doubles have a double bed, a sofa and armchair, and an en suite shower. Grab room 9 if you fancy sleeping on one of two single mattresses on the tatami mat floor, Japanese-style. There's also a BBQ area, a TV room, a laundry, and Internet access.

✪ **Tricketts Luxury Bed & Breakfast.** 270 Glebe Point Rd., Glebe, NSW 2037. ☎ **02/9552 1141**. Fax 02/9692 9462. 7 units. A$140 (U.S.$98) double; A$175 (U.S.$122.50) honeymoon suite. Rates include continental breakfast. No credit cards. Free parking. Bus: 431 from George Street, or Airport Express bus 352 from airport.

As soon as I walked into this atmospheric old place, I wanted to ditch my modern Sydney apartment and move in. Your first impression as you enter the tessellated tiled corridor of this 1880s Victorian mansion is the amazing jumble of plants and ornaments, the high ceilings, the Oriental rugs, and the leaded windows. Guests play billiards over a decanter of port, or relax among magazines and wicker furniture on the balcony overlooking the fairly busy Glebe Point Road. The bedrooms are quiet and homey (no TVs). My favorites are number 2, with its wooden floorboards and king-size bed, and number 7, with its queen-size bed, extra single bed, and very large bathroom. Rooms all have showers. There's a nice courtyard out the back with a barbecue.

8 In Bondi

Bondi Beach is a good place to stay if you want to be close to the surf and sand, though if you're getting around by public transport you'll need to catch a bus to Bondi Junction, then a train to the city center (you can stay on the bus all the way, but it takes forever).

The Hotel Bondi. 178 Campbell Parade, Bondi Beach, NSW 2026. ☎ **02/ 9130 3271**. Fax 02/9130 7974. 50 units, 40 with bathroom. TV. A$100 (U.S.$70) double (all with bathroom); A$120–$150 (U.S.$84–$105) suite.

AE, BC, MC, V. Free secured parking. CityRail: Bondi Junction; then bus 380. Bus: 380 from Circular Quay or George St., or Airport Express bus 351 from airport.

This white-stucco Bondi landmark is adequate for a few days' stay if you don't mind the creaks of the vintage wooden elevator and the brusque front-desk service. The corridors are generally in need of a lick of paint, and the rooms are slightly disheveled, but overall it still retains a fairly healthy slap of 1920s grandeur. Double rooms are basic and small, with gray carpeting, a springy double bed, a shower, a small refrigerator, and a TV. The six suites are nicer, and have their own balconies looking out to sea. Downstairs there are seven bars, which frequently seem to attract aggressive drunks. Given the choice (Bondi hotels are often booked well in advance) I'd stay at the far friendlier Ravesi's on Bondi Beach (see below).

Ravesi's on Bondi Beach. Corner of Hall St. and Campbell Parade, Bondi Beach (P.O. Box 198, Bondi Junction, NSW 2022). ☎ **02/9365 4422.** Fax 02/ 9365 1481. 16 units. A/C TV TEL. A$105 (U.S.$73.50) standard double; A$160– $165 (U.S.$112–$115.50) double with side view; A$190 (U.S.$133) 1-bedroom suite; A$215 (U.S.$150.50) split-level 1-bedroom; A$190–$215 (U.S.$133– $150.50) 1-bedroom suite with ocean view. Extra person A$20 (U.S. $14). Two children under 12 stay free in parents' room. AE, BC, DC, MC, V. Parking at the Swiss-Grand Hotel nearby for A$5 (U.S.$3.50) for 24 hours. CityRail: Bondi Junction; then bus 380. Bus: 380 from Circular Quay.

Right on Australia's most famous golden sands, this art-deco boutique property offers Mediterranean-influenced rooms with a beachy decor. Standard doubles are spacious, quite basic, and don't have air-conditioning—though you hardly need it with the ocean breeze. The one-bedroom suite is good for families, with two sofa beds in the living room. The split-level one-bedroom room has a bedroom upstairs and a single sofa bed in the living area. Rooms 5 and 6 and the split-level suite have the best views of the ocean. All rooms have Juliet balconies, and the split-level suite has its own terrace. If you're a light sleeper, request a room on the top floor because the popular Ravesi's Restaurant can cook up quite a bit of noise on busy nights.

Swiss-Grand Hotel. Corner of Campbell Parade and Beach Rd. (P.O. Box 219, Bondi Beach, NSW 2026). ☎ **1800/655 252** in Australia, 800/344-1212 in the U.S., 0800/951 000 in the U.K., 0800/056 666 in New Zealand, or 02/9365 5666. Fax 02/9365 9710. 230 units. A$260 (U.S.$182) double, A$300 (U.S.$210) double with ocean view; A$320–$380 suite (U.S.$224–$399); A$570–$670 (U.S.$399–$469) premium suite. Extra person A$40 (U.S.$28). AE, BC, DC, MC, V. Free parking. Bus: 380 from Circular Quay.

Situated right on Bondi Beach, overlooking the Pacific, the Swiss-Grand is the best hotel in Bondi. The lobby is grand indeed, with high ceilings and stylish furniture. Rooms are spacious, and all come with a separate tub and shower in a rather luxurious bathroom. All rooms have two TVs; some have spas. All ocean-fronting rooms have balconies.

Dining: The Garden Terrace has good views over the beach, and the stylishly elegant Epic Brasserie offers an impressive buffet.

Amenities: Rooftop and indoor swimming pools, spa, fitness center.

9 In Manly

If you decide to stay at my favorite beachside suburb, keep in mind that the ferries from the city stop running at midnight. Taxi fare from the city is around A$30 (U.S.$21), or can catch a night bus from the stand behind Wynyard Station.

If you're looking for a super-cheap place to stay, consider the **Manly Backpackers Beachside,** 28 Ragland St., (☎ **02/ 9977 3411**), where a double with a bathroom goes for A$55 (U.S.$38.50); or the ✪ **Wharf Backpackers,** 48 East Esplanade (☎ **02/9977 2800**), opposite the ferry terminal, with doubles for A$40 (U.S.$28).

EXPENSIVE

✪ **Manly Pacific Parkroyal.** 55 North Steyne, Manly, NSW 2095. ☎ **800/ 835-7742** in the U.S. and Canada, or 02/9977 7666. Fax 02/9977 7822. 169 units. A/C MINIBAR TV TEL. A$250–$290 (U.S.$175–$203) double, depending on view; A$400–$440 (U.S.$280–$308) suite. Extra person A$25 (U.S.$17.50). AE, BC, DC, JCB, MC, V. Parking: $8 (U.S.$5.60). Ferry or JetCat: Manly.

If you could bottle the views from this top-class hotel—across the sand and through the Norfolk Island Pines to the Pacific Ocean— you'd make a fortune. Standing on your private balcony in the evening with the sea breeze in your nostrils and the chirping of hundreds of lorikeets is nothing short of heaven. The Manly Pacific is the only hotel of its class in this wonderful beachside suburb. There's nothing claustrophobic here, from the broad expanse of glittering foyer to the wide corridors and spacious rooms. Each standard room is light and modern with two double beds, a balcony, limited cable TV, and all the necessities from bathrobes to an iron and ironing board. Views over the ocean are really worth the extra money. The hotel is a 10-minute stroll, or an A$4 (U.S.$2.80) taxi ride, from the Manly ferry.

Dining/Diversions: Gilbert's Restaurant has fine dining and views of the Pacific. Nells Brasserie & Cocktail Bar serves a buffet breakfast and dinner daily. The Charlton Bar and Grill has live bands every evening from Wednesday to Sunday and attracts a young crowd.

Amenities: Rooftop spa, pool, gym, sauna, concierge, 24-hour room service, laundry.

MODERATE

Manly Lodge. 22 Victoria Parade, Manly, NSW 2095. ☎ **02/9977 8655.** Fax 02/9976 2090. 24 units. A/C TV. Standard double A$120–A$140 (U.S.$84–$98) peak season, A$98–$120 (U.S.$68.60–$84) off-season; deluxe double A$140–$180 (U.S.$98–$126) peak season, A$120–$140 (U.S.$84–$98) off-season; family suite with spa A$240–$300 (U.S.$168–$210) peak season, A$170–$240 (U.S.$119–$168) off-season. Peak season is Christmas, Easter, and school holidays. Rates include continental breakfast. Extra person A$28 (U.S.$19.60); children under 10 A$15 (U.S. $10.50) extra. Ask about weekly rates; management will also negotiate off-season prices. AE, BC, MC, V. Free parking. Ferry or JetCat: Manly.

At first sight, this ramshackle building halfway between the main beach and the harbor doesn't look like much—especially the cramped hostel-like foyer bristling with tourist brochures. But don't let the taint of tattiness put you off. Some of the rooms here are lovely, and the whole place has a nice atmosphere about it and plenty of character. Standard double rooms are not exceptional and come with a double bed, stone or carpet floors, a TV and VCR, a small kitchen area, and either a spa or a tub/shower combination. Family rooms have a set of bunk beds and a double in one room, and a shower. Family suites are very classy; each has a small kitchen area, one double and three singles in the bedroom, and two sofa beds in the living area. The lodge also has a communal spa, sauna, gym, laundry, table tennis, and even an Olympic-size trampoline.

Manly Paradise Motel and Beach Plaza Apartments. 54 North Steyne, Manly, NSW 2095. ☎ **1800/815 789** in Australia or 02/9977 5799. Fax 02/9977 6848. 40 units. A/C TV TEL. A$95–$145 (U.S.$66.50–$101.50) double motel unit; A$265 (U.S.$185.50) 2-bedroom apt. Extra person A$20 (U.S.$14). Ask about lower rates for long-term stays. AE, BC, DC, MC, V. Free secured parking. Ferry or JetCat: Manly.

I walked into this place after taking a good look around the modern Manly Waterfront Apartment Hotel next door and immediately felt more at home here. The motel and the apartment complex are separate, but share the same reception area. Though there is one motel room that goes for A$90 (U.S.$63), it's a bit small for my liking; the rest of the irregularly shaped rooms are big yet cozy, and come with a shower (no tub) and a springy double bed. Though there is no restaurant, you can get breakfast in bed. My only concern is that the traffic outside can make it a little noisy during the day. Some rooms have glimpses of the sea. A swimming pool (with views) on the roof is shared with the apartment complex.

The apartments are magnificent—very roomy, with thick carpets. They're stocked with everything you need, including a private laundry, a full kitchen with dishwasher, and two bathrooms (one with a tub). The sea views from the main front balcony are heart-stopping.

10 At the Airport

The two airport hotels listed below also accommodate guests for short-term stays between flights. Sample costs for the Sheraton are A$60 (U.S.$42) for two hours and A$70 (U.S.$49) for four hours.

Sheraton Sydney Airport Hotel. Corner of O'Riordan and Robey sts. (P.O. Box 353, Mascot, Sydney, NSW 2020). ☎ **1800/073 535** in Australia, 800/325-3535 in the U.S. and Canada, 0800/353 535 in the U.K., 0800/ 443 535 in New Zealand, or 02/9317 2200. Fax 02/9317 3855. 314 units. A/C MINIBAR TV TEL. A$240–$265 double (U.S.$168–$185.50); from A$390 (U.S.$273) and up for suites. Extra person A$25 (U.S.$17.50). Children under 17 stay free in parents' room. Ask about discount packages and weekend rates. AE, BC, DC, JCB, MC, V. A$5 (U.S.$3.50) self-parking fee for up to 10 days.

This is the best airport hotel. Opened in 1992, it has the largest rooms, each with a king-size bed or two doubles, in-house movies, access to airport information, and a good-size bathroom with tub. It's just seven minutes from the airport via a free pickup service. There's also a fine gym and a good outdoor swimming pool.

Sydney Airport Parkroyal. Corner of O'Riordan St. and Bourke Rd., Mascot, NSW 2020. ☎ **1800/621 859** in Australia or 02/9330 0600. Fax 02/ 9667 4517. 244 units. A/C MINIBAR TV TEL. A$185 (U.S.$129.50) double; A$390 (U.S.$273) suite. Extra person A$25 (U.S.$17.50). Children under 15 stay free in parents' room. Ask about special weekend rates and packages. AE, BC, DC, JCB, MC, V. Free parking.

The Parkroyal is a modern hotel with all the facilities you'd expect except a swimming pool. Rooms are of a moderate size, with either a king- or queen-size bed, in-house movies, and facilities to access the airport arrival and departure information. Free shuttle buses take five minutes to and from the airport.

5

Dining

Sydney is a gourmet paradise, with an abundance of fresh seafood, a vast range of vegetables and fruit always in season, prime meats at inexpensive prices, and top-quality chefs making international names for themselves. You'll find that Asian and Mediterranean cooking have had a major influence on Australian cuisine, with spices and herbs finding their way into most dishes. Immigration has brought with it almost every type of cuisine you could imagine, from African to Tibetan, from Russian to Vietnamese, with whole areas of the city dedicated to one type of food, while other areas are a true melting pot of styles.

Sydney is a great place to try "Modern Australian," or "Mod Oz," cuisine, which has been applauded by chefs and food critics around the world as one of the most important food trends going. Modern Australian cuisine emphasizes very fresh ingredients and a creative blend of simple European styles with touches of Asian influence. (Some foodies complain, however, that restaurants are using the label "Modern Australian" as an excuse to serve skimpy portions—like one lamb chop atop a miniscule mound of mashed potatoes.)

The Sydney dining world was turned on its head in 1999 when the new **Cockle Bay Wharf complex,** on the city-side of Darling Harbour, really began making its mark after its opening in late 1998. Leading the fabulous array of new restaurants are **Ampersand** (see section 4), and the Southern Mediterranean–influenced **Coast** (☎ 02/ 9267 6700). Other marvelous restaurants here include **Chinta Ria, The Temple of Love** (see section 4); the bustling **Blackbird** (☎ 02/ 9283 7385), a cafe with gourmet pizzas; the fiery south Indian **Tandoori Connection** (☎ 02/9283 6707); and the **Tiara Japanese Brasserie** (☎ 02/9264 5822).

Sydney's **cheap eats** are congregated in inner-city areas such as along King Street in Newtown, Crown Street in Darlinghurst, and Glebe Point Road in Glebe. There are also inexpensive joints scattered among the more upscale restaurants in Kings Cross and along trendy Oxford Street. There are some good food courts around Chinatown, including the **Sussex Street Food Court,** on Sussex

Central Sydney Dining

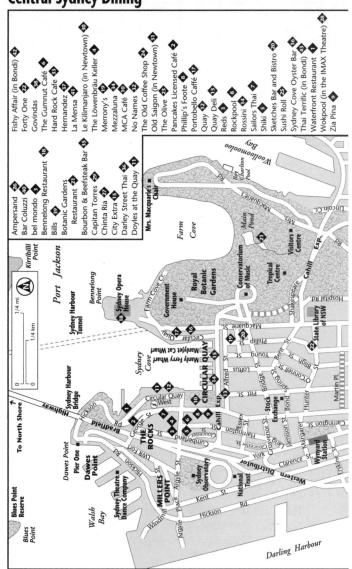

Ampersand 29
Bar Coluzzi 40
bel mondo 6
Bennelong Restaurant 18
Bills 39
Botanic Gardens
Restaurant 21
Bourbon & Beefsteak Bar 3
Capitan Torres 35
Chinta Ria 27
City Extra 15
Darley Street Thai 31
Doyles at the Quay 16

Fishy Affair (in Bondi) 42
Forty One 22
Govindas 41
The Gumnut Café 6
Hard Rock Café 33
Hernandez 37
La Mensa 38
Le Kilimanjaro (in Newtown) 4
The Löwenbräu Keller 1
Merrony's 24
Mezzaluna 34
MCA Café 12
No Names 32

The Old Coffee Shop 23
Old Saigon (in Newtown) 36
The Olive 11
Pancakes Licensed Café 2
Phillip's Foote 8
Portobello Caffé 17
Quay 12
Quay Deli 13
Reds 8
Rockpool 9
Rossini 14
Sailors Thai 7
Shiki 11
Sketches Bar and Bistro 20
Sushi Roll 25
Sydney Cove Oyster Bar 19
Thai Terrific (in Bondi) 10
Waterfront Restaurant 5
Wokpool (in the IMAX Theatre) 28
Zia Pina 9

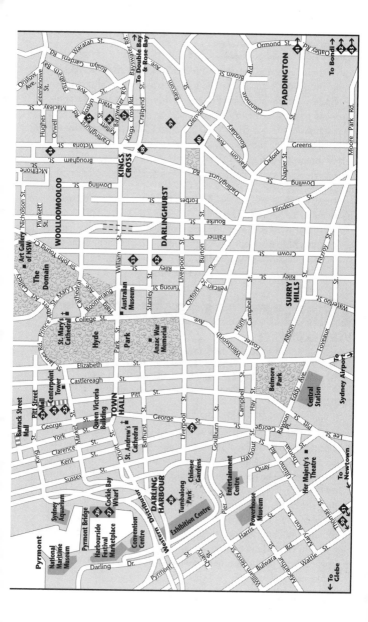

101

What to Know about BYO

Most moderate and inexpensive restaurants in Sydney are **BYO,** as in "bring your own" bottle, though some places may also have extensive wine and beer lists of their own. More and more moderately priced restaurants are introducing "corkage" fees, which mean you pay anywhere from A\$1 to \$4 (U.S.70¢ to \$2.80) per person for the privilege of the waiter opening your bottle of wine. Very expensive restaurants discourage BYO.

Street, which offers Chinese, Malay, Thai, Japanese, and Vietnamese meals for between A\$4 and A\$7 (U.S.\$2.80 and U.S.\$4.90).

I would avoid the takeout booths settled among the ferry wharves at Circular Quay; recent revelations showed that some of them harbor nasty bugs. **Quay Seafoods,** the fish-and-chip shop opposite the bottle shop is an exception; it serves up some of the best French fries in Sydney.

1 Near Circular Quay

VERY EXPENSIVE

Bennelong Restaurant. In the Sydney Opera House, Bennelong Point. ☎ **02/9250 7548** or 02/9250 7578. Reservations recommended. Main courses A\$30–\$37 (U.S.\$21–\$25.90). AE, BC, DC, MC, V. Fri noon–2:30pm; Mon–Sat 7–10:30pm. CityRail, bus, or ferry: Circular Quay. MODERN AUSTRALIAN.

If you go to Bondi, you have to swim in the Pacific; if you see the Harbour Bridge, you have to walk across it; if you visit the Opera House, you have to eat at the Bennelong—that's if by the time you get there the arrogant service I keep hearing about has been dispensed with. The restaurant is as uniquely designed as the building itself, with tall glass windows furrowing around in an arch and grabbing the harbor and Circular Quay by the throat. Diners munch on main course such as roasted tuna steak and roasted tomato with tomato-and-chili jam, or red emperor with sweet and sour eggplant baked in clay. Many patrons would rather miss the first half of the opera they've paid a fortune to see rather than leave the Bennelong before eating dessert.

✪ **Forty One.** Level 41, Chifley Tower, 2 Chifley Sq. ☎ **02/9221 2500.** Reservations required. Lunch main courses Mon–Fri A\$28 (U.S.\$19.60). Sun lunch: 3 courses A\$70 (U.S.\$49), 4 courses A\$80 (U.S.\$56), 5 courses A\$90 (U.S.\$63). Mon–Sat dinner: 3 courses A\$75 (U.S.\$52.50), 4 courses A\$85 (U.S.\$59.50),

A Word about Smoking

Smoking is allowed in the vast majority of Sydney's restaurants, but if you do light up you'll find you won't be the most popular person in the place. Some restaurants have a no-smoking section.

5 courses A$95 (U.S.$66.50). AE, BC, DC, MC, V. Sun–Fri noon–4pm; Mon–Sat 6:30pm–late. CityRail: Wynyard. MODERN AUSTRALIAN.

Powerful people, international celebrities, and average Sydneysiders out for a special celebration all come here to feel exclusive. It's won some 32 awards from 1994 to 1998 for its cooking, including the Restaurant and Catering Association's best Restaurant Award, Sydney 1998. The views over the city are terrific, the service is fun, the cutlery is the world's best, and Swiss chef Dietmar Sawyere has given the food a wickedly good Asian slant. In all, it's a very glamorous place to experience the best of Australian cuisine. Try the specialty crown roast wild hare, with braised Belgian endive and chartreuse jus. The seared yellowfin tuna on sesame and miso English spinach is another favorite. If there are 6 to 10 people in your group, rent one of the three special private dining rooms.

Merrony's. 2 Albert St., Circular Quay. ☎ **02/9247 9323.** Reservations recommended for lunch any day and dinner Fri–Sat. Main courses A$28–$34 (U.S.$19.60–$23.80). AE, BC, DC, MC, V. Mon–Fri noon–2:30pm; Mon–Sat 5:45pm–11pm. Closed public holidays. CityRail, bus, or ferry: Circular Quay. MODERN AUSTRALIAN.

Come here for great views across Sydney Harbour toward the Harbour Bridge and the highly acclaimed bistro-style food from master chef Paul Merrony. The signature dishes are the grilled sirloin with marrowbone and the veal fillet with roast beetroot, garlic, and spinach. The blue-eyed cod with saffron-braised potatoes and a tomato sauce is a fine meal. Follow the locals by coming here before or after a show at the Opera House. The wine list is extensive. If you need to drive, the restaurant has a parking arrangement with the adjacent Ritz-Carlton hotel for A$5 (U.S.$3.50).

EXPENSIVE

Botanic Gardens Restaurant. In the Royal Botanic Gardens. ☎ **02/9241 2419.** Reservations recommended. Main courses A$18–$25 (U.S.$12.60–$17.50). AE, BC, DC, MC, V. Daily noon–2:30pm. Bus or ferry: Circular Quay. MEDITERRANEAN.

You couldn't ask for a better walk to get to a restaurant than through the Royal Botanic Gardens, next to the Sydney Opera House.

Enjoying lunch on the wisteria-covered balcony in the middle of Sydney's most beautiful park is a treat every visitor should enjoy. Main courses include the very popular roast loin of lamb with warm salad and couscous. Just reminiscing about the desserts, such as the rhubarb compote with zabaglione and shortbread, makes my mouth water.

Sydney Cove Oyster Bar. No. 1 Eastern Esplanade, Circular Quay East. ☎ **02/9247 2937.** Main courses A$20–$23.50 (U.S.$14–$16.45). 10% surcharge weekends and public holidays. AE, BC, DC, MC, V. Mon–Sat 11am–11pm, Sun 11am–8pm. CityRail, bus or ferry: Circular Quay. SEAFOOD.

Just before you reach the Sydney Opera House you'll notice a couple of small shedlike buildings with tables and chairs set up to take in the stunning views of the harbor and the Harbour Bridge. The first of these buildings is a Sydney institution, serving some of the best oysters in town. Light meals such as Asian-style octopus and seared tuna steak are also on the menu.

MODERATE

City Extra. Shop E4, Circular Quay. ☎ **02/9241 1422.** Main courses A$10.30–$17.65 (U.S.$7.20–$12.35). 10% surcharge midnight–6am, Sundays, and public holidays. Daily 24 hours. AE, BC, DC, MC, V. CityRail, bus, or ferry: Circular Quay. ITALIAN/AUSTRALIAN.

Because this place stays open 24 hours, it's convenient if you get the munchies at a ridiculous hour. It's also nicely placed right next to the Manly ferry terminal. The plastic chairs and tables placed outside make it a pleasant spot to while away an inexpensive meal. A range of pastas are on offer as well as salads, pies, steaks, ribs, fish, and Asian-influenced dishes. There's also a fat selection of deserts. That said, I agree with several friends of mine who believe the food is much nicer and a better value next door at Rossini (see below).

✪ **MCA Café.** Museum of Contemporary Art, Circular Quay West. ☎ **02/9241 4253.** Main courses A$19–$20 (U.S.$13.30–$14). 10% surcharge weekends and public holidays. AE, BC, DC, MC, V. Daily noon–2:30pm. CityRail, bus, or ferry: Circular Quay. SEAFOOD.

If you find yourself sitting at one of the 16 outside tables here, count yourself as one of the most fortunate people lunching in Sydney. The views over the ferries and the Opera House are wonderful, and you are far enough away from the crowds at Circular Quay to watch the action without feeling a spectacle yourself. Whether you sit outside or in, the food is great. Eighty percent of the dishes are seafood, but there are some pasta and meat dishes on the menu. The signature dishes are the trevally with a lemon, olive, and parsley salad, and the smoked salmon lasagna with eggplant caviar.

Sketches Bar and Bistro. In the Hotel Inter-Continental, 117 Macquarie St. (enter from Bridge St.). ☎ **02/9240 1210.** Reservations recommended. Pasta A$10.90–$17 (U.S.$7.65–$11.90). AE, BC, DC, MC, V. Mon–Fri 5:30–9:30pm, Sat 5:30–10:30pm. CityRail, bus, or ferry: Circular Quay. PASTA.

Sketches is a favorite with people on their way to the Opera House and those who really know a good cheap meal when they taste one. Here's how it works: After getting the barman's attention, point to one of three different sized plates stuck to the bar above your head—the small size is adequate if you're an average eater, the medium plate is good for filling up after a hard day of sightseeing (and no lunch), but I've yet to meet a man who can handle the large serving with its accompanying bread, pine nuts, and parmesan cheese. Then, with ticket in hand, head toward the chefs in white hats and place your order. There are 12 pastas to choose from and several sauces, including carbonara, marinara, pesto, vegetarian, and some unusual ones to dishearten pasta purists, such as south Indian curry. Meals are cooked in a few minutes while you wait.

INEXPENSIVE

✪ **Freckle Face Café.** 32A Burton St., Kirribilli. ☎ **02/9957 2116.** Main courses A$6.50 (U.S.$4.55) eat in, A$5.90 (U.S.$4.15) takeout. No credit cards. Mon–Sat 7am–4pm. CityRail or ferry: Milsons Point. Take the left exit from the Milsons Point CityRail station, walk downhill to the traffic lights, cross the road, and it's in the street opposite. CAFE.

There's no better to place to refuel after a walk across the Harbour Bridge than this intimate cafe near the Milsons Point CityRail station on the north side of Sydney Harbour. Freckle Face specializes in sandwiches, bagels, Turkish bread, foccacia, and very good coffee. The smoked salmon, baby spinach, and cream cheese on toasted Turkish bread is one of my favorites, and the biscuits and cakes (especially the flourless orange and almond cake) are gorgeous. There are good breakfasts here for A$6.90 (U.S.$4.85), including fruit salads, muesli, fruit bread, and egg dishes. Everything is made on the premises. The staff is very friendly, so say hello to Jackie and Victoria—two freckle-faced sisters.

Portobello Caffé. No.1 Eastern Esplanade, Circular Quay East. ☎ **02/9247 8548.** Main courses A$8 (U.S. $5.60). 10% surcharge Sundays and public holidays. AE, BC, DC, JCB, MC, V. Minimum credit card purchase A$30 (U.S.$21). Daily 8am–11:50pm. CityRail, bus, or ferry: Circular Quay. PIZZA/ SANDWICH.

Sharing the same address as the Sydney Cove Oyster Bar (and the same priceless views), the Portobello Caffé offers first-class gourmet sandwiches on Italian wood-fired bread, small but delicious gourmet pizzas, breakfast croissants, snacks, cakes, and hot and cold drinks.

Walk off with sensational ice cream in a cone for around A$3 (U.S.$2.10).

Quay Deli. E5 Alfred St. (next to the pharmacy underneath the Circular Quay CityRail station). ☎ **02/9241 3571.** Menu items A$1.80–$4.50 (U.S.$1.25–$3.15). No credit cards. Mon–Fri 5am–6:45pm, Sat 9am–4pm. DELI.

If you're looking for a sandwich or something to take with you on a harbor cruise or on your walk through the Royal Botanic Gardens then you can't go wrong buying it here. Everything is fresh and tasty, and there are all sorts of goodies to choose from, including gourmet sandwiches and simple take-away foods such as olives, Greek dishes, pasta, fruit salads, green salads, homemade rissoles, meat, pies and the best English-style custard tarts around. The shop also carries a stock of biscuits, tea, coffee, and other supplies. Plenty of tourists simply buy a couple of fresh bread rolls and a piece of cheese from here, pick up a bottle of wine from the bottle shop just around the corner, and then take off somewhere for a cheerful meal.

✪ **Rossini.** Shop W5, Circular Quay. ☎ **02/9247 8026.** Main courses A$7–$14 (U.S.$4.90–$9.80). Cash only. Daily 7am–10pm. CityRail, bus, or ferry: Circular Quay. ITALIAN.

This cafeteria-style Italian restaurant opposite ferry wharf 5 at Circular Quay is wonderfully positioned for people watching. The outside tables are perfect spots for breakfast or a quick bite before a show at the Opera House. Breakfast croissants, Italian donuts, muffins, and gorgeous Danish pastries cost just A$2 (U.S. $1.40), and bacon and eggs just A$8 (U.S. $5.60). Wait to be seated for dinner, make your choice, pay your money at the counter, take a ticket, and then pick up your food. Meals, including veal parmigiana, cannelloni, ravioli, chicken crêpes, and octopus salad, are large and tasty. Coffee fanatics I know rate the Rossini brew as only average.

2 In The Rocks

VERY EXPENSIVE

bel mondo. 3rd floor in the Argyle Department Store, 18–24 Argyle St., The Rocks. ☎ **02/9241 3700.** Reservations recommended well in advance. Main courses A$33–$39 (U.S.$23.10–$27.30). 10% surcharge Sun and public holidays. AE, BC, DC, MC, V. Mon–Fri noon–2:30pm; Mon–Thurs 6:30–10:30pm, Fri–Sat 6:30–11pm, Sun 6:30–10pm. CityRail, bus, or ferry: Circular Quay. NORTHERN ITALIAN.

With its uncomplicated northern Italian cuisine, bel mondo has deservedly positioned itself alongside the very best of Sydney's upscale restaurants. At this family-run affair, chef Stefano Manfredi is

Dining in The Rocks

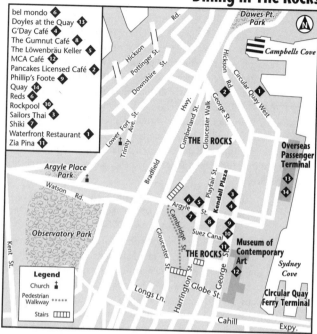

bel mondo 6
Doyles at the Quay 13
G'Day Café 4
The Gumnut Café 8
The Löwenbräu Keller 5
MCA Café 12
Pancakes Licensed Café 2
Phillip's Foote 9
Quay 14
Reds 6
Rockpool 10
Sailors Thai 3
Shiki 7
Waterfront Restaurant 1
Zia Pina 11

helped out in the kitchen by his mum, Franca, a pasta diva in her own right. The restaurant is large and long with high ceilings, and the energetic pace and the banging and clashing coming from the open kitchen give the place a New York feel. Standout appetizers include grilled sea scallops with soft polenta and pesto. Favorite main courses include roast suckling pig cutlets with beans and olives, and roast pigeon with Italian couscous and potato. The wine list is very extensive. bel mondo's **Antibar** is cheaper and more relaxed; it offers a good selection of antipasto and lighter meals and features jazz on Friday evenings from 5:30 to 7:30pm.

✪ **Quay.** On the upper level of the Overseas Passenger Terminal, Circular Quay West, The Rocks. ☎ **02/9251 5600.** Reservations recommended well in advance. Main courses A$40–$50 (U.S.$28–$35). A$6 (U.S.$4.20) per person surcharge Sun and public holidays. AE, BC, DC, JCB, MC, V. Mon–Fri noon–3pm; Mon–Sun 6–10pm. CityRail, bus, or ferry: Circular Quay. SEAFOOD.

Without question, Quay (formerly known as Bilson's) is Sydney's best fish and seafood restaurant—and with its enviable location on top of the cruise-ship terminal, it offers perhaps the loveliest view in

Sydney, too. In good weather the sun sparkles off the water and through the large glass windows the Opera House, the city skyline, the North Shore suburbs, and the Harbour Bridge all look magnificent. At night, when the lights from the city wash over the harbor and the bridge and the Opera House's sails are all lit up, the view is even better. The signature dishes are the basil-infused tuna, the Kangaroo Island roast chicken with ravioli and truffles (which the *Sydney Morning Herald* named the city's best dish in 1999), and the popular char-grilled beef tenderloin on mashed potatoes. The service is exemplary. Expensive, yet select, this restaurant has tempted all the big-name visitors to Sydney. Believe me, they tell all their friends.

✪ **Rockpool.** 109 George St., The Rocks. ☎ **02/9252 1888.** Reservations required. Main courses A$38 (U.S.$26.60). AE, BC, DC, MC, V. Mon–Sat 6–11pm. CityRail, bus, or ferry: Circular Quay. MODERN AUSTRALIAN.

The Rockpool is an institution in Sydney, known for its inventive food. It's approached by a steep ramp and opens up into two stories of ocean-green carpet, designer chairs, and stainless steel. Along with the bar, the kitchen—with its busy chefs and range of copper pots and pans—is very much at the center of things. Menus change regularly, but you can expect to find anything from a dozen fresh oysters and spanner crab with lemon ravioli to fish cooked with coconut milk and Indian garam masala and served with snow peas and semolina noodles. On my last visit, the desserts were a letdown after the fabulous main courses.

EXPENSIVE

Doyles at the Quay. Overseas Passenger Terminal, Circular Quay. ☎ **02/9252 3400.** Main courses A$20–$33 (U.S.$14–$23.10). BC, DC, JCB, MC, V. Daily 11:30am–2:45pm; Mon–Sat 5:30–9:30pm,, Sun 5:30–9pm. CityRail, bus, or ferry: Circular Quay. SEAFOOD.

Just below Quay (see above) is Doyles, a name synonymous with seafood in Sydney. Most customers sit outside to enjoy the fabulous views across the harbor, though a set of thick green railings does somewhat interrupt the view of the Opera House. Businesspeople and tourists come here if they don't want to lay out the cash for Quay or if they fancy a more relaxed style. The most popular dish here is basically pricey fish-and-chips (choose between ocean trout, garfish, John Dory, swordfish, whiting, and salmon). You can also pick up a dozen oysters for A$20 (U.S.$14) or a lobster for A$65 (U.S.$45.50). A second Doyles, **Doyles on the Beach** (☎ **02/9337 2007**), at Watsons Bay, serves fabulous food. Nearby is a third

Doyles, **Doyles Fisherman's Wharf** (☎ **02/9337 1572**), located on the ferry wharf; it used to be a take-out joint, but now has sit-down service.

Reds. Next to the Argyle Department Store, 12 Argyle St., The Rocks. ☎ **02/9247 1011**. Reservations recommended. Main courses A$24–$49.50 (U.S.$16.80–$34.65). AE, BC, DC, MC, V. Daily noon–3pm and 5–10pm. CityRail, bus, or ferry: Circular Quay. MODERN AUSTRALIAN.

Revamped from its days as a barbecue restaurant, Reds is located in an 1828 bond store and warehouse. The light and airy dining area has a beachy feel. Light jazz trickles over the lemon-and-tangerine carpets to a bar area heaving with wooden beams. Contemporary starters include Sydney rock oysters and scallops with angel-hair pasta, while you'll find char-grilled kangaroo strip loin with sweet potato on the limited selection of main courses. Native herbs, nuts and berries, and exotic dairy produce are also featured. The food is really great, and the chef has to be highly commended, but last time I ate here for lunch, the service left much to be desired.

Shiki. Clock Tower Square, corner of Argyle and Harrington sts., The Rocks. ☎ **02/9252 2431**. Reservations recommended well in advance. Meals around A$30 (U.S.$21) per person. AE, BC, DC, JCB, MC, V. Mon–Fri noon–2:30pm; Mon–Sun 6–10pm. TRADITIONAL JAPANESE.

Shiki is making a name for itself as a top-flight traditional Japanese eatery. Though you can eat at Western-style tables, or the sushi bar, there are also five tatami rooms available, where you sit around a raised table on Japanese mats. Either way you can enjoy some good views over The Rocks (it's especially magical at night when the ferry lights strung across the area's trees are lit up). There is plenty of sushi, sashimi, and sukiyaki dishes on the menu, but "pot-cooking" at the table is very popular. Of these the Tobanyaki, where customers simmer a combination of beef and seafood on their own burner, steals the show. If you want your main meal during the day, consider the lunch menu, costing between A$13.50 (U.S.$9.45) and A$20 (U.S.$14). The sushi plate—with seven pieces of sushi, six pieces of tuna roll, a salad, and miso soup—costs A$20 (U.S.$14).

Waterfront Restaurant. In Campbell's Storehouse, 27 Circular Quay West, The Rocks. ☎ **02/9247 3666**. Reservations recommended. Main courses A$23.90–$42.50 (U.S.$16.75–$29.75). A$3 (U.S.$2.10) per person surcharge weekends and public holidays. AE, BC, DC, JCB, MC, V. Daily 11am–10pm. CityRail, bus, or ferry: Circular Quay.

You can't help but notice the mast, rigging, and sailing ship sails that mark this restaurant in the line of four right next to the water below the main spread of The Rocks. It's very popular at lunchtime when businesspeople snap up the best seats outside in the sunshine, but at night with the colors of the city washing over the harbor it can be magical. Most main courses cost a hefty A$25 (U.S.$17.50) or so, but for that you get a choice of such things as steaks, mud crab, fish fillets, prawns, or a seafood platter. The food is nice and simple, with the markup added for the glorious position and views.

In the same building you'll find the Waterfront's sister restaurants **Wolfie's Grill** (☎ **02/9241 5577**), which serves good char-grilled beef and seafood dishes for A$22 to $26 (U.S.$15.40 to $18.20), and **The Italian Village** (☎ **02/9247 6111**), which serves regional Italian cuisine for A$22 to $30 (U.S.$15.40 to $21). The third in the line is an excellent Chinese restaurant, the ✪ **Imperial Peking** (☎ **02/9247 7073**), which serves excellent food for similar prices. All four restaurants offer fantastic water views and indoor and outdoor dining.

MODERATE

The Löwenbräu Keller. 18 Argyle St. (at Playfair St.), The Rocks. ☎ **02/ 9247 7785.** Reservations recommended. Main courses A$15–$21.50 (U.S. $10.50–$15.05). AE, BC, DC, JCB, MC, V. Daily 9:30am–2am (kitchen closes at 11pm.) CityRail, bus, or ferry: Circular Quay. BAVARIAN.

Renowned for celebrating Oktoberfest every day for the past 20 years, this is the place to come to watch Aussies let their hair down. You can come for lunch and munch a club sandwich or focaccia in the glassed-off atrium while watching the daytime action of The Rocks. For a livelier scene, head here on a Friday or Saturday night, when mass beer-sculling (chugging) and yodeling are accompanied by a brass band, and costumed waitresses ferry foaming beer steins about the atmospheric, cellarlike bowels. Hearty southern German and Austrian fare and no less than 17 varieties of German beers in bottle or on draught (tap), are served. There's a good wine list, and, surprisingly, vegetarians are well catered for, too.

Pancakes Licensed Café. 10 Hickson Rd. (enter from Hickson Rd. or George St.), The Rocks. ☎ **02/9247 6371.** Reservations not accepted. Main courses A$12.95–$21.95 (U.S.$9.10–$15.35); breakfast (served 24 hours) A$8.95– $11.95 (U.S.$6.25–$8.35). AE, BC, DC, JCB, MC, V. Daily 24 hours. CityRail, bus, or ferry: Circular Quay. AMERICAN COFFEESHOP FARE/PANCAKES.

Buttermilk and chocolate pancakes, and French crêpes filled with seafood, chicken and mushrooms, vegetables in a basil-cream sauce, or smoked ham and cheese are the most popular dishes served up in this old warehouse done up in art-deco style. The beef ribs, pastas, and pizzas are also good sellers.

Phillip's Foote. 101 George St., The Rocks. ☎ **02/9241 1485.** Main courses A$20 (U.S.$14). AE, BC, JCB, MC, V. Mon–Sat noon–midnight, Sun noon–10pm. CityRail, bus, or ferry: Circular Quay. BARBECUE.

Venture behind this historic pub and you'll find a popular courtyard strung with tables and benches and large barbecues. Choose your own steak, lemon sole, trout, chicken, or pork and throw it on the "barbie." It's fun, it's filling, and you might even meet some new friends while your meal's sizzling.

Sailors Thai. 106 George St., The Rocks. ☎ **02/9251 2466.** Reservations required well in advance in restaurant; not accepted in canteen. Main courses A$14–$34 (U.S. $9.80–$23.80) in restaurant, A$11–$16 (U.S.$7.70–$11.20) in canteen. AE, BC, DC, MC, V. Restaurant Mon–Fri noon–2pm, Mon–Sat 6pm–10pm; canteen daily noon–8pm. CityRail, bus, or ferry: Circular Quay. THAI.

With a reputation as hot as the chilies in its jungle curry, Sailors Thai canteen attracts lunchtime crowds who come to eat noodles, clams, curries, and Thai salads at its single, stainless steel table lined with some 40 chairs. Four other tables overlook the cruise ship terminal and the quay. Downstairs, the a la carte restaurant serves simple and cutting-edge food, like a pineapple curry of mussels and steamed duck soup with pickles.

Zia Pina. 93 George St., The Rocks. ☎ **02/9247 2255.** Reservations recommended well in advance. Main courses A$7.80–$19 (U.S.$5.50–$13.30). AE, BC, DC, JCB, MC, V. Daily noon–3pm; Sun–Mon 5–9pm, Tues–Thurs 5–10:30pm, Fri–Sat 5–11:30pm. CityRail, bus, or ferry: Circular Quay. PIZZA/PASTA.

With 10 tables crammed downstairs and another 24 upstairs, there's not much room to breathe in this cramped traditional pizzeria and spaghetti house. But squeeze in between the close-fit bare-brick walls and wallow in the clashes and clangs coming from the hard-working chefs in the kitchen. Pizzas come in two sizes; the larger feeds two people. Servings of delicious gelato go for a cool A$4 (U.S.$2.80).

INEXPENSIVE

G'Day Café. 83 George St., The Rocks. ☎ **02/9241 3644.** Main courses A$2–$6 (U.S.$1.40–$4.20). AE. Sun–Thurs 5am–midnight, Fri–Sat 5am–3am. CityRail, bus or ferry: Circular Quay. CAFE.

According to the manager, about half the tourists who visit Sydney visit this little place in the heart of The Rocks. That's not surprising considering it offers simple but satisfying food at around half the price you'd expect to pay in such a tourist precinct. The interior is uninspiring, but out the back there's a pleasant leafy courtyard. Among the offerings are foccacia sandwiches, hearty soups, salads, burgers, lasagne, chili con carne, and beef curry.

The Gumnut Cafe. 28 Harrington St., The Rocks. ☎ **02/9247 9591.** Main courses A$6.90–$13 (U.S.$4.85–$9.10). AE, BC, DC, MC, V. Daily 8am–5pm. CityRail, bus, or ferry: Circular Quay. MODERN AUSTRALIAN.

A hearty lunch in a courtyard shaded from the sun by giant cream umbrellas—ah, heaven. With a great location in the heart of The Rocks, this restaurant also has an extensive indoor seating area, so it's a perfect place to take a break from all that sightseeing. The breakfast specials (A$7.90/U.S.$5.55) are very popular with guests from surrounding hotels, while at lunchtime it's always bustling with tourists and local office workers. Lunchtime blackboard specials cost A$10 (U.S. $7). More regular fare includes the disappointing Ploughman's Lunch (why spoil a traditional English meal of bread, cheese, and pickles by limiting the bread and adding unappealing vegetables and salad?), the better chicken and leek pies, and pasta and noodle dishes. Filling Turkish bread sandwiches cost between A$6.90 and $8.20 (U.S.$4.85 and 5.75). The courtyard is heated in winter, making it quite cozy.

3 Near Town Hall

✪ **Capitan Torres.** 73 Liverpool St., (just past the cinema strip on George St., near Town Hall). ☎ **02/9264 5574.** Main courses A$16.50–$19 (U.S.$11.55–$13.30); tapas A$5–$9 (U.S.$3.50–$6.30). AE, BC, DC, JCB, MC, V. Daily noon–3pm; Mon–Sat 6–11pm, Sun 6–10pm. CityRail: Town Hall. SPANISH.

Sydney's Spanish quarter, based on Liverpool Street (a 10-minute walk from Town Hall station and just past Sydney's main cinema strip) offers some great restaurants, of which Capitan Torres is my favorite. Downstairs is a tapas bar with traditional stools, Spanish serving staff, and lots of authentic dark oak. Upstairs on two floors is a fabulous restaurant with heavy wooden tables and chairs and an atmosphere thick with sangria and regional food. The garlic prawns are incredible, and the whole snapper a memorable experience. The tapas are better, though, at **Asturiana** (☎ **02/9264 1010**), another Spanish restaurant a couple of doors down on the same street.

The Olive. Shop 18, Strand Arcade. ☎ **02/9231 2962.** Main courses A$4–$6.30 (U.S.$2.80–$4.40). Cash only. Mon–Sat 6am–4pm. CityRail, bus, or monorail: Town Hall. ITALIAN/SANDWICHES.

This tiny little sandwich shop in the Strand Arcade, just of the Pitt Street Mall between Town Hall and the AMP Centerpoint Tower, is a tasty lunch option if you find yourself in the city. You can feast on authentic Italian pastas and pizzas, focaccias, and spicy rissoles, or gourmet sandwiches filling enough to last you through a hectic afternoon of sightseeing.

Something Fishy

If you like fresh seafood at cheap prices, then saunter down to the **Sydney Fishmarket,** on the corner of Bank Street and Pyrmont Bridge Road, Pyrmont (☎ **02/9660 1611,** or call the **Fishline** at ☎ **02/9552 2180** for information on special events such as sea-food cooking classes). The major fish retailers here sell sashimi at the cheapest prices in Sydney, but if you prefer your seafood cooked then don't miss out on these two fabulous outlets.

First off there's **Musumeci Seafoods,** found outside the large blue retail arcade. It's little more than a stall with a hotplate, but you won't find baby octopus cooked better in any of Sydney's glitzy restaurants. Seafood combinations are also offered, with a small plate (easily enough for one person) costing just A$5 (U.S.$3.50), and a large plate A$10 (U.S.$7). Musumeci's is open Friday and Sunday from 7am to 4pm and Saturday from 6am to 4pm.

Also mouthwatering are the stir-fries at nearby **Christies,** a seafood retailer inside the main retail building. Here you pick your own seafood, such as fresh calamari or mussels, and your own sauce, and they just throw it straight in a wok and cook it for you on the spot. Stir-fries or great Asian-style seafood noodle dishes cost just A$5 (U.S.$3.50). Christies cooks are on the job daily from 7am to 7pm.

To get to the Fishmarket, take the light rail (tram) from Central Station, Chinatown, or Darling Harbour to the Fishmarket stop, or you can walk from Darling Harbour (follow the signs).

✪ **Sushi Roll.** Sydney Central Plaza (downstairs in the food hall next to Grace Brothers dept. store on Pitt Street Mall). ☎ **02/9233 5561.** Sushi rolls A$1.50 (U.S.$1.05) each. No credit cards. Mon–Wed and Sat 8am–7pm, Thurs 8am–10pm, Sun 10am–6pm. SUSHI.

The fresh and simple food served up at this bargain-basement take-out booth is certainly a healthy alternative to the greasy edibles with which many travelers end up satisfying their hunger. A large range of sushi dishes peek out from behind the counter here, each one virtually a meal in itself for the price of a donut. Sit at the tables provided.

4 At Darling Harbour & Cockle Bay Wharf

✪ **Ampersand.** Cockle Bay Wharf Complex. ☎ **02/9264 6666.** Reservations essential. Main courses A$32–$39.50 (U.S.$22.40–$27.65). AE, BC, DC, MC, V.

Mon–Fri noon–3pm, Mon–Sat 6–11pm. Monorail or ferry: Darling Harbour.
MODERN AUSTRALIAN.

The upscale Ampersand was an immediate hit following its opening in late 1998. It's the premier restaurant at the new Cockle Bay
Wharf development on the city side of Darling Harbour. Its team
of world-renowned chefs is lead by Sydney icon Tony Bilson. The
food can be stunning and reflects Bilson's views on using the finest
and freshest ingredients. The restaurant itself is light and contemporary and has sparkling views across the harbor. Sample dishes
include the confit of ocean trout with prawn cannelloni and the
spiced duck breast with quince mousseline.

✪ **Chinta Ria, The Temple of Love.** Cockle Bay Wharf Complex.
☎ **02/9264 3211.** Main courses A$12–$25 (U.S.$8.40–$17.50). AE, BC, DC,
MC, V. Daily noon–2:30pm and 6–11pm. Ferry or monorail: Darling Harbour.
MALAYSIAN.

Cockle Bay's star attraction for those who appreciate good food and
a fun ambiance without paying a fortune, Chinta Ria is on the roof
terrace of the three-story Cockle Bay development. In a round building dominated by a giant golden Buddha in the center, Chinta Ria
serves up fairly good "hawker-style" (read: cheap and delicious)
Malaysian food. While the food is indeed good, the atmosphere is
even more memorable. The service is slow, but who cares in such an
interesting space, with plenty of nooks and crannies and society folk
to look at. There are seats outside (some get the noise of the highway), but the best views unfold inside. The hot-and-sour soup—a
broth made with tofu, mushrooms, bamboo shoots, and preserved
cabbage—makes an interesting starter, and I recommend the chili
prawns and the *Hokkeien Char* (soft-cooked egg noodles with extras)
as main dishes.

Wockpool. Imax Theatre, Southern Promenade, Darling Harbour. ☎ **02/
9211 9888.** Main courses upstairs A$22–$38 (U.S.$15.40–$26.60); noodle-bar
dishes A$8–$16 (U.S.$5.60–$11.20). AE, BC, DC, MC, V. Daily noon–3pm, Sun–
Thurs 6–10pm, Fri–Sat 6–11pm. Ferry: Darling Harbour. Monorail: Convention
Center. MODERN ASIAN.

The best restaurant with the best views in Darling Harbour, this
adventuresome child of co-owners Neil Perry and chef Kylie Kwong
has taken off big-time. Upstairs, the main dining room is light and
spacious with glass walls opening up across the water. The essence
up here is Chinese with a twist, and the Sechuan duck and stir-fried
spanner-crab omelet are always on the menu. Other dishes to go for
are whole steamed snapper with ginger and shallot, rock lobster, and

mud crab. Downstairs, the noodle bar is always happening, with tourists, locals, and business types crunched up along the bar or around the tables, tucking into light meals such as beef curry and stir-fried Shanghai noodles with spicy chicken.

5 In Kings Cross & the Suburbs Beyond
EXPENSIVE

✪ **Darley Street Thai.** 28–30 Bayswater Rd., Kings Cross. ☎ **02/9358 6530.** Reservations recommended. Main courses A$27 (U.S.$18.90). 8-course set meal A$80 U.S.$56). AE, DC, MC, V. Daily 6:30–10:30pm. CityRail: Kings Cross. MODERN THAI.

So trendy is this place that the only signage outside is a small plaque about knee height. This Thai-inspired restaurant highlights the dizzying heights cooking has reached in Australia. Though the place doesn't look like much—a Spartan affair with simple wooden floor boards and noisy fans in summer—I guarantee you've never tasted anything quite so exquisite. Flavors and textures are so delicate and perfectly matched that, course after course, your taste buds virtually leap out of your mouth. The menu changes regularly, but some of the dishes offered might include green jungle curry of quail and smoked trout sausage. The desserts—especially the sticky rice pudding with mango—are out of this world. Next door is a cheaper but equally flavorful Darley Street Thai take-out and bar-stool eatery.

✪ **Mezzaluna.** 123 Victoria St., Potts Point. ☎ **02/9357 1988.** Reservations recommended. Main courses A$19.50–$31 (U.S.$13.65–$21.70). A$3 surcharge Sun. AE, BC, DC, MC, V. Tues–Sun noon–3pm; Tues–Sun 6pm–11pm. Closed public holidays. CityRail: Kings Cross. MODERN ITALIAN.

Exquisite food, flawless service, and an almost unbeatable view across the city's western skyline have all helped Mezzaluna position itself firmly among Sydney's top restaurants. A cozy, candlelit place with plain white walls and polished wooden floorboards, the main dining room opens up onto a huge, all-weather terrace kept warm in winter by giant overhead fan heaters. The restaurant's owner, well-known Sydney culinary icon Beppi Polesi, provides an exceptional wine list to complement an extravagant menu that changes daily. You could indulge in an unbeatable salmon risotto to start, followed by fillets of fish with scampi, scallops, mussels, oysters, and Morton Bay bugs, or succulent roasted lamb with grilled eggplant and sheep's yogurt. Whatever you choose, you can't go wrong. I highly recommend this place.

MODERATE

Bourbon & Beefsteak Bar. 24 Darlinghurst Rd., Kings Cross. ☎ **02/ 9358 1144.** Reservations recommended Fri–Sun. Main courses A$8.50–$23.95 (U.S.$7.70–$16.80). A$2 (U.S.$1.40) surcharge weekends and public holidays. AE, BC, DC, MC, V. Daily 24 hours (happy hour 4–7pm). CityRail: Kings Cross. INTERNATIONAL.

The Bourbon & Beefsteak has been a popular Kings Cross institution for more than 30 years, and it still attracts everyone from visiting U.S. sailors and tourists to businesspeople and ravers. The fact that it's open 24 hours means many people never seem to leave—occasionally you'll find someone taking a nap in the bathroom. The American-themed restaurant is busy at all hours, churning out steaks, seafood, salads, Tex-Mex, ribs, seafood specials, and pasta. Breakfast is served daily from 6 to 11am.

Every night there's live music in the Piano Bar from 5 to 9pm, followed by a mixture of jazz, Top 40, and rock'n'roll until 5am. A disco downstairs starts at 11pm every night (finishing at 6am), and a larger one takes off in The Penthouse at the Bourbon bar on Friday and Saturday nights. The music is geared toward the 18 to 25 crowd of locals and tourists.

INEXPENSIVE

Govindas. 112 Darlinghurst Rd., Darlinghurst. ☎ **02/9380 5155.** Dinner A$13.90 (U.S.$9.75), including free movie. AE, BC, MC, V. Daily 6–11pm. CityRail: Kings Cross. VEGETARIAN.

When I think of Govindas, I can't help smiling. Perhaps it's because I'm reliving the happy vibe from the Hare Krishna center it's based in, or maybe it's because the food is so cheap! Or maybe it's because they even throw in a decent movie with the meal (the movie theatre is on a different floor). The food is simple vegetarian, served buffet style and eaten in a basic room off black lacquer tables. Typical dishes include pastas and salads, lentil dishes, soups and casseroles. It's BYO and doctrine-free.

6 In Darlinghurst

Hard Rock Cafe. 121–129 Crown St., Darlinghurst. ☎ **02/9331 1116.** Reservations not accepted. Main courses A$9.95–$19.95 (U.S.$6.95–$13.95). 10% surcharge weekends and public holidays. AE, BC, DC, JCB, MC, V. Daily noon–midnight. Shop daily 10am–midnight. Closed Christmas. CityRail: Museum; then walk across Hyde Park, head down the hill past the Australian Museum on William St., and turn right onto Crown St. Sydney Explorer Bus: Stop 7. AMERICAN.

The obligatory half a Cadillac through the wall beckons you into this shrine to rock-and-roll. Among the items on display are costumes worn by Elvis, John Lennon, and Elton John, as well as guitars from Sting and the Bee Gees, drums from Phil Collins and The Beatles, and one of Madonna's bras. The mainstays here are the burgers, with ribs, chicken, fish, and salads, and T-bone steaks on the menu, too. Most meals come with french fries or baked potatoes and a salad. It's really busy on Friday and Saturday evenings from around 7:30pm to 10:30pm, when you might have to queue to get a seat.

✪ **No Names.** 2 Chapel St. (or 81 Stanley St.), Darlinghurst. ☎ **02/9360 4711.** Main courses A\$6–\$14 (U.S.\$4.20–\$9.80). Cash only. Daily noon–2:30pm and 6–10pm. CityRail: Kings Cross or Town Hall, then a 10-minute walk. ITALIAN.

This fabulous cafeteria-style Italian joint is the place to go in Sydney for a cheap and cheerful meal. Downstairs you can nibble on cakes or drink good coffee, but upstairs you have a choice between spaghetti and several meat or fish dishes. The servings are enormous and often far more than you can eat. You get free bread, and simple salads are cheap. Help yourself to water and cordials.

7 In Newtown

The inner-city suburb of Newtown is three stops from Central Station by CityRail train, and 10 minutes by bus from central Sydney. Its main drag, King Street, is clustered with inexpensive restaurants offering food from around the world.

Le Kilimanjaro. 280 King St., Newtown. ☎ **02/9557 4565.** Reservations not accepted. Main courses A\$8.50–\$9.50 (U.S.\$5.95–\$6.65). No credit cards. CityRail: Newtown. AFRICAN.

With so many excellent restaurants to choose from in Newtown—they close down or improve quick enough if they're bad—I picked Kilimanjaro because it's the most unusual. It's a tiny place, with very limited seating on two floors. Basically, you enter, choose a dish off the blackboard menu (while standing), and then you are escorted to your seats by one of the waiters. On a recent visit I had couscous, some African bread (similar to an Indian chapatti), and the *Saussougor di guan* (tuna in a rich sauce). Another favorite dish is *Yassa* (chicken in a rich African sauce). All meals are served on traditional wooden plates.

✪ **Old Saigon.** 107 King St., Newtown. ☎ **02/9519 5931.** Reservations recommended. Main courses A\$10–\$40 (U.S.\$7–\$28). AE, BC, DC, MC, V. Wed–Fri noon–3pm; Tues–Sun 6–11pm. BYO only. CityRail: Newtown. VIETNAMESE.

Another Newtown establishment bursting with atmosphere, the Old Saigon was owned until 1998 by a former American Vietnam War correspondent who loved Vietnam so much he ended up living there and marrying a local, before coming to Australia. Just to make sure you know about it, he's put up his own photos on the walls, and strewn the place with homemade tin helicopters. His Vietnamese brother-in-law has taken over the show, but the food is still glorious, with the spicy squid dishes among my favorites. A popular pastime is grilling your own thin strips of venison, beef, wild boar, kangaroo, or crocodile over a burner at your table, then wrapping the meat up in rice paper with lettuce and mint, then dipping it in a chili sauce. I highly recommend this place for a cheap night out.

8 In Paddington/Oxford Street

The top end of Oxford Street, which runs from Hyde Park in central Sydney towards Bondi, has a profusion of trendy bars and cafes, with a scattering of cheaper places among the more glamorous ones. In addition to La Mensa, my other favorite places in the area are **Claudes,** 10 Oxford St., Woolhara (☎ **02/9331 2325**), which offers expensive French cuisine in a hushed, intimate atmosphere, and ✪ **Grand National,** 161 Underwood St., Paddington (☎ **02/9363 3096**), which offers fabulous Modern Australian food at moderate prices in elegant surrounds (try the fish pie!). Claudes is open for dinner Tuesday to Saturday, and Grand National is open for dinner daily and lunch Wednesday to Friday and Sunday.

La Mensa. 257 Oxford St., Paddington. ☎ **02/9332 2963.** Reservations recommended. Main courses A$14.50–$19.50 (U.S.$10.15–$13.65). AE, BC, DC, MC, V. Mon–Thurs 11am–10pm, Fri 11am–11pm, Sat 9am–11pm, Sun 9am–10pm. Bus: Oxford St. ITALIAN/MEDITERRANEAN.

Though I find clean-cut, minimal interiors like the one here to be increasingly boring, at La Mensa it has the added zest of a gourmet food and vegetable store tacked on. There's a communal table seating about 20 people, as well as other smaller tables both inside and out. The stand-out main courses are roast beef rib-eye with lentils and garlic puree, veal with spinach and onions, and braised lamb shanks with soft polenta. The couple of vegetarian items include roast banana chilies filled with risotto.

9 In Bondi

Fishy Affair. 152–162 Campbell Parade, Bondi Beach. ☎ **02/9300 0494.** Main courses A$14.40–$21 (U.S.$10.10–$14.70) AE, BC, JCB, MC, V. Mon–Sat noon–3pm; Mon–Thurs 6–10pm, Fri–Sat 6–10:30pm; Sun noon–10pm. Bus: Bondi Beach. SEAFOOD.

Jumping Java Joints

Debate rages over which cafe serves the best coffee in Sydney, which has the best atmosphere, and which has the tastiest snacks. The main cafe scenes are centered around Victoria Street in Darlinghurst, Stanley Street in East Sydney, and King Street in Newtown. Other places, like Balmoral Beach on the north shore, Bondi Beach, and Paddington, all have their favored hangouts, too. If you're American, keep in mind that, unlike in the States, it's very rare to have free refills of coffee in Australian restaurants and cafes.

Here are some of my favorite spots: **The Old Coffee Shop,** ground floor of the Strand Arcade (☎ **02/9231 3002**), Sydney's oldest coffee shop with an old-world feel and tasty snacks; ✪ **Bills,** 433 Liverpool St., Darlinghurst (☎ **02/9360 9631**), a bright and airy (and a bit pretentious) hangout serving nouveau cafe–style food; **Hernandez,** 60 Kings Cross Rd., Potts Point (☎ **02/ 9331 2343**), a tiny, zany, cluttered cafe serving 20 types of coffee; **Cafe Niki,** 544 Bourke St., Surry Hills (☎ **02/9319 7517**), where you can munch on light Italian meals in the cozy booths; **Bar Coluzzi,** 322 Victoria St., Darlinghurst (☎ **02/9380 5420**), the first cafe in Sydney to serve real espresso when the rest of the city was still drinking Nescafé; and last but not least, ✪ **Balmoral Boatshed Kiosk,** 2 The Esplanade, Balmoral Beach (☎ **02/ 9968 4412**), a beautiful rustic cafe right on the water that's popular with families on weekend mornings.

Just one of many good restaurants, cafes and takeaways along the Beach's main drag, the Fishy Affair is nevertheless a standout. Sitting outside watching the beach bums saunter past while tucking into great fish-and-chips is a great way to spend an hour or so. The herb-crusted Atlantic salmon steak and the smoked salmon salad are both truly delicious.

✪ **Thai Terrific.** 147 Curlewis St., Bondi Beach. ☎ **02/9365 7794.** Reservations recommended on Fri and Sat nights. Main courses A$10–$18 (U.S.$7– $12.60). Cash only. Daily noon–11pm. Bus: 380 to Bondi Beach. THAI.

Thai Terrific by name, terrific Thai by nature. This truly superb place just around the corner from the Bondi Hotel is run with flair and coolly efficient service. The large back room can be quite noisy, so if you prefer less din with your dinner sit at one of the small sidewalk tables outside. Servings are enormous; two mains are easily enough to fill three people. The *tom yum* soups and the prawn or seafood *laksa* noodle soups are the best I've tasted in Australia and are very filling. I also highly recommend the red curries.

Equally nice (and quieter) is the Bangkok-style **Nina's Ploy Thai Restaurant,** 132 Wairoa Ave. (☎ **02/9365 1118**), at the corner of Warners Avenue at the end of the main Campbell Parade strip. Main courses here go for A$8 to $12.50 (U.S. $5.60 to $8.75); it's cash only.

10 In Manly

Manly is 30 minutes from Circular Quay by ferry, or 15 minutes by JetCat. Take-out shops lining **the Corso,** the pedestrian mall between the ferry terminal and the main Manly Beach, offer everything from Turkish kebabs to Japanese noodles. If you've got a hankering for french fries, don't miss **Manly Ocean Foods,** three shops down from the main beach on The Corso; they serve the best in Sydney. Steer away from the fish-and-chips at A$5.95 (U.S.$4.15) though (the shark is not the best in my opinion) and spend a couple of dollars extra on barramundi, salmon, perch, or snapper. Another excellent take-out option is **Shakespeares,** at 13 The Corso (☎ **02/9977 5909**), on the left side of the Corso as you walk toward the main beach (one block up from the ferry terminal). It sells a wide range of fabulous gourmet pies including several excellent vegetarian options, for around A$4.20 (U.S.$2.95) each.

○ **Ashiana.** 2 Sydney Rd., Manly. ☎ **02/9977 3466.** Reservations recommended. Main courses A$9.90–$15.90 (U.S.$6.95–$11.15). AE, BC, MC, V. Daily 5:30–11pm. Ferry or JetCat: Manly. INDIAN.

You'll be hard pressed to find a better cheap Indian restaurant in Sydney. Tucked away up a staircase next to the Steyne Hotel (just off the Corso and near the main beach), Ashiana has won a few prizes for its traditional spicy cooking. Portions are large and filling, and the service is very friendly. The butter chicken is magnificent, while the *Malai Kofta* (cheese and potato dumplings in a mild, creamy sauce) is the best this side of Bombay. Beer is the best drink with everything. My only gripe is that it's hard to avoid cigarette smoke in such a cozy place, especially on Friday and Saturday nights when the place is heaving. Clear your lungs and work off the heavy load in your stomach with a beach-side stroll afterwards. Check out the soda machine in Woolworth's just across the road for A80¢ (U.S.56¢) cold drinks—the cheapest in Sydney.

Café Tunis. 30/31 South Steyne, Manly. ☎ **02/9976 2805.** Main courses (big enough for two) A$17–$21 (U.S.$11.90–$14.70). AE, BC, DC, MC, V. Daily 7am–10pm. Ferry or JetCat: Manly. TUNISIAN.

Right on the beach with fabulous views across the ocean, Café Tunis dishes out huge, value-for-money portions of North African special-ties. My favorite to start is the fresh tuna with vegetables and egg deep-fried in pastry. It's big enough for a main dish. Real main courses include couscous royale, with lamb, chicken, and spicy sau-sage. It's large enough for two. The grilled seafood platter is very popular and is also big enough for you and a friend. Café Tunis is open for breakfast—eggs, especially the egg Benedict, are a spe-cialty—and for lunchtime when fish-and-chips is the favorite (but you can still try the authentic Tunisian desserts).

Green's Eatery. 1–3 Sydney Rd., Manly. ☎ **02/9977 1904.** Menu items A$2–$6.20 (U.S.$1.40–$4.35). Cash only. Daily 8am–6pm. Ferry or JetCat: Manly. VEGETARIAN.

Of the many eateries in Manly, this nice little vegetarian place, just off the Corso on the turnoff just before the Steyne Hotel, does the best lunchtime business. The food is healthy and of good quality. The menu includes eleven different vegetarian burgers, vegetable curries and noodle dishes, patties and salads, soups, smoothies, and wraps. They serve some exceptionally nice cakes here, too, which despite being incredibly wholesome are still surprisingly tasty.

6

Exploring Sydney

*T*he only problem with visiting Sydney is fitting in everything you want to do and see. A well-planned itinerary can easily be upset by countless other sights and experiences that suddenly become "must sees" and "must dos" once you arrive. Of course, you won't want to miss the "icon" attractions—the Opera House and the Harbour Bridge— but you should also check out the native Aussie wildlife in the Taronga Zoo and the Sydney Aquarium and get a dose of Down Under culture at the not-too-large Australian Museum. Also try to take time out to visit one of the nearby national parks for a taste of the Australian bush, and if it's hot take your swimsuit and towel to Bondi Beach.

Whatever you decide to do, you won't have enough time. So, don't be surprised if you find yourself planning ahead for your next visit before your first visit is even finished.

SIGHTSEEING SUGGESTIONS FOR FIRST-TIME VISITORS

If You Have 1 Day

In the morning, make your way down to **Circular Quay** to look around the **Opera House** and admire the **Sydney Harbour Bridge.** Then head over to **The Rocks,** stopping off at The Rocks Visitors Centre to pick up maps and extra information and check out the fascinating exhibits on the top two floors. Have lunch around Circular Quay or The Rocks, or jump on a ferry, to Darling Harbour or Manly perhaps, and eat it on board. A guided walking tour around The Rocks should be at the top of your agenda for the early afternoon (see "Harbor Cruises & Other Organized Tours," in section 9 below). The rest of the afternoon I'd spend browsing around the stores, or I'd head to **Taronga Zoo** by ferry to at least get a glimpse of some Australian wildlife. An option for the late afternoon, or dinner, is to take a **harbor cruise.**

If You Have 2 Days

On the second day, head down to Circular Quay again and take the ferry that travels beneath the Harbour Bridge and across to **Darling Harbour.** At Darling Harbour, visit **Sydney Aquarium,** for its giant sharks, seals, underwater ocean tunnels, and Barrier Reef displays.

Great Deals on Sightseeing

The **Privileges Card** is a great way to save money if you plan to visit Sydney's biggest attractions. The card costs A$25 (U.S.$17.50), is good for up to one month, and can be used in Sydney, Canberra, and Melbourne. In Sydney, all the major attractions offer some sort of discount if you show a Privileges Card, such as two-for-one admission or reduced-price admission if you're traveling alone. With the card you'll also get discounts on harbor cruises (typically 20%), as well as discounts at certain restaurants (sometimes a free main course if two of you are dining, or a 20% rebate off the total bill for the cardholder and three others). To get a card, you'll need to fill out an application form, available on the Internet (www.privilegescard.com) or at tourist information centers in Sydney; you'll receive a booklet with details on where you can save. Call Privileges at ☎ **02/6254 1375,** or fax 02/6254 8788. If you book in advance, the company can arrange to have the card sent to your hotel.

Another money-saving option is the **Sydney Bonus Ticket,** which includes admission to the AMP Centerpoint Tower and the Sydney Aquarium, as well as a morning or afternoon harbor cruise with Captain Cook Cruises. You can also use the card to receive discounts while shopping in the AMP Centerpoint Tower shopping complex. The card costs A$39 (U.S.$27.50) for adults and A$29 (U.S.$20.30) for children. You can get the ticket from any of the participating operators or at the desk as you enter Centerpoint from Pitt Street Mall.

If you plan to hit the sights in Darling Harbour, you'll want to know about the **Super Ticket.** It includes a ride on the monorail, entry to both the Sydney Aquarium and the Chinese Gardens, a two-hour cruise on the Matilda Harbour Express, a meal at the Sydney Aquarium cafe, and discounts on a coach tour of the site of the Sydney Olympic Games at Homebush Bay. The Super Ticket costs A$29.90 (U.S.$20.95) for adults and A$19.90 (U.S.$13.95) for children 3 to 15. It's available at monorail stations, the Sydney Aquarium, and Darling Harbour information booths.

Then visit the **National Maritime Museum,** or one of the other attractions that dot this tourist precinct. Take the monorail to Town Hall in time for sunset at the top of the **AMP Centerpoint Tower.**

If You Have 3 Days

If the weather's fine, head to the beach. Go to either **Bondi Beach,** where you can take the cliff walk to Bronte Beach and back, or take the ferry to **Manly** (see "Getting Around," in chapter 2) and hang out on the beach there. If you have time in the afternoon, I highly recommend visiting the **Featherdale Wildlife Park**—it's in the suburbs, but it's really worth the trek. Have dinner at Circular Quay with a view of the harbor and the lights of the Opera House and Harbour Bridge.

1 The Sydney Opera House & Sydney Harbour

Sydney Opera House. Bennelong Point. ☎ **02/9250 7111** for guided tours and inquiries. Fax 02/9250 7624. www.soh.nsw.gov.au. For bookings, call ☎ 02/9250 7777; fax 02/9251 3943; e-mail bookings@soh.nsw.gov.au. Box office open Mon–Sat 9am–8:30pm, Sun 2 hrs. before performance. Tour prices A$10 (U.S.$7) adults, A$7 (U.S.$4.90) children (family prices available on application). Regular 1-hr. tours Mon–Sat 9am–4pm, subject to theater availability (tour sizes are limited, so be prepared to wait). See more information on tours and tickets below. Parking daytime A$9 (U.S.$6.30) per hr.; evening A$19 (U.S.$13.30) flat rate. CityRail, bus, or ferry: Circular Quay. Sydney Explorer bus: Stop 2.

Only a handful of buildings around the world are as architecturally and culturally significant as the Sydney Opera House. But the difference between, say, the Taj Mahal, the Eiffel Tower, and the Great Pyramids of Egypt, for example, is that this great, white-sailed construction caught mid-billow over the waters of Sydney Cove is a working building, not just a monument. Most people are surprised to learn that its not just an Opera House, but a full-scale performing arts complex with five major performance spaces. The biggest and grandest of the lot is the 2,690-seat **Concert Hall,** which has just about the best acoustics of any man-made building of its type in the world. Come here to experience opera, of course, but also chamber music, symphonies, dance, choral performances, and even on occasion rock and roll. The **Opera Theatre** is smaller, seating 1,547, and is home to operas, ballets, and dance. The **Drama Theatre,** seating 544, and the **Playhouse,** seating 398, specialize in plays and smaller-scale performances. In March 1999 a new theater, the Boardwalk, seating 300, opened on the site of the old library. It will be used for dance and experimental music.

The history of the building is as intriguing as the design. The New South Wales Government raised the money needed to build it from a public lottery. Danish Architect Jørn Utzon won an international competition to design it. From the start, the project was controversial, with many Sydneysiders believing it was a monstrosity. Following a disagreement, Utzon returned home, without ever seeing his finished project, and the interior fell victim to a compromise design, which, among other things, left too little space to perform full-scale operas. And the cost? Initially the project was budgeted at a cool A$7 million (U.S.$5.6 million), but by the time it was finished in 1973 it had cost a staggering A$102 million (U.S.$71.4 million), most raised through a series of lotteries. Since then, continual refurbishment and the major task of replacing the asbestos-infected grouting between the hundreds of thousands of white tiles that make up its shell has cost many millions more.

Tours & Tickets: Guided tours of the Opera House last about an hour and are conducted daily from 9am to 4pm, except Good Friday and Christmas. Though guides try to take groups into the main theaters and around the foyers, if you don't get to see everything you want it's because the Opera House is not a museum but a workplace, and there's almost always some performance, practice, or setting up going on. Reservations are essential. Tours include approximately 200 stairs (tours for people with disabilities can be arranged). Specialized tours, focusing on the building's architectural and engineering configurations, for example, can also be arranged.

The Tourism Services Department at the Sydney Opera House can book combination packages, including dinner and a show; a tour, dinner, and a show; or a show and champagne. Prices vary depending on shows and dining venues. Visitors from overseas can buy tickets by credit card and then pick them up at the box office on arrival, or contact a local tour company specializing in Australia. Tickets for performances vary from as little as A$9.50 (U.S.$6.65) for children's shows to A$150 (U.S.$105) for good seats at the opera. Plays cost between A$35 (U.S.$24.50) and A$45 (U.S.$31.50) on average.

Free performances are given outside on the Opera House boardwalks on Sunday afternoons and during festival times. The shows range from musicians and performance artists, to school groups.

Sydney Harbour. Officially called Port Jackson.

Sydney Harbour is the focal point of Sydney and one of the features—along with the beaches and the easy access to surrounding national parks—that makes this city so special. It's entered through the Heads, two bush-topped outcrops (you'll see them if you take a ferry or JetCat to Manly), beyond which the harbor laps at some 240 kilometers (149 miles) of shoreline before stretching out into the Parramatta River. Visitors are often awestruck by the harbor's

Central Sydney Attractions

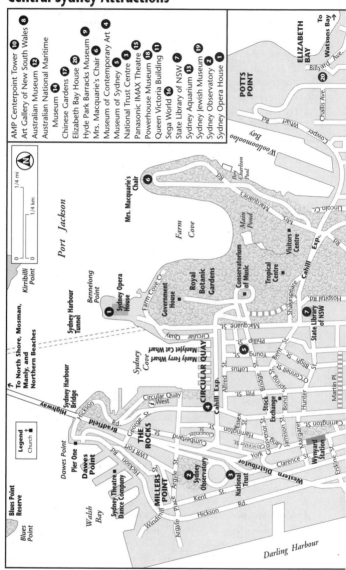

AMP Centerpoint Tower 10
Art Gallery of New South Wales 8
Australian Museum 12
Australian National Maritime Museum 14
Chinese Gardens 17
Elizabeth Bay House 20
Hyde Park Barracks Museum 9
Mrs. Macquarie's Chair 6
Museum of Contemporary Art 4
Museum of Sydney 5
National Trust Centre 3
Panasonic IMAX Theatre 15
Powerhouse Museum 18
Queen Victoria Building 11
Sega World 16
State Library of NSW 7
Sydney Aquarium 13
Sydney Jewish Museum 19
Sydney Observatory 2
Sydney Opera House 1

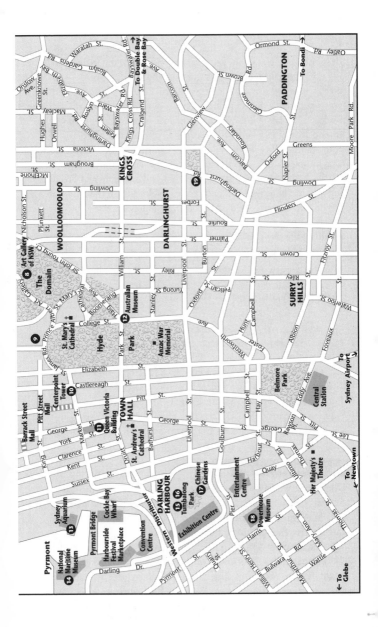

Pyrmont

National Maritime Museum **14**

Sydney Aquarium **13**

Pyrmont Bridge

Cockle Bay Wharf

Harbourside Festival Marketplace

Convention Centre

Exhibition Centre

DARLING HARBOUR

Tumbalong Park **15** **16**

Chinese Gardens **17**

Pier Entertainment Centre

Powerhouse Museum **18**

Her Majesty's Theatre

Convention Centre

Darling Dr.

Pyrmont St.

Quay St.

Harris St.

Bulwara Rd.

William Henry St.

Mary Ann St.

Thomas St.

Macarthur St.

Wattle St.

← To Glebe

← To Newtown

Barrack Street

Pitt Street Mall

Centrepoint Tower **10**

Queen Victoria Building **11**

St. Andrew's Cathedral

TOWN HALL

George St.

York St.

Clarence St.

Kent St.

Sussex St.

King St.

Market St.

Druitt St.

Bathurst St.

Liverpool St.

Goulburn St.

Hay St.

Campbell St.

Pitt St.

Castlereagh St.

Elizabeth St.

Art Gallery of NSW **8**

The Domain

St. Mary's Cathedral

9

Hyde Park

College St.

Park St.

Prince Albert Rd.

Art Gallery Rd.

Mrs. Macquaries Rd.

Cathedral St.

Sir John Young Cr.

Boomerang St.

Australian Museum **12**

Anzac War Memorial

William St.

Stanley St.

Yurong St.

Riley St.

Liverpool St.

Oxford St.

Pelican St.

Wentworth Ave.

Foster St.

Hunt St.

Campbell St.

Belmore Park

Eddy Ave.

Central Station

Pitt St.

George St.

Lee St.

Regent St.

To Sydney Airport →

WOOLLOOMOOLOO

Nicholson St.

Plunkett St.

Dowling St.

Forbes St.

Bourke St.

Palmer St.

Crown St.

McElhone St.

Brougham St.

Victoria St.

KINGS CROSS

DARLINGHURST

Darlinghurst Rd.

Flinders St.

Burton St.

Fitzroy St.

19

SURRY HILLS

Riley St.

Crown St.

Waterloo St.

Albion St.

Foveaux St.

To Sydney Airport →

Elizabeth Bay Rd.

Greenknowe Ave.

Onslow Ave.

Roslyn Gardens Rd.

Macleay St.

Hughes St.

Orwell St.

Ward Ave.

Darlinghurst Rd.

Kellett St.

Roslyn St.

Bayswater Rd.

Craigend St.

Barcom Ave.

Waratah St.

Elizabeth Bay Rd.

To Double Bay & Rose Bay →

Bayswater Rd.

PADDINGTON

Ormond St.

Brown St.

Glenmore Rd.

Glenview St.

Gurner St.

Oxford St.

Napier St.

Dowling St.

Greens Rd.

Moore Park Rd.

To Bondi →

Oatley Rd.

beauty, especially at night when the sails of the Opera House and the girders of the Harbour Bridge are lit up, and the waters are swirling with the reflection of lights from the abutting high-rises—reds, greens, blues, yellows, and oranges. During the day, it buzzes with green-and-yellow ferries pulling in and out of busy Circular Quay, sleek tourist craft, tall ships, giant container vessels making their way to and from the wharves of Darling Harbour, and hundreds of white-sailed yachts. The greenery along the harbor's edges is perhaps a surprising feature, and all thanks to the Sydney Harbour National Park, a haven for native trees and plants, and a feeding and breeding ground for lorikeets and nectar-eating bird life. In the center of the harbor is a series of islands, the most impressive being the tiny isle supporting Fort Denison, which once housed convicts and acted as part of the city's defense.

Sydney Harbour Bridge.

One thing so few tourists do, but which only takes an hour or so, is to walk right across the Harbour Bridge. The bridge, completed in 1932, is 1,150 meters (3,795 ft.) long and spans the 503-meter (1,600-ft.) distance from the south shore to the north. It accommodates pedestrian walkways, two railway lines, and an eight-lane road. The 30-minute stroll across offers some excellent harbor views. Once on the other side, you can take a CityRail train from Milsons Point train station back to the city (to Wynyard, Town Hall, or Central stations).

As you walk across the bridge, you should stop off at the **Pylon Lookout** (☎ **02/9247 3408**), located at the southeastern pylon. Admission is just A$2 (U.S.$1.40). From the top of this bridge support, you are 89 meters (591 feet) above the water and get

The Harbour on the Cheap

The best way to see Sydney Harbour, of course, is from the water. Several companies operate tourist craft for fare-paying customers (see "Harbor Cruises & Other Organized Tours," later in this chapter), but it's easy enough just to hop on a regular passenger ferry (one-way tickets are just $3.20/U.S.$2.25; see "Getting Around," in chapter 2). The best ferry excursions are over to the beachside suburb of **Manly** (come back after dusk to see the lights ablaze around The Rocks and Circular Quay); to **Watsons Bay,** where you can have lunch and wander along the cliffs; to **Darling Harbour,** for all the area's entertainment and the fact that you travel right under the Harbour Bridge; and to **Mosman,** just for the ride and to see the grand houses that overlook exclusive harbor inlets.

A Walk on the Wild Side: Climbing the Harbour Bridge

At one time, only bridge workers employed in the full-time job of painting the Harbour Bridge had the opportunity to view Sydney from the top of the main bridge arch. But since October 1998, Sydneysiders and tourists have been able to experience the spectacular view and the exhilarating achievement of climbing to the top of one of Australia's icons. The experience takes 3 hours from check-in at the **BridgeClimb** base at 5 Cumberland St., The Rocks (☎ **02/9240 1100;** fax 02/9240 1122; e-mail: admin@bridgeclimb.com), to the completion of the climb. The office is open daily from 8am to 6pm, and climbers leave in small groups every 10 minutes or so. Climbers wear specially designed "Bridge Suits" and are harnessed to a static line. Participants are also breath-tested for alcohol and are banned from carrying anything on the climb, including cameras or video recorders. Climbs cost A$98 (U.S.$68.60) for adults and A$79 (U.S.$55.30) for children ages 12 to 16 on weekdays; A$120 (U.S.$84) for adults and A$98 (U.S.$68.60) for children on weekends and Thursday and Friday evenings; and A$140 (U.S.$98) for adults and A$118 (U.S.$82.60) for children on Saturday evenings. Children under 12 are not allowed to climb.

excellent views of Sydney Harbour, the ferry terminals of Circular Quay, and beyond. An interesting museum here charts the building of the bridge. Reach the pylon by walking to the far end of George Street in The Rocks toward the Harbour Bridge. Just past the Mercantile Pub on your left you'll see some stone steps that take you onto Cumberland Street. From there, it's a 2-minute walk to the steps underneath the bridge on your right. Climb four flights of stairs to reach the bridge's Western Footway, then walk along to the first pylon. *Note:* Climbing up inside the pylon involves 200 steps. The Pylon Lookout is open daily from 10am to 5pm (closed Christmas).

2 Darling Harbour

Many tourists head to Darling Harbour for the **Harbourside Festival Marketplace,** a huge structure beside the Pyrmont pedestrian and monorail bridge that's crammed full of cheap eateries and a few interesting shops. However, Sydney's tourist precinct has a lot more to offer.

✪ **Australian National Maritime Museum.** Darling Harbour. ☎ **02/ 9552 7777.** Admission A$9 (U.S.$6.30) adults, A$4.50 (U.S.$3.15) children, A$19.50 (U.S.$13.65) families. Daily 9:30am–5pm (until 6:30pm in Jan). Ferry: Darling Harbour. Monorail: Harbourside. Sydney Explorer bus: Stop 18.

Modern Australia owes almost everything to the sea, so it's not surprising that there's a museum dedicated to the ships, from Aboriginal vessels to submarines, that overcame the tyranny of the waves. Here you'll also find ships' logs, all sorts of things to pull and tug at, as well as the Americas Cup–winning vessel *Australia II.* Docked in the harbor outside is an Australian Naval Destroyer, *The Vampire,* which you can clamber all over, and an Oberon Class submarine. Two fully rigged tall ships were installed in 1999. Allow at least two hours.

Chinese Garden. Darling Harbour (adjacent to the Entertainment Centre). ☎ **02/9281 6863.** Admission A$4 (U.S.$2.80) adults, A$2 (U.S.90¢) children, A$10 (U.S.$4.20) families. Daily 9:30am–dusk. Ferry: Darling Harbour. Monorail: Convention. Sydney Explorer bus: Stop 19.

The largest Chinese garden of its type outside China offers a pleasant escape from the city concrete. It was designed by expert gardeners from China's Guangdong Province to embody principals of garden design dating back to the 5th century.

Panasonic IMAX Theatre. Southern Promenade, Darling Harbour. ☎ **02/ 9281 3300.** Admission A$13.95 (U.S.$9.70) adults, A$9.95 (U.S.$7) children 3–15, A$42.95 (U.S.$30) families. Daily 9:45am–10pm (until 11:30pm Fri and Sat). Ferry: Darling Harbour. Monorail: Convention. Sydney Explorer bus: Stop 20.

Four different IMAX films are usually showing on the gigantic eight-story-high screen. Each flick lasts about 50 minutes or so. If you've ever been to an IMAX theater before, you know what to expect. As you watch, your mind is tricked into feeling that it's right in the heart of the action. Also shown are 3-D movies, which cost A$1 (U.S.70¢) extra.

Powerhouse Museum. 500 Harris St, Ultimo (near Darling Harbour). ☎ **02/ 9217 0111.** Admission A$8 (U.S.$5.60) adults, A$2 (U.S.$1.40) children, A$18 (U.S.$12.60) families. Free admission first Sat of every month. Daily 10am–5pm. Ferry: Darling Harbour. Monorail: Harbourside. Sydney Explorer bus: Stop 17.

Sydney's most interactive museum is also one of the largest in the Southern Hemisphere. Inside the post-modern industrial interior you'll find all sorts of displays and gadgets relating to the sciences, transportation, human achievement, decorative art, and social history. The many hands-on exhibits make this fascinating museum worthy of a couple of hours of your time.

Sega World. Darling Harbour (between the IMAX Theatre and Chinese Gardens). ☎ **02/9273 9273.** www.segaworld.com.au. Admission Mon–Fri A$22 (U.S.$15.40) adults, A$15 (U.S.$10.50) children; Sat–Sun A$25 (U.S.$17.50) adults, A$20 (U.S.$14) children. Entry includes all rides. Mon–Fri 11am–10pm, Sat–Sun 10am–10pm. Ferry: Darling Harbour. Monorail: Convention.

If you fancy a few hours break from the kids, if you're just a big kid yourself, or if it's raining outside, then you might like to give this indoor theme park a try. Simulators, 3-D rides, computer games, and the like are fun, but occasionally a little limp. It's good for a couple of hours. Avoid the huge queues on Friday nights and weekends.

✪ **Sydney Aquarium.** Aquarium Pier, Darling Harbour. ☎ **02/9262 2300.** Admission A$15.90 (U.S.$11.15) adults, A$8 (U.S.$5.60) children. The Aquarium Link ticket, available from CityRail train stations, is a combined rail and Aquarium ticket that includes a ferry ride. It costs A$15.90 (U.S.$11.15) adults, A$8.20 (U.S.$5.75) children, and A$42 (U.S.$29.50) families. Daily 9:30am–10pm. Seal Sanctuary closes at 7pm in summer. CityRail: Town Hall. Ferry: Darling Harbour. Sydney Explorer bus: Stop 20.

This is one of the world's best aquariums and should be near the top of any Sydney itinerary. The main attractions are the underwater walkways through two enormous tanks—one containing an impressive collection of creatures you can find in Sydney Harbour, and the other full of giant rays and Grey Nurse Sharks. Other excellent exhibits include a giant Plexiglas room suspended inside a pool patrolled by rescued seals, and a truly magnificent section on the Great Barrier Reef, where thousands of colorful fish school around coral outcrops. Also on display are a couple of saltwater crocodiles and some tiny fairy penguins. Try to visit during the week when it's less crowded.

3 Other Top Attractions: A Spectacular View, Sydney's Convict History & More

AMP Centerpoint Tower. Pitt and Market sts. ☎ **02/9229 7444.** Admission A$10 (U.S.$7) adults, A$4.50 (U.S.$3.15) children. Sun–Fri 9am–10:30pm, Sat 9am–11:30pm. CityRail: St. James or Town Hall. Sydney Explorer bus: Stop 14.

The tallest building in the Southern Hemisphere is not hard to miss—it resembles a giant steel pole skewering a golden marshmallow. Standing more than 300 meters (1,860 ft.) tall, it offers stupendous 360-degree views across Sydney and as far as the Blue

Mountains. Fortunately, an elevator takes you to the indoor viewing platform. Don't be too concerned if you feel the building tremble slightly, especially in a stiff breeze—I'm told it's perfectly natural. Below the tower are three floors of stores and restaurants. The giant sporting figures on top of the tower are temporary constructions celebrating the Sydney Olympic Games.

Hyde Park Barracks Museum. Queens Sq., Macquarie St. ☎ **02/ 9223 8922.** Admission A$6 (U.S.$4.20) adults, A$3 (U.S.$2.10) children, A$15 (U.S.$10.50) families. Daily 9:30am–5pm. CityRail: St. James or Martin Place. Sydney Explorer bus: Stop 4.

These Georgian-style barracks were designed in 1819 by the convict/ architect Francis Greenway. They were built by convicts and inhabited by fellow prisoners. These days they house relics from those early days in interesting, modern displays, including log books, early settlement artifacts, and a room full of ships' hammocks in which visitors can lie and listen to fragments of prisoner conversation. If you are interested in Sydney's early beginnings, then I highly recommend a visit. The courtyard cafe is excellent.

Museum of Contemporary Art (MCA). 140 George St., Circular Quay West. ☎ **02/9252 4033.** www.mca.com.au. Admission A$9 (U.S.$7.60) adults, A$6 (U.S.$4.20) children, A$18 (U.S.$12.60) families. Daily 10am–6pm (5pm in winter). CityRail, bus, ferry: Circular Quay. Sydney Explorer bus: Stop 1.

This imposing sandstone museum set back from the water on The Rocks–side of Circular Quay offers wacky, entertaining, inspiring, and befuddling displays of what's new (and dated) in modern art. It houses the J. W. Power Collection of more than 4,000 pieces, including works by Andy Warhol, Christo, Marcel Duchamp, and Robert Rauschenberg, as well as temporary exhibits. Guided tours are offered Monday to Saturday at noon and 2pm, and Sunday at 2pm.

The Sydney International Aquatic and Athletic Centres. Sydney 2000 Olympic Site, Olympic Park, Homebush Bay. ☎ **02/9752 3666.** Tours A$14 (U.S.$9.80) adults, A$9 (U.S.$6.30) children, A$40 (U.S.$28) families. Tours Mon–Fri 10am, noon, and 2pm; Sat–Sun, noon, and 2pm. CityRail: Olympic Park.

A tour of the best Olympic swimming complex in the world, as well as the athletic center where the Olympic athletes will train, is fast becoming an essential thing to do for any visitor to Sydney. Tours last 90 minutes. If you fancy putting in a few laps afterwards, then be prepared to pay an additional A$4.50 (U.S.$3.15) for adults, and A$3.50 (U.S.$2.45) for children.

Gledswood Homestead. Camden Valley Way, Catherine Field. ☎ **02/ 9606 5111**. Fax 02/9606 5897. Farm activities A$12 (U.S.$8.40) adults, A$6 (U.S.$4.20) children, A$20 (U.S.$14) families. Homestead tour A$6 (U.S.$4.20) adults, A$4.50 (U.S.$3.15) children. Horseback riding A$16 (U.S.$11.20) for 30 min. Daily 10am–4pm. Several tour operators offer tips from Sydney. By car: Take the M5 to Camden Valley Way (Exit 89), an hr. from Sydney. By CityRail: Campbelltown station and then transfer to local Busways service 891 from outside station (20-min. trip).

If you have a day to spare, then you might consider the long trek to Gledswood, a sort of theme agricultural property set on 61.5 hectares (150 acres). You can try your hand at boomerang throwing, catch a sheep shearing demonstration, learn how to crack a stockman's whip, watch working sheepdogs in action, and milk a cow. The homestead tour is interesting if you're into colonial relics and architecture, and the gardens are nice (take a hat in summer). A hearty lunch and snacks are served by costumed staff in the restaurant. You can also sample billy tea and damper (bread made in the embers of a campfire). You'll come home feeling you've had a good taste of rural Australia.

❂ **Old Sydney Town.** Pacific Hwy., Somersby. ☎ **02/4340 1104.** Admission A$18 (U.S.$12.60) adults, A$10.50 (U.S.$7.35) children. Wed–Sun 10am–4pm; daily during school holidays. Somersby is near the town of Gosford, 84km (52 miles) north of Sydney. To reach Gosford by car, take the Pacific Highway and the Sydney-Newcastle Freeway (F3); the trip takes about an hr. **CityRail** trains leave from Central Station for Gosford every 30 min. From Gosford, take the bus marked OLD SYDNEY TOWN (15-min. ride).

You can spend quite a few hours on a nice day wandering around this outdoor theme park bustling with actors dressed up like convicts, sailors, and the like. You'll see plenty of stores, buildings, and ships from the old days of the colony, and performances are put on throughout the day. It's the Australian version of an American Wild West–theme town.

Wonderland Sydney. Wallgrove Rd., Eastern Creek. ☎ **02/9830 9100.** Admission (includes all rides and entrance to the Australian Wildlife Park) A$37 (U.S.$25.90) adults, A$26 (U.S.$18.20) children, A$115 (U.S.$80.50) families. Daily 10am–5pm. CityRail: Rooty Hill (trip takes less than an hr.); Wonderland buses leave from Rooty Hill station every half hr. on weekends, and at 8:55am, 9:32am; 10:10am, 11:35am, and 12:14pm weekdays.

If you're used to big Disneyesque extravaganzas, then this theme park (until recently called Australia's Wonderland) might be a bit of a disappointment—though I guarantee The Demon roller coaster will more than satisfy in the terror department. Other big rides are Space Probe 7, which is basically a heart-stopping drop, and a cute and rattly wooden roller coaster called the Bush Beast. Live shows and bands round out the entertainment options. The entry ticket also includes admission to a wildlife park, with all the old favorites—koalas, wombats, kangaroos, wallabies, and more.

4　Where to See 'Roos, Koalas & Other Aussie Wildlife

The world-class Sydney Aquarium is discussed above in section 2, " Darling Harbour."

Australian Reptile Park. Pacific Hwy., Somersby. ☎ **02/4340 1022.** Admission A$11.95 (U.S.$8.35) adults, A$5.95 (U.S.$4.15) children. Daily 9am–5pm. Closed Christmas. Somersby is near the town of Gosford, 84km (52 miles) north of Sydney. To reach Gosford by car, take the Pacific Highway and the Sydney-Newcastle Freeway (F3); the trip takes about an hr. CityRail trains leave from Central Station for Gosford every 30 min. From Gosford, take the bus marked AUSTRALIAN WILDLIFE PARK (10-min. ride).

What started off as a one-man operation supplying deadly snake antivenom in the early 1950s has ended up a nature park teeming with the slippery-looking creatures. But it's not all snakes and lizards here. You'll also find Eric, a 15-foot-long saltwater crocodile; an alligator lagoon with some 50 American alligators; and as well as plenty of somewhat cuddlier creatures, such as koalas, platypus, wallabies, dingoes, and flying foxes. The park is set in beautiful bushland dissected by nature trails.

Taronga Zoo. Bradley's Head Rd, Mosman. ☎ **02/9969 2777.** Admission A$16 (U.S.$11.20) adults, A$8.50 (U.S.$5.95) children 4–15, and A$41.50 (U.S.$29.05) families. Zoopass (includes entry, round-trip ferry from Circular Quay, and Aerial Safari cable car ride from ferry terminal to upper entrance of zoo) A$21 (U.S.$14.70) adults, A$10.50 (U.S.$7.35) seniors and children. Daily 9am–5pm (January 9am–9pm). Ferry: Taronga Zoo. At the Taronga Zoo wharf, a bus to the upper zoo entrance costs A$1.20 (U.S. 85¢), or you can take a cable car to the top for A$2.50 (U.S.$1.75). The lower zoo entrance is a 2-min. walk up the hill from the wharf, but it's better on the legs to explore the zoo from the top down.

Taronga has the best view of any zoo in the world. Set on a hill, it looks out over Sydney Harbour, the Opera House, and the Harbour Bridge. The main attractions here are the fabulous chimpanzee exhibit, the gorilla enclosure, and the Nocturnal Houses, where you can see some of Australia's many nighttime marsupials out and about, including the platypus and the cuter-than-cute bilby (the official Australian Easter bunny). There's an interesting reptile display, a couple of rather impressive Komodo dragons, a scattering of indigenous Australian beasties—including a few koalas, echidnas, kangaroos, dingoes, and wombats—and lots more. The kangaroo and wallaby exhibit is very unimaginative; you'd be better off going to Featherdale Wildlife Park (see below) for happier-looking animals. Animals are fed at various times during the day. The zoo can get very crowded on weekends, so I strongly advise visiting during the week or going very early in the morning on weekends. Interestingly, the three sun bears near the lower ferry entrance/exit were rescued by an Australian businessman, John Stephens, from a restaurant in Cambodia, where they were to have their paws cut off one by one and served up as an expensive soup.

✪ **Featherdale Wildlife Park.** 217 Kildare Rd., W. Pennant Hills. ☎ **02/ 9622 1644.** Admission A$12 (U.S.$8.40) adults, A$6 (U.S.$4.20) children 4–14. Daily 9am–5pm. CityRail: Blacktown station, then take bus 725 to park (ask driver to tell you when to get off). By car: take the M4 motorway to Reservoir Rd., turn off, travel 4km (2¹⁄₂ miles), then turn left at Kildare Rd.

If you only have time to visit one wildlife park in Sydney, make it this one. The selection of native Australian animals is excellent, and, most importantly, the animals are very well cared for. You could easily spend a couple of hours here despite the park's compact size. You'll have the chance to hand feed plenty of friendly kangaroos and wallabies, and get a photo taken next to a koala (there are many here, both the New South Wales variety and the much larger Victorian type). The park offers twice-daily bus tours, which include hotel pickup and drop-off.

Koala Park. 84 Castle Hill Rd., West Pennant Hills. ☎ **02/9484 3141,** or 02/ 9875 2777. Admission A$10 (U.S.$7) adults, A$5 (U.S.$3.50) children. Daily 9am–5pm. Closed Christmas. CityRail: Pennant Hills station via North Strathfield (45 min.), then take bus 651–655 to park.

Unless you want to go all the way to Kangaroo Island in South Australia, it's unlikely you're going to spot as many koalas in the trees as you can find here. In all, there are around 55 koalas roaming within the park's leafy boundaries. Koala cuddling sessions are free, and take place at 10:20am, 11:45am, 2pm, and 3pm daily. There are also wombats, dingoes, kangaroos, wallabies, emus, and native birds here, too. You can hire a private guide to take you around for A$70 (U.S.$49) for a two-hour session, or hitch onto one of the free "hostess" guides who wander around the park like Pied Pipers.

Oceanworld. West Esplanade, Manly. ☎ **02/9949 2644.** Admission A$14.50 (U.S.$10.15) adults, A$7.50 (U.S.$5.25) children, A$39 (U.S.$27.30) families. Daily 10am–5:30pm. Ferry or JetCat: Manly.

Though not as impressive as the Sydney Aquarium, Oceanworld can be combined with a visit to the wonderful Manly beach (see section 5 below) for a nice day's outing. There's a pretty good display of Barrier Reef fish, a pool of giant saltwater turtles, and yet more giant sharks.

5   Hitting the Beach

One of the big bonuses of visiting Sydney in the summer months (December, January, and February) is that you get to experience the beaches in their full glory.

Most major city beaches, such as Manly and Bondi, have lifeguards on patrol, especially during the summer months. They check the water conditions and are on the lookout for "rips"—strong ocean currents that can easily pull a swimmer far out to sea. Safe places to swim are marked by red and yellow flags. You must always swim between these flags, never outside them. If you are using a foam or plastic body board or "boogie board" it's also advisable to use them between the flags. Fiberglass surfboards must generally be used outside the flags.

Another common problem off Sydney's beaches are **"blue bottles"**—small blue jellyfish, often called "stingers" in Australia, and "Portuguese-Man-o'-Wars" elsewhere. You'll often find these creatures washed up along the tide line on the beach; they become a hazard for swimmers when there's a strong breeze coming off the ocean and they're blown in to shore (watch out for warning signs erected on the shoreline). Minute individual stinging cells often break off the main body of the creature, and they can cause minor itching or stinging. Other times, you might be hit by the full force

What about Sharks?

One of the first things visitors wonder when they hit the water in Australia is, "Are there sharks?" The answer is yes, but fortunately they are rarely spotted inshore. In reality, sharks have more reason to be scared of us than we of them, as most of them end up as the fish portion in your average packet of fish and chips (you might see shark fillets sold as "flake"). Though some beaches, such as the small beach next to the Manly ferry wharf in Manly and a section of Balmoral Beach, have permanent shark nets, most rely on portable nets that are moved from beach to beach periodically to prevent territorial sharks setting up home alongside bathers.

of a whole blue bottle, which will often stick to your skin and wrap its tentacles around you. Blue bottles deliver a hefty punch from their many stinging cells, and you will feel a severe burning sensation almost immediately. If you are stung, ask a lifeguard for some vinegar to neutralize any stinging cells that haven't yet sprung into action. Otherwise, a very hot bath or shower can help relieve the pain, which can be very intense and last for up to a day.

SOUTH OF SYDNEY HARBOUR

Sydney's most famous beach is **Bondi.** In many ways it's a raffish version of a Californian beach, with plenty of tanned skin and in-line skaters. Though the beach is nice, it's cut off from the cafe and restaurant strip that caters to beachgoers by a big ugly road that pedestrians have to funnel across in order to reach the sand. To reach Bondi Beach, take the CityRail train to Bondi Junction, then transfer to bus 380. You can also catch bus 380 directly from Circular Quay.

If you follow the water along to your right at Bondi, you'll come across a very scenic cliff-top track that takes you to **Bronte Beach** (a 20-min. walk), via gorgeous little **Tamarama,** a boutique beach known for its dangerous rips. Bronte has better swimming than Bondi. To get to Bronte, catch bus 378 from Circular Quay, or pick up the bus at the Bondi Junction CityRail station.

Clovelly Beach, farther along the coast, is blessed with a large rock pool carved into a rock platform and sheltered from the force of the Tasman Sea. This beach is accessible for visitors in wheelchairs via a series of ramps. To reach Clovelly, take bus 339 from Circular Quay.

The cliff walk from Bondi will eventually bring you to **Coogee,** which has a pleasant strip of sand with a couple of hostels and hotels nearby. To reach Coogee, take bus 373 or 374 from Circular Quay (via Pitt, George, and Castlereagh streets, and Taylor Square on Oxford Street) or bus 314 or 315 from Bondi Junction.

NORTH OF SYDNEY HARBOUR

On the north shore you'll find ❂ **Manly,** a long curve of golden sand edged with Norfolk Island Pines. (Don't be fooled into thinking the two small beaches found on either side of the ferry terminal are Manly Beach. Many people have made this mistake, including novelist Arthur Conan Doyle, who traveled to Manly by ferry and, presuming the small beach near the ferry station was the best the suburb had to offer, did not bother to disembark.) Follow the crowds shuffling through the pedestrians-only **Corso** to the main ocean beach. You'll find one of Sydney's nicest walks here, too: As

Grin & Bare It

If getting an all-over tan is your scene, you have a couple of options in Sydney. You can either head to the nudist beach at **Lady Jane Bay,** which is a short walk from Camp Cove beach (accessed from Cliff Street in Watsons Bay). Or, you can try **Cobblers Beach,** which is accessed via a short but steep bush track that leads from the far side of the playing field oval next to the main *HMAS Penguin* naval base at the end of Bradley's Head Road in Mosman. Be prepared for a largely male-orientated scene—as well as the odd boatload of beer-swigging peeping toms.

you face the ocean, head right along the beachfront and follow the coastal path to the small and sheltered **Shelly Beach,** a nice area for snorkeling and swimming. There's also a small take-out outlet here, next to the beachfront restaurant, selling drinks and snacks. Follow the paved path up the hill to the parking lot. Here, a track cuts into the bush and leads toward a fire wall, which marks the entrance to **Sydney Harbour National Park.** Around here you'll get some spectacular ocean views across to Manly and the northern beaches. The best way to reach Manly is on a ferry or JetCat from Circular Quay.

Farther along the north coast are a string of ocean beaches, including the surf spots of **Curl Curl, Dee Why, Narrabeen, Mona Vale, Newport, Avalon,** and finally ✪ **Palm Beach,** a very long and beautiful strip of sand, cut from the calmer waters of **Pittwater** by sand dunes and a golf course. Here you'll also find the Barrenjoey Lighthouse, which offers fine views along the coast. Bus numbers 136 and 139 run from Manly to Curl Curl, while bus L90 runs from Wynyard to Newport and to the other northern beaches as far as Palm Beach. There's no direct bus from Manly to Palm Beach, although you can take bus 132, 155, 156, or 169 to Warringah Mall (ask the driver to tell you when to get off) and catch the L90 from there.

INSIDE SYDNEY HARBOUR

The best harbor beach is ✪ **Balmoral,** a wealthy North Shore hangout complete with its own little island and some excellent cafes and an upscale restaurant. The beach itself is split into three separate parts. As you look toward the sea, the middle section is the most popular, whereas the wide expanse of sand to your left and the sweep of surreally beautiful sand to your right have a mere scattering of sunbathers. To reach Balmoral, take the Taronga Zoo ferry and then catch one of connecting buses from the ferry wharf for the 5-minute ride to Balmoral. In summer, you can take one of the special summer ferries to Balmoral that also stop at Watsons Bay and Manly).

6 Museums, Galleries, Historic Houses & More

Art Gallery of New South Wales. Art Gallery Rd., The Domain. ☎ **02/ 9225 1744.** www.artgallery.nsw.gov.au. Free admission to most galleries. Special exhibitions vary, though expect to pay around A$12 (U.S.$8.40) adults, A$7 (U.S.$4.90) children. Daily 10am–5pm. Tours of general exhibits Tues–Fri 11am, noon, 1pm, and 2pm. Call for weekend times. Tours of Aboriginal galleries Tues–Fri 11am. Free Aboriginal performance Tues–Sat at noon. CityRail: St. James. Sydney Explorer bus: Stop 6.

The numerous galleries here present some of the best of Australian art and many fine examples by international artists, including good displays of Aboriginal and Asian art. You enter from The Domain parklands on the third floor of the museum. On the fourth floor you will find an expensive restaurant and a gallery often showing free photography displays. On the second floor is a wonderful cafe overlooking the wharves and warships of Wooloomooloo. Every January and February there is a fabulous display of the best work created by school students throughout the state.

Australian Museum. 6 College St. ☎ **02/9320 6000.** www.austmus. gov.au. Admission A$5 (U.S.$3.50) adults, A$2 (U.S.$1.40) children, A$12 (U.S.$8.40) families. Special exhibits cost extra. Daily 9:30am–5pm. Closed Christmas. CityRail: Museum, St. James, or Town Hall. Sydney Explorer bus: Stop 15.

Though nowhere near as impressive as, say, the Natural History Museum in London or similar museums in Washington or New York, Sydney's premier natural history museum still ranks in the top five of its kind in the world. Displays are presented thematically. The best displays are in the Aboriginal section, with its traditional clothing, weapons, and everyday implements. There are some sorry examples of stuffed Australian wildlife, too. Temporary exhibits run from time to time.

Customs House. Alfred St., Circular Quay. ☎ **02/9320 6429.** Free general admission. Admission to Djamu Gallery A$8 (U.S.$5.60) adults, A$2 (U.S.$1.40) children. Open daily 9:30am–5pm. CityRail, bus, or ferry: Circular Quay.

This new museum, across the large square opposite the Circular Quay CityRail station and the ferry wharves, opened in December 1998. It's worthwhile to take a look inside just for the stunning architecture. Once inside, I'm sure you'll be hooked on the interesting series of modern art objects displayed on the ground floor, and the traveling exhibits on the third floor (the history of chairs was the big thing in early 1999). The Djamu Gallery, on the second floor, has four small rooms of Aboriginal and South Pacific items—the overspill from the Australian Museum. Outside in the square is a cafe selling reasonably priced coffee, cakes, sandwiches, and the like.

Elizabeth Bay House. 7 Onslow Ave, Elizabeth Bay. ☎ **02/9356 3022.** Admission A$6 (U.S.$4.20) adults, A$3 (U.S.$2.10) children, A$15 (U.S.$10.50) families. Tues–Sun 10am–4:30pm. Closed Good Friday and Christmas. Bus: 311 from Circular Quay. Sydney Explorer bus: Stop 10.

This magnificent example of colonial architecture was built in 1835 and was described at the time as the "finest house in the colony." Visitors can tour the whole house and get a real feeling of the history of the fledgling settlement. The house is situated on a headland and has some of the best harbor views in Sydney.

Museum of Sydney. 37 Phillip St. ☎ **02/9251 5988.** Admission A$6 (U.S.$4.20) adults, A$3 (U.S.$2.10) children under 15, A$15 (U.S.$10.50) families. Daily 9:30am–5pm. CityRail, bus, or ferry: Circular Quay. Sydney Explorer bus: Stop 3.

You'll need your brain in full working order to make the most of the contents of this three-story post-modern building that encompasses the remnants of Sydney's first Government House. This place is far from being a conventional showcase of history; instead, it's a rather minimalist collection of first-settler and Aboriginal objects and multimedia displays that invite the museum-goer to discover Sydney's past for him or herself. By the way, that forest of poles filled with hair, oyster shells, and crab claws in the courtyard adjacent to the industrial-design cafe tables is called *Edge of Trees.* It's a metaphor for the first contact between Aborigines and the British.

Sydney Jewish Museum. 148 Darlinghurst Rd. (at Burton St.), Darlinghurst. ☎ **02/9360 7999.** Admission A$6 (U.S.$4.20) adults, A$3 (U.S.$2.10) children, A$15 (U.S.$10.50) families. Cash only. Mon–Thurs 10am–4pm; Fri 10am–2pm; Sun 11am–5pm. Closed Jewish holidays, Christmas, and Good Friday. CityRail: Kings Cross.

Harrowing exhibits here include documents and objects relating to the Holocaust and the Jewish culture, mixed with soundscapes, audiovisual displays, and interactive media. There's also a museum shop, a resource center, a theatrette, and a traditional kosher cafe. It's considered one of the best museums of its type in the world.

Sydney Observatory. Observatory Hill, Watson Rd., Millers Point. ☎ **02/ 9217 0485.** Free admission in daytime; guided night tours (reservations essential), A$8 (U.S.$5.60) adults, A$3 (U.S.$2.10) children, and A$18 (U.S.$12.60) families. Daily 10am–5pm. CityRail, bus, or ferry: Circular Quay.

The city's only major museum of astronomy offers visitors a chance to see the southern skies through modern and historic telescopes. The best time to visit is during the night on a guided tour, when you can take a close-up look at some of the planets. Night tours are offered at 8:15pm from the end of May to the end of August and at 6:15 and 8:15pm the rest of the year; be sure to double-check the times when you book your tour. The planetarium and hands-on exhibits are also interesting.

State Library of NSW. Macquarie St., ☎ **02/9273 1414.** Free admission. Mon–Fri 9am–9pm; Sat, Sun, and selected holidays 11am–5pm. Closed New Year's Day, Good Friday, Christmas, and Boxing Day (Dec 26). CityRail: Martin Place. Sydney Explorer bus: Stop 4.

The state's main library is divided into two sections, located next door to one another. The newer reference library complex has two floors of reference materials, local newspapers, and microfiche viewers. Leave your bags in the free lockers downstairs. If you are over in this area of town at lunchtime, I highly recommend the library's leafy Glasshouse Café, in my opinion one of the best lunch spots in Sydney. The older building contains many older and more valuable books on the ground floor, and often hosts free art and photography displays in the upstairs galleries. A small library section in the Sydney Town Hall building has international newspapers.

Vaucluse House. Wentworth Rd., Vaucluse. ☎ **02/9337 1957.** Admission A$6 (U.S.$4.20) adults, A$3 (U.S.$2.10) children, A$15 (U.S.$10.50) families. House Tues–Sun 10am–4:30pm. Grounds daily 7am–5pm. Free guided tours. Closed Good Friday and Christmas. Bus: 325 from Circular Quay.

Also overlooking Sydney Harbour, this house includes lavish entertainment rooms and impressive stables and outbuildings. It was built in 1803 and was the home of Charles Wentworth, the architect of the Australian Constitution. It's set in 27 acres of gardens, bushland and beach frontage—perfect for picnics.

7 Parks & Gardens

IN SYDNEY

ROYAL BOTANIC GARDENS   If you are going to spend time in one of Sydney's green spaces, then make it the Royal Botanic Gardens (☎ **02/9231 8111**), next to Sydney Opera House. The gardens were laid out in 1816 on the site of a farm dedicated to supplying food for the fledgling colony. It's informal in appearance with a scattering of duck ponds and open spaces, though there are several areas dedicated to particular plant species, such as the rose garden, the cacti and succulent display, and the central palm and the rain forest groves. **Mrs. Macquarie's Chair,** along the coast path, offers superb views of the Opera House and the Harbour Bridge (it's a favorite stop for tour buses). The giant sandstone building dominating the gardens nearest to the Opera House is **Government House,** which was once the official residence of the Governor of New South Wales (he moved out in 1996 in the spirit of republicanism). The pleasant gardens are open to the public daily from 10am to 4pm, and the house is open for inspection Friday to Sunday from 10am to 3pm. Entrance to both is free. If you plan to park around here it's well to note that parking meters cost upwards of A$3 (U.S.$2.10) per hour, and you need A$1 coins.

A popular walk takes you through the Royal Botanic Gardens to the **Art Gallery of New South Wales.**

The botanic gardens are open daily from 6:30am to dusk. Admission is free.

HYDE PARK   In the center of the city is Hyde Park, a favorite with lunching business people. Of note here are the **Anzac Memorial** to Australian and New Zealand troops killed in the wars, and the **Archibald Fountain,** complete with spitting turtles and sculptures of Diana and Apollo. At night, avenues of trees are lit up with twinkling lights giving the place a magical appearance.

MORE CITY PARKS   Another Sydney favorite is the giant **Centennial Park** (☎ **02/9339 6699**), usually accessed from the top of Oxford Street. It was opened in 1888 to celebrate the centenary of European settlement, and today encompasses huge areas of lawn, several lakes, picnic areas with outdoor grills, cycling and running paths, and a cafe. It's open from sunrise to sunset. To get there, take bus 373, 374, 377, 380, 396, or 398 from the city.

A hundred years later, **Bicentennial Park,** at Australia Avenue, in Homebush Bay, came along. Forty percent of the park's total 100 hectares (247 acres) is general parkland reclaimed from a city rubbish tip; the rest is the largest remaining remnant of wetlands on the Parramatta River and is home to many species of both local and migratory wading birds, cormorants, and pelicans. At 1:30pm Monday through Friday, a tractor train takes visitors around the park on a 1 to 1$\frac{1}{2}$-hour guided trip. Tours cost A$6 (U.S.$4.20) per person. Follow park signs to the **visitor information office** (☎ **02/9763 1844**), open Monday through Friday from 10am to 4pm, and Saturday and Sunday from 9:30am to 4:30pm. To reach the park, you can either take a CityRail train to Strathfield and then take bus

401 to Homebush Bay (ask the driver when to get off), or take a CityRail train directly to the Homebush CityRail station.

BEYOND SYDNEY

SYDNEY HARBOUR NATIONAL PARK   You don't need to go far to experience Sydney's nearest national park. The Sydney Harbour National Park stretches around parts of the inner harbor and includes several small harbor islands (many first-time visitors are surprised at the amount of bushland still remaining in prime real estate territory). The best walk through the Sydney Harbour National Park is the **Manly to Spit Bridge Scenic Walkway** (☎ 02/ 9977 6522). This 10-kilometer (6-mile) track winds its way from Manly (it starts near the Oceanarium), via Dobroyd Head to Spit Bridge (where you can catch a bus back to the city). The walk takes between 3 and 4 hours, and the views across busy Sydney Harbour are fabulous. Maps are available from the **Manly Visitors Information Bureau,** right opposite the main beach (☎ 02/9977 1088).

Other access points to the park include tracks around Taronga Zoo (ask the zoo staff to point you toward the rather concealed entrances), and above tiny Shelly Beach, opposite the main beach at Manly.

Also part of the national park is the recently restored **Fort Denison,** the easily recognizable fortified outcrop in the middle of the harbor between Circular Quay and Manly. The fort was built during the Crimean War due to fears of a Russian invasion, and later acted as a penal colony. One- to two-hour **Heritage Tours** of the island leave from Cadmans Cottage, in The Rocks (☎ 02/ 9247 5033). Call for times. Tours cost A$12 (U.S.$8.40) for adults, A$8 (U.S.$5.60) for children, and A$32 (U.S.$22.40) for a family of four. Sunset Tours leave at 5:30pm on Thursday and Friday, and 6pm on Saturday and cost A$14 (U.S.$9.80) for adults, A$11 (U.S.$7.70) for children, and A$41 (U.S.$28.70) for a family.

Pick up maps of Sydney Harbour National Park at Cadmans Cottage.

Another great walk in Sydney can be combined with lunch or a drink at Watsons Bay. A 15-minute bush stroll to **South Head** is accessed from the small beach outside the Watson's Bay Hotel. Walk to the end of the beach (to your right as you look at the water) then up the flight of steps and bear left. There are some great views of the harbor from the lighthouse here.

MORE NATIONAL PARKS   Forming a semicircle around the city are Sydney's biggest parks of all. To the west is the Blue

---

Bushwalking Safety Tips

Bushwalking (hiking) in Australia can be a tough business. You'll need to take plenty of water, a hat, sunscreen, and insect repellent to ward off the flies in summer. It's always wise to tell someone where you're going, too.

Mountains National Park, to the northeast is **Ku-ring-gai Chase National Park,** and to the south is the magnificent **Royal National Park.** All three parks are home to marsupials such as echidnas and wallabies, numerous bird and reptile species, and a broad range of native plant life. Walking tracks, whether they stretch for half an hour or a few days, make each park accessible to the visitor.

Ku-ring-gai Chase National Park (☎ **02/9457 9322** or 02/9457 9310), is a great place to take a bushwalk through gum trees and rain forest on the lookout for wildflowers, sandstone rock formations, and Aboriginal art. There are plenty of tracks through the park, but one of my favorites is a relatively easy 2.5-kilometer (1.5-mile) tramp to **The Basin** (Track 12). The well-graded dirt path takes you down to a popular estuary with a beach and passes some significant Aboriginal engravings. There are also some wonderful water views over Pittwater from the picnic areas at **West Head.** Pick up a free walking guide at the park entrance, or gather maps and information in Sydney at the National Parks & Wildlife Service's center at **Cadmans Cottage,** 110 George St., The Rocks (☎ **02/9247 8861**). The park is open from sunrise to sunset, and admission is A$9 (U.S.$6.30) per car. You can either drive to the park or catch a ferry from Palm Beach to McMasters Beach or The Basin (both inside the park). Ferries run on the hour (except at 1pm) from 9am to 5pm daily and cost A$7 (U.S.$4.90) one-way; call ☎ **02/9918 2747** for details. Shorelink bus 577 runs from the Turramurra CityRail station to the nearby park entrance every hour on weekdays and every two hours on weekends; call ☎ **02/9457 8888** for details. There is no train service to the park. Camping is allowed only at The Basin (☎ **02/9457 9853**), and costs A$10 (U.S.$7) for two people booked in advance. An excellent place to dine in the park is the Akuna Bay Restaurant.

While in the area you could visit the **Ku-ring-gai Wildflower Garden,** 420 Mona Vale Rd., St Ives (☎ 02/9440 8609), which is essentially a huge area of natural bushland and a center for urban bushland education. There are plenty of bushwalking tracks, self-guided walks, and a number of nature-based activities. It's open daily from 8am to 4pm. Admission is A\$2.50 (U.S.\$1.75) for adults, A\$1 (U.S.70¢) for children, and A\$6 (U.S.\$4.20) for families.

To the south of Sydney is the remarkable **Royal National Park,** Farrell Avenue, Sutherland (☎ **02/9542 0648**). It's the world's oldest national park, having been gazetted as such in 1879 (the main competitor to the title is Yellowstone in the United States, which was established in 1872 but not designated as a national park until 1883). Severe bushfires almost totally destroyed the whole lot in early 1994, but the trees and bush plants have recovered remarkably. There's no visitor center, but you can pick up park information at park entrances, where you'll have to pay a A\$9 (U.S.\$6.30) per car entry fee.

There are several ways to access the park, but my favorites are the little-known access points from Bundeena and Otford. To get to Bundeena, take a CityRail train from Central Station to Cronulla. Just below the train station you'll find Cronulla Wharf. From there, hop on the delightful ferry run by **National Park Ferries** (☎ **02/ 9523 2990**) to Bundeena; ferries run hourly on the half hour (except 12:30pm). After you get off the ferry, the first turn on your left just up the hill will take you to **Bundeena Beach.** It's another 5 kilometers (3 miles) or so to the wonderfully remote **Little Marley Beach,** via Marley Beach (which has dangerous surf). The ferry returns to Cronulla from Bundeena hourly on the hour (except 1pm). The fare is A\$2.40 (U.S.\$1.68) each way.

An alternative way to reach the park is to take the train from Central Station to **Otford,** then climb the hill up to the sea cliffs. If you're driving, you might want to follow the scenic cliff edge road down into Wollongong. The entrance to the national park is a little tricky to find, so you may have to ask directions. A 2-hour walk from the sea cliffs through beautiful and varying bush land and a palm forest will take you to **Burning Palms Beach.** There is no water along the route. The walk back up is steep, so only attempt this trek if you're reasonable fit. Trains to the area are irregular, and the last one departs around 4pm, so give yourself at least 2¹/₂ hours for the return trip back to the train station to make sure you don't get stranded. It's possible to walk the 26 kilometers (16 miles) from Otford to Bundeena, or vice versa, in two days (take all your food, water and camping gear).

8 Especially for Kids

There are plenty of places kids can have fun in Sydney, but the recommendations below are particularly suitable for youngsters (all of the places are reviewed in full above).

Taronga Zoo (see p. 134) is an all-time favorite with kids, where the barnyard animals, surprisingly, get as much attention as the koalas. If your kids want hands-on contact with the animals, though, then you'd better head to **Featherdale Wildlife Park** (see p. 135), where they can get their photo taken next to a koala, and hand feed and stroke kangaroos and wallabies.

Sega World (see p. 131 in Darling Harbour will no doubt entertain them for a few hours, but the trouble is adults can't resist the rides, too. Just as interactive are the exhibits just crying out to be touched and bashed at the **Powerhouse Museum** (see p. 130).

The sharks at **Oceanworld** (see p. 135) in Manly and at the **Sydney Aquarium** (see p. 131) in Darling Harbour are big lures for kids, too, and the thrill of walking through a long plexiglass tunnel as giant manta rays perch over their heads will lead to more squeals of excitement.

Another fascinating outing for both adults and children is to crawl around inside a navy destroyer at the **Australian National Maritime Museum** (see p. 130)—if you're lucky there may even be a submarine to explore, too.

And, of course, what kid wouldn't enjoy a day at the beach, and Sydney's got plenty to choose from, like **Bondi** or **Manly.**

9 Harbor Cruises & Organized Tours

For details on the Red Sydney Explorer bus, see "Getting Around" in chapter 2, "Getting to Know Sydney."

HARBOR CRUISES

The best thing about Sydney is the harbor, so you shouldn't leave without taking a harbor cruise. **Sydney Ferries** (☎ **13 15 00**) offers a 1-hour morning harbor cruise with commentary departing Circular Quay, wharf 4, daily at 10am and 11:15am. It costs A$12 (U.S.$8.40) for adults, A$8 (U.S.$5.60) for children under 16, and A$32 (U.S.$22.40) for families (any number of children under 16). A $2^1/_2$-hour afternoon cruise explores more of the harbor and leaves from wharf 4 at 1pm on weekdays and 1:30pm on weekends and public holidays. This tour costs A$17.50 (U.S.$12.25) for adults, A$12 (U.S.$8.40) for children, and A$47 (U.S.$32.90) for families.

The highly recommended 1¹/₂-hour **evening harbor tour,** which takes in the city lights as far east as Double Bay and west to Goat Island, leaves Monday through Saturday at 8pm from wharf 5. The evening tour costs A$15 (U.S.$10.50) for adults, A$10 (U.S.$7) for children, and A$40 (U.S.$28) for families.

If you are missing the Mississippi, another option is a trip on a paddle-steamer. The **Sydney Showboat** (☎ 02/9552 2722; fax 02/ 9552 1934) departs from Campbells Cove in The Rocks. A daily lunch cruise running from 12:30 to 2pm costs A$50 (U.S.$35) for adults and A$30 (U.S.$21) for children 5–12; it includes a good buffet lunch, a jazz band, and commentary. Daily coffee cruises depart at 10:30am, 2:30pm, and 5:15pm, and cost A$17 (U.S.$11.90) for adults and A$11 (U.S.$7.70) for children. A daily dinner cruise that runs from 7:30pm to 10pm costs A$116 (U.S.$81.20) for adults and A$67 (U.S.$46.90) for children; it includes a three-course meal, cabaret, dancers, a magician, singers, and a juggler. A Starlight dinner cruise without entertainment on the same boat costs A$74 (U.S.$51.80) for adults, and A$44 (U.S.$30.80) for children. You can buy tickets at the no. 2 jetty in Circular Quay.

If you're going to splurge on a cruise, though, the best are aboard the fully rigged replica of **Captain Bligh's Bounty** (☎ 02/ 9247 1789). The boat was built for the movie *Mutiny on the Bounty,* which starred Mel Gibson, Anthony Hopkins, Daniel Day Lewis, and Liam Neeson. Standard two-hour lunch cruises run Monday through Friday and cost A$55 (U.S.38.50) for adults and A$33 (U.S.$23.10) for children. Two-and-a-half hour dinner cruises depart daily and cost A$85 (U.S.$59.50) for adults and A$51 (U.S.$35.70) for children. On Saturday and Sunday, a 2¹/₂-hour buffet lunch sail costs A$80 (U.S.$56) for adults and A$48 (U.S.$33.60) for children, and a 1¹/₂-hour predinner sail costs A$45 (U.S.$31.50) for adults and A$27 (U.S.$18.90) for children.

Harbor Cruise Tickets & Info

The one-stop shop for tickets and information on all harbor cruises is the **Australian Travel Specialists** (☎ 02/9247 5151; www. atstravel.com.au). Find outlets at jetties no. 2 and no. 6 at Circular Quay; at Manly Wharf in Manly; at the Harbourside Festival Marketplace at Darling Harbour; and inside the Oxford Koala Hotel on Oxford Street.

Alternatively, you can cruise like a millionaire aboard the **MV Oceanos** (☎ **02/9555 2701**), a 72-foot luxury motor cruiser. A 2¹/₂-hour cruise, which leaves the Eastern Pontoon at Circular Quay at 1pm daily, costs A$69 (U.S.$48.30) per person and includes a quality seafood lunch. **Sail Venture Cruises** (☎ **02/9262 3595**) also has a range of cruises aboard their catamarans.

Captain Cook Cruises. Departing jetty no.6, Circular Quay. ☎ **02/9206 1111**. Fax 02/9251 1281. www.captcookcrus.com.au.

This major cruise company offers several harbor excursions on its sleek vessels, with commentary along the way.

The Harbour Highlights cruise runs at 9:30am, 11am, 12:30pm, 2:30pm, and 4pm daily and takes in most of the main points of interest in 1¹/₄ hours. Cruises cost A$18 (U.S.$12.60) for adults and A$13 (U.S.$9.10) for children. The 1¹/₂-hour Sundowner cruise takes in the last of the sun's rays starting out at 5:30pm daily; it costs the same as the Harbour Highlights cruise.

The *Sydney Harbour Explorer* departs at 9:30am, 11:30am, 1:30pm, and 3:30pm and combines visits to five major Sydney attractions with a two-hour cruise. You can get off where you want and join the boat again later. Tickets cost A$20 (U.S.$14) for adults and A$12 (U.S.$8.40) for children. An Aquarium Cruise, costing A$32 (U.S.$22.40) for adults and A$18 (U.S.$12.60) for children, includes the *Sydney Harbour Explorer* cruise and admission to the Sydney Aquarium.

The company also offers a 1¹/₂-hour Luncheon Cruise, which leaves daily at noon. It costs A$47 (U.S.$32.90) for adults and A$35 (U.S.$24.50) for children. A Showtime Dinner Cruise leaves nightly at 7:30pm and includes a cabaret and dinner; it costs A$89 (U.S.$62.30) for adults and A$50 (U.S.$35) for children.

Superior meals are served aboard the **John Cadman Cruising Restaurant boat.** A nightly 1¹/₂-hour Sunset Dinner cruise departs at 5:15pm and costs A$65 (U.S.$45.50) for adults and A$30 (U.S.$21) for children, which includes a two-course meal and drinks. A second dinner cruise leaves at 7:30pm nightly and takes about 2¹/₂ hours to cruise the harbor, while guests indulge in a fine three-course meal and bop away on the dance floor. Adults cost A$89 (U.S.$62.30), and children A$50 (U.S.$35). Reservations are essential.

Matilda Cruises. Departing Aquarium Wharf, Darling Harbour. ☎ **02/9264 7377**. Fax 02/9261 8483. www.matilda.com.au.

The modern Matilda fleet is based at Darling Harbour and offers 1-hour sightseeing tours, morning and afternoon coffee cruises, and daily lunch and dinner cruises. One-hour sightseeing cruises leave Darling Harbour eight times daily beginning at 9:30am (six times daily in winter beginning at 10:30am) and cost A$18 (U.S.$12.60) for adults and A$9 (U.S.$6.30) for children 5 to 12. Two-hour coffee cruises leave Darling Harbour at 9am and 3:05pm and cost A$24 (U.S.$16.80) for adults and A$12 (U.S.$8.40) for children. Two-hour lunch cruises leave at 12:15pm daily and cost A$49.95 (U.S.$35) for adults and A$24.95 (U.S.$17.50) for children. Three-hour dinner cruises leave at 7pm and cost A$94.95 (U.S.$67) for adults and A$47.50 (U.S.$33.25) for children. All boats dock at Circular Quay's Eastern Pontoon (near The Oyster Bar, before you get to the Sydney Opera House), 20 minutes after picking up passengers at Darling Harbour.

WALKING TOURS

The center of Sydney is surprisingly compact, and you'll find you can see a lot in a day on foot. If you want to learn more about Sydney's early history, then you should book a guided tour with **The Rocks Walking Tour** (☎ 02/9247 6678), based at the Sydney Visitor Centre, 106 George St. Excellent walking tours leave Monday through Friday at 10:30am, 12:30pm, and 2:30pm, and Saturday and Sunday at 11:30am and 2pm. The 1¹/₂-hour tour costs A$12 (U.S.$8.40) for adults, A$8 (U.S.$5.60) for children 10 to 16, and A$30 (U.S.$21) for families. Accompanied children under 10 are free.

For other historical walks, contact **Sydney Guided Tours** (☎ 02/9660 7157; fax 02/9660 0805). The company's owner, Maureen Fry, has been in the business for over 12 years and employs trained guides qualified in specific disciplines, such as history, architecture, and botany. She offers a range of tours including an introductory tour of Sydney, a tour of historic Macquarie Street, and many others. Walking tours cost A$15 (U.S.$10.50) for two hours as part of a group (call in advance to find out what's available), or A$150 (U.S.$105) for a 2-hour personalized tour (for 1 to 10 people).

A walking tour with a difference is **Unseen Sydney's History, Convicts, and Murder Most Foul** (☎ 02/9555 2700). Th⸱ is fascinating and fun, with the guide dressed up in ol ⸱ and theatrical storytellers spinning yarns about Sydn⸱

and intrigue. The 1¹/₂-hour tour leaves at 6:30pm sharp from Circular Quay Tuesday, and Thursday through Saturday. It costs A$17 (U.S.$11.90) for adults and A$13 (U.S.$9.10) for children.

MOTORCYCLE TOURS

Blue Thunder Motorcycle Tours (☎ **02/9977 7721;** fax 02/ 4578 5033) runs chauffeured Harley-Davidson tours of Sydney, the Blue Mountains, and other places around New South Wales. A 1-hour ride (you sit on the back of the bike) around the city costs A$80 (U.S.$56). A half-day trip to the northern beaches or down the south coast through the Royal National Park costs A$230 (U.S.$161), including lunch. Full day trips cost A$360 (U.S.$252) including lunch and snacks, and go to either the Hunter Valley, the south coast, Bathurst, or the Blue Mountains.

Another Harley-Davidson tour specialist is **Dream Legends Motor Cycle Tours** (☎ **02/9584 2451**). One-hour city trips cost A$60 (U.S.$42), half-day jaunts go for A$180 (U.S.$126), and a full-day excursion "wherever you want to go" costs A$300 (U.S.$210).

A third mean-machine operator is **Eastcoast Motorcycle Tours** (☎ **02/9247 5151**). One-hour city tours cost A$80 (U.S.$56), and 4-hour trips to the south coast, Ku-ring-gai Chase National Park, or Wisemans Ferry cost A$240 (U.S.$168).

10 Staying Active

CYCLING   The best place to cycle in Sydney is in **Centennial Park.** Rent bikes from **Centennial Park Cycles,** 50 Clovelly Rd., Randwick (☎ **02/9398 5027**), which is 200 meters from the Musgrave Avenue entrance. (The park has five main entrances). Standard bikes cost A$6 (U.S.$4.20) for the first hour, A$10 (U.S.$7) for 2 hours, and A$14 (U.S.$9.80) for 3 or 4 hours. Mountain bikes can be hired for the day to take on bush trails elsewhere. They cost A$30 (U.S.$21) for 8 hours, or A$40 (U.S.$28) for 24 hours.

Bicycles & Adventure Sports Equipment, 722 George St. (near Central Station) (☎ **02/9252 2229**), rents mountain bikes from A$5 (U.S.$3.50) per hour, or A$20 to $25 (U.S.$14 to $17.50) per day. You can rent in-line skates here, too, for the same daily rate with all protective clothing.

Helmets are compulsory in Australia.

FITNESS CLUBS   The **City Gym,** 107 Crown St., East Sydney (☎ 02/9360 6247), is a busy gym near Kings Cross. Drop-in ʼre A$8 (U.S.$5.60), and it's open daily 24 hours.

GOLF   Sydney has more than 90 golf courses and plenty of fine weather. The 18-hole championship course at **Moore Park Golf Club,** at Cleveland Street and Anzac Parade, Waterloo (☎ **02/ 9663 1064**), is the nearest to the city. Visitors are welcome at all times except Sunday mornings and all day on Fridays. Green fees are A$24 (U.S.$16.80) Monday through Thursday, and A$27 (U.S.$18.90) Saturday and Sunday.

One of my favorite courses is **Long Reef Golf Club,** Anzac Avenue, Colloroy (☎ **02/9982 2943**). This northern beaches course is surrounded by the Tasman Sea on three sides and has gorgeous views. Green fees are A$25 (U.S.$17.50) midweek, and A$30 (U.S.$21) on weekends.

For general information on courses call the **New South Wales Golf Association** (☎ **02/9264 8433**).

IN-LINE SKATING   The best places to go in-line skating are along the beachside promenades at Bondi and Manly beaches and in Centennial Park. **Manly Blades,** 49 North Steyne (☎ **02/9976 3833**), rents skates for A$10 (U.S.$7) for the first hour and A$5 (U.S.$3.50) for each subsequent hour, or A$20 (U.S.$14) per day. Lessons are A$20 (U.S.$14) including 1-hour skate hire and a half-hour lesson. **Bondi Boards & Blades,** 148 Curlewis St., Bondi Beach (☎ **02/9365 6555**), offers the same hourly rates, with daily rentals costing A$28 (U.S.$19.60). There's a free lesson at Bondi Boards & Blades every Tuesday afternoon. **Total Skate,** 36 Oxford St., Paddington, near Centennial Park (☎ **02/9380 6356**), also has the same hourly rates, with a whole day costing A$30 (U.S.$21). Lessons at 5pm on Sundays are free if you rent skates.

JOGGING   The **Royal Botanic Gardens, Centennial Park,** or any **beach** are the best places to kick start your body. You can also run across the Harbour Bridge, though you'll have to put up with the car fumes. Another popular spot is along the sea cliffs from Bondi Beach to Bronte Beach.

PARASAILING   If being strapped to a harness and a parachute 100 meters above Sydney Harbour while being towed along by a speed boat is your idea of fun, contact **Sydney Harbour Parasailing and Scenic Tours** (☎ **02/99776781**). A regular flight will see you in the air for 6 to 7 minutes at the end of a 100-meter line. Flights cost A$39 (U.S.$27.30) per adult. For A$49 (U.S.$34.30), you can get 8 to 10 minutes in the air and 150 meters of line on a "super flight." Tandem rides, for children and adults, are also available. The boat departs next to the Manly ferry wharf in Manly.

SURFING **Bondi Beach** and **Tamarama** are the best surf beaches on the south side of Sydney Harbour, while **Manly, Narrabeen, Bilgola, Colloroy, Long Reef,** and **Palm Beach** are the most popular on the north side. Most beach suburbs have surf shops where you can rent a board. At Bondi Beach, the **Bondi Surf Co.,** 72 Campbell Parade (☎ **02/9365 0870**), rents surfboards and body boards for A$20 (U.S.$14) for three hours. In Manly, **Aloha Surf,** 44 Pittwater Rd., Manly (☎ **02/9977 3777**) rents surfboards for A$30 (U.S.$21) per day. Call **Manly Surf School** (☎ **0418 717 313** mobile phone) for information on surf lessons.

SWIMMING The best place to swim indoors in Sydney is the **Sydney International Aquatic Centre,** at Olympic Park, Homebush Bay (☎ **02/9752 3666**). It's open Monday through Friday from 5am to 9:45pm, and Saturday, Sunday, and public holidays from 7am to 7pm (but not during the Olympics, of course). Entry costs A$4.50 (U.S.$3.15) for adults and A$3.50 (U.S.$2.45) for children.

Another popular place is the **Andrew (Boy) Charlton Pool,** at Mrs. Macquarie's Point (☎ **02/9358 6686**), near the Art Gallery of New South Wales. It has great views over the finger wharves of Wooloomooloo Bay. The pool is open in summer only, Monday through Friday from 6am to 8pm, and Saturday and Sunday from 6am to 7pm. Entry costs A$2.50 (U.S.$1.75) for adults and A$1.20 (U.S.84¢) for children.

Another good bet is the **North Sydney Olympic Pool,** Alfred South St., Milsons Point (☎ 02/9955 2309). Swimming here costs A$3 (U.S.$2.10) for adults and A$1.40 (U.S.$1) for children. More world records have been broken in this pool than in any other pool in the world. In 1999, the pool went through major renovations, so the prices may go up.

TENNIS There are hundreds of places around the city to play one of Australia's most popular sports. A nice spot is the **Miller's Point Tennis Court,** Kent St., The Rocks (☎ **02/9256 2222**). It's run by the Observatory Hotel and is open daily from 8am to 9:30pm. The court costs A$20 (U.S.$14) per hour. The **North Sydney Tennis Centre,** 1a Little Alfred St., North Sydney (☎ **02/9371 9952**), has three courts available daily from 7am to 10pm. They cost A$14 (U.S.$9.80) until 5pm on weekdays and A$18 (U.S.$12.60) at other times.

WINDSURFING My favorite spot to learn to windsurf or to set out onto the harbor is at **Balmoral Beach,** in Mosman on the North

Shore. Rent boards at **Balmoral Windsurfing, Sailing and Kayaking School & Hire,** 3 The Esplanade, Balmoral Beach (☎ **02/9960 5344**). Windsurfers cost A$25 (U.S.$17.50) per hour, and lessons cost A$145 (U.S.$101.50) for five hours teaching over a weekend. This place also rents fishing boats.

YACHTING   Balmoral Boat Shed, Balmoral Beach (☎ **02/ 9969 6006**) rents catamarans, 12-foot aluminum run-abouts, canoes, and surf skis. The catamarans and run-abouts cost A$30 (U.S.$21) for the first hour (with an A$80/U.S.$56 deposit); a full-day costs A$110 (U.S.$77). Other vessels cost A$10 (U.S.$7) per hour with an A$10 (U.S.$7) deposit.

Sydney by Sail (☎ **02/9552 7561,** or 0419/367 180 mobile phone) offers daily introductory sailing cruises on the harbor aboard luxurious 34- and 38-foot yachts. A maximum of six people sail aboard each boat, which leave from the National Maritime Museum at Darling Harbour. Ninety-minute introductory sails cost A$39 (U.S.$27.30) per person. Reservations are essential.

Elizabeth Bay Marina (☎ **02/9358 2057**), close to Kings Cross, rents boats with outboard motors for A$65 (U.S.$45.50) for half a day.

11 Catching a Cricket Match & Other Spectator Sports

CRICKET   The **Sydney Cricket Ground,** at the corner of Moore Park and Driver Avenue, is famous for its one-day and test matches, played generally from October to March. Phone the **New South Wales Cricket Association** at ☎ **02/9261 5155** for match details. **Sportspace Tours** (☎ **02/9380 0383**) run tours of the stadium, the Sydney Cricket Ground Museum, and the Football (rugby league) Stadium next door. Tours run Monday through Saturday at 10am, 1pm, and 3pm, and cost A$18 (U.S.$12.60) for adults, A$12 (U.S.$8.40) for children, and A$48 (U.S.$33.60) for families.

FOOTBALL   In this city, "football" means rugby league. If you want to see burley chaps pound into each other while chasing an oval ball, then be here between May and September. The biggest venue is the **Sydney Football Stadium,** Moore Park Rd., Paddington (☎ **02/9360 6601**). Match information is available at ☎ **0055 63 133.** Buy tickets at **Ticketek** (☎ **02/9266 4800**).

HORSE RACING   Sydney has four horse racing tracks, Randwick, Canterbury, Rosehill, and Warwick Farm. The most central and most well known is **Randwick Racecourse,** Alison St., Randwick (☎ **02/9663 8400**). The biggest race day of the week is Saturday. Entry costs A$6 (U.S.$4.20) per person. Call the **Sydney Turf Club** at ☎ **02/9799 8000** with questions about Rosehill and Canterbury, and the Randwick number above for Warwick Farm.

SURFING CARNIVALS   Every summer these uniquely Austra-lian competitions bring large crowds to Sydney's beaches, as surf clubs compete against each other in various water sports. Contact the **Surf Lifesaving Association** (☎ **02/9663 4298;** fax 02/9662 2394) for times and locations. Other beach events include Iron Man and Iron Woman competitions, during which Australia's fit-test struggle it out in combined swimming, running, and surfing events.

YACHT RACING   While sailing competitions take place on the harbor most summer weekends, the start of the **Sydney to Hobart Yacht Race** on Boxing Day (December 26) is something not to be missed. The race starts from the harbor near the Royal Botanic Gardens. Contact **Tourism New South Wales** (☎ **02/9931 1111;** fax 02/9931 1490) or **Tourism Tasmania** (☎ **03/6230 8169;** fax 03/6230 8353) for more information.

7

Shopping

Sydney's shopping is not as good as Melbourne's, but you'll still find plenty of places to keep your credit cards in action. Most shops of interest to the visitor are located in The Rocks and along George and Pitt streets (including the shops below the AMP Centerpoint Tower and along the Pitt Street Mall). Other shopping precincts worth checking out are Mosman on the North Shore and Double Bay in the eastern suburbs for exclusive boutique shopping, Chatswood for its general shopping centers, the Sydney Fishmarket for the sake of it, and the various weekend markets (listed below).

1 The Shopping Scene

You won't want to miss the **Queen Victoria Building (QVB),** on the corner of Market and George streets. This Victorian shopping arcade is one of the prettiest in the world and has some 200 boutiques—mostly men's and women's fashion—on four levels. The arcade is open 24 hours, but the shops do business Monday to Saturday from 9am to 6pm (Thursday to 9pm) and Sunday 11am to 5pm.

Several other arcades in the city center also offer good shopping potential, including the **Royal Arcade** under the Hilton Hotel; the **Imperial Arcade** near the AMP Centerpoint Tower; **Sydney Central Plaza,** beside the Grace Brothers department store on Pitt Street Mall; and the **Skygarden Arcade,** which runs from Pitt Street Mall to Castlereagh Street. The **Strand Arcade** (running between Pitt Street Mall and George Street) was built in 1892 and is interesting for its architecture and small boutiques, food stores and cafes, and the Down Town Duty Free store on the basement level.

On **Pitt Street Mall** you'll find record shops, including HMV; a branch of The Body Shop; and fashion boutiques such as Just Jeans, Jeans West, Katies, and Esprit.

If you're looking for bargains, head to **Foveraux Street** between Elizabeth and Waterloo streets in Surry Hills for factory clearance shops selling end-of-the-run, last season's fashions, and seconds at deep discounts. If you're really keen on bargain shopping you might want to consider joining up with **Shopping Spree Tours** (☎ **1800/ 625 969** in Australia, or 02/9360 6220; fax 02/9332 2641), which offers tours to factory outlets and warehouses selling everything from clothes to cookware to electrical appliances. Full-day tours cost A$50 (U.S.$35) for adults and A$15 (U.S.$10.50) for children 3 to 12 and include pick up at your hotel, visits to 8 to 10 outlets and warehouses, and a two-course lunch at a good restaurant. Tours depart at 8:15am daily except Sunday and public holidays.

2 Sydney Shopping from A to Z

ABORIGINAL ARTIFACTS & CRAFTS

Aboriginal & Tribal Art Centre. 1st Floor, 117 George St., The Rocks. ☎ **02/9247 9625.** Fax 02/9247 4391.

This center carries a wide range of desert paintings and bark paintings, mostly of very high quality. Collectibles such as didjeridoos, fabrics, books, and boomerangs are on sale, too. Open daily from 10am to 5pm.

Coo-ee Aboriginal Art Gallery and Shop. 98 Oxford St., Paddington. ☎ **02/9332 1544.** Fax 02/9360 1109.

The proprietors of Coo-ee collect artifacts and fine art from more than 30 Aboriginal communities and dozens of individual artists throughout Australia. The gallery also stocks the largest collection of limited-edition prints in Australia. There are also plenty of hand-painted fabrics, T-shirts, didjeridoos, boomerangs, sculpture, bark paintings, jewelry, music, and books. Don't expect bargain prices, though; you pay for the quality here. Open Monday to Saturday from 10am to 6pm, and Sunday from 11am to 5pm.

Didj Beat Didjeridoo's. Shop 2, The Clock Tower Square, Corner of Argyle and Harrington sts. ☎ **02/9251 4289.**

Here you'll find the best selection of didjeridoos in Sydney. The pieces are authentic and well priced. Open daily from 9:30am to 6pm.

Shopping Hours

Regular shopping hours are generally Monday to Wednesday and Friday from 8:30 or 9am to 6pm, Thursday from 8:30 or 9am to 9pm, Saturday from 9am to 5 or 5:30pm, and Sunday from 10 or 10:30am to 5pm. Exceptions are noted in the store listings below.

Gavala Aboriginal Art & Cultural Education Centre. Harbourside Festival Marketplace, Darling Harbour. ☎ **02/9212 7232.** Fax 02/9211 7009.

I'd head here first if I were in the market for a decent boomerang or didjeridoo. Gavala is entirely owned and operated by Aborigines, and there are plenty of authentic Aboriginal crafts for sale, including carved emu eggs, grass baskets, cards, and books. A first-rate painted didjeridoo will cost anywhere from A$160 (U.S.$112) to A$265 (U.S.$185.50). Gavala also sponsors cultural talks, didjeridoo-making and emu egg–carving lessons, and storytelling sessions. Open daily from 10am to 9pm.

Original & Authentic Aboriginal Art. 79 George St., The Rocks. ☎ **02/9251 4222.**

Quality Aboriginal art is on offer here from some of Australia's best-known painters, including Paddy Fordham Wainburranga whose paintings even hang in the White House in Washington, and Janet Forrester Nangala, whose work has been exhibited in the Australian National Gallery in Canberra. Expect to pay in the range of A$1,000 (U.S.$700) to A$4,000 (U.S.$2,800) for the larger paintings. There are some nice painted pots here, too, costing from A$30 (U.S.$21) to A$80 (U.S.$56). Open daily from 9:30am to 7pm.

ART PRINTS & ORIGINALS

Done Art and Design. 1 Hickson Rd., The Rocks. ☎ **02/9247 2740.**

The art is by Ken Done, who's well known for having designed his own Australian flag, which he hopes to raise over Australia should it abandon its present one following the formation of a republic. The clothing designs—which feature printed sea and beachscapes, the odd colorful bird, and lots of pastels—are by his wife Judy. Ken Done's Gallery is in Hickson Road, just off George Street, in the Rocks. Open daily from 10am to 5:30pm.

Ken Duncan Gallery. 73 George St., The Rocks (across from The Rocks Visitor Centre). ☎ **02/9241 3460.** Fax 02/9241 3462.

This photographer-turned-salesman is making a killing from his exquisitely produced large-scale photographs of Australian scenery. Open daily from 9am to 8pm.

BOOKS

You'll find a good selection of specialized books on Sydney and Australia for sale at the **Art Gallery of New South Wales,** the Garden Shop in the **Royal Botanic Gardens,** the **Museum of Sydney,** the **Australian Museum,** and the **State Library of New South Wales.**

Abbey's Bookshop. 131 York St. (behind the Queen Victoria Building). ☎ **02/9264 3111.**

This interesting, centrally located bookshop specializes in literature, history, crime, and mystery, and has a whole floor on language and education.

Angus & Robertson Bookworld. Pitt Street Mall, 168 Pitt St. ☎ **02/9235 1188.**

One of Australia's largest bookshops, with two stories of books—including a good guidebook and Australiana section—and games. Open Monday to Wednesday and Friday from 8:30am to 6pm, Thursday from 8:30am to 9pm, Saturday from 9am to 5:30pm, and Sunday from 10:30am to 5pm.

Dymocks. 424–428 George St. (just north of Market St.). ☎ **02/9235 0155.**

The largest of four book department stores in the city, Dymocks has three levels of general books and stationary. There's a reasonable travel section here with plenty of guides. Open Monday to Wednesday and Friday from 9am to 6pm, Thursday from 9am to 9pm, Saturday from 9am to 5pm, and Sunday from 10am to 5pm.

Gleebooks Bookshop. 49 Glebe Point Rd, Glebe. ☎ **02/9660 2333.**

Specializing in art, general literature, psychology, sociology, and women's studies, Gleebooks also has a second-hand store (with a large children's department) down the road at 191 Glebe Point Rd. Open daily 8am to 9pm.

✪ **Goulds Book Arcade**. 32–38 King St., Newtown. ☎ **02/9519 8947.**

Come here to search for unusual dusty volumes. Located about a 10-minute walk from the Newtown CityRail station, the place is bursting at the seams with many thousands of second-hand and new books. You can browse for hours here. Open daily from 8am to midnight.

✪ **Travel Bookshop**. Shop 3, 175 Liverpool St. (across from the southern end of Hyde Park, near the Museum CityRail station). ☎ **02/9261 8200.**

Hundreds of travel guides, maps, Australiana titles, coffee-table books, and travel accessories line the shelves of this excellent bookshop. Open Monday to Friday from 9am to 6pm and Saturday from 10am to 5pm.

CRAFTS

Australian Craftworks. 127 George St., The Rocks. ☎ **02/9247 7156.**

This place showcases some of Australia's best arts and crafts, collected from some 300 Australian artists from around the country. It's all displayed in a former police station built in 1882, a time of economic depression when mob riots and clashes with police were common in this area. The cells and administration areas are today used as gallery spaces. Open daily from 9am to 7pm.

✪ **The puppet shop at the rocks.** 77 George St., The Rocks. ☎ **02/9247 9137.** Fax 02/9418 4157.

I can't believe I kept walking past the sign outside this place for so many years without looking in. Deep down in the bowels of a historic building, I eventually came across several cramped rooms absolutely packed with puppets, costing from a couple of dollars to a couple of hundred. The owners make their own puppets—mostly Australian in style (emus, koalas, and that sort of thing)—as well as import things from all over the world. Wooden toys abound, too. It's the best shop in Sydney! Open daily from 10am to 5:30pm.

Telopea Gallery. Shop 2 in the Metcalfe Arcade, 80–84 George St., The Rocks. ☎ **02/9241 1673.**

This shop is run by the New South Wales Society of Arts and Crafts, which exhibits works made by its members, all of whom are New South Wales residents. There are some wonderful glass, textile, ceramic, jewelry, fine metal, and wood-turned items for sale. Open daily from 9:30am to 5:30pm.

DEPARTMENT STORES

The two big names in Sydney shopping are David Jones and Grace Brothers. **David Jones** (☎ 02/9266 5544) is the city's largest department store, selling everything from fashion to designer furniture. You'll find the women's section on the corner of Elizabeth and Market streets, and the men's section on the corner of Castlereigh and Market streets.

   Grace Brothers (☎ 02/9238 9111) is similar to David Jones, but the building is newer and flashier. It's located on the corner of George and Market streets. Both stores are open Monday to Wednesday and Friday from 9am to 5:30pm, Thursday from 9am to 9pm, Saturday from 9am to 5pm, and Sunday from 11am to 5pm.

DUTY-FREE SHOPS

Sydney has several duty-free shops selling goods at a discount. To take advantage of the bargains, you need a passport and a flight ticket, and you must export what you buy. The duty-free shop with the best buys is **Downtown Duty Free,** which has two city outlets, one on the basement level of the Strand Arcade, off Pitt Street Mall

(☎ **02/9233 3166**); and one at 105 Pitt St. (☎ **02/9221 4444**). Five more stores are found at Sydney International Airport and are open from the first to the last flight of the day.

FASHION

The best places to shop for fashion are the Queen Victoria Building and the Sydney Central Plaza (on the ground floor of the mall next to the Grace Brothers department store on Pitt Street Mall). Otherwise, the major department stores and Pitt Street Mall outlets will keep you up to date.

AUSTRALIAN OUTBACK CLOTHING

R.M. Williams. 389 George St. (between Town Hall and Central CityRail stations). ☎ **02/9262 2228.**

Moleskin trousers may not be the height of fashion at the moment, but you never know. R.M. Williams boots are famous for being both tough and fashionable. You'll find Akubra hats, Driza-bone coats, and kangaroo-skin belts here, too. Open Monday to Wednesday and Friday from 9am to 5:30pm, Thursday from 9am to 9pm, Saturday from 9am to 5pm, and Sunday from 11am to 4pm.

Thomas Cook Boot & Clothing Company. 790 George St., Haymarket. ☎ **02/9212 6616.** www.thomascookclothing.com.au.

Located on George Street between Town Hall and central CityRail stations, this place specializes in Australian boots, Driza-bone coats, and Akubra hats. Open Monday to Wednesday and Friday from 9am to 5:30pm, Thursday from 9am to 7pm, Saturday from 9am to 5pm, and Sunday from noon to 4pm. There's another shop at 129 Pitt St., near Martin Place (☎ **02/9232 3334**).

UNISEX FASHIONS

Country Road. 142–146 Pitt St. ☎ **02/9394 1818.**

This chain store has outlets all across Australia as well as in the United States. The clothes, for both men and women, are good quality but tend to be quite expensive (though you might find something smart if you forgot to pack something). You'll find other branches in the Queen Victoria Building and the Skygarden Arcade, and in Bondi Junction, Darling Harbour, Double Bay, Mosman, and Chatswood. Open Monday to Wednesday and Friday from 9am to 5:30pm, Thursday from 9am to 9pm, Saturday from 9am to 6pm, and Sunday from 11am to 5pm.

Mostrada. Store 15G, Sydney Central Plaza, 450 George St. ☎ **02/ 9221 0133.**

If you're looking for good-quality leather items at very reasonable prices, then this is your place. Leather jackets for men and women go for between A$199 (U.S.$139.30) and A$899 (U.S.$629.30), with an average price of around A$400 (U.S.$280). There are also bags, belts, and other leather accessories on offer. Open Monday to Friday from 9am to 6pm, Saturday from 10am to 6pm, and Sunday from 11am to 5pm.

MEN'S FASHIONS

Esprit Mens. Shop 10G, Sydney Central Plaza, 450 George St. ☎ **02/ 9233 7349.**

Not so cheap, but certainly colorful clothes come out of this designer store where bold hues and fruity patterns are the in thing. Quality designer shirts cost around A$60 (U.S.$42). Open Monday to Wednesday, Friday, and Saturday from 9am to 6pm; Thursday from 9am to 9pm; and Sunday from 11am-5pm.

Gowings. 45 Market St. ☎ **02/9264 6321.**

Probably the best all-round men's clothing store in Sydney, Gowings sells quality clothing on two levels, with more formal attire sold in the basement. Upstairs, things go weird, with an eclectic mix of gardening equipment, gourmet camping gear, odds and ends for the extrovert, a good range of Australian bush hats, and R.M. Williams boots (well-priced at around A$200/U.S.$140 a pair). Open Monday to Wednesday and Friday from 8:30am to 6pm, Thursday from 8:30am to 9pm, Saturday from 9am to 6pm, and Sunday from 10am to 5pm. There's a similar store at 319 George St., near Wynyard CityRail station.

Outdoor Heritage. Shop 13G, Sydney Central Plaza, 450 George St. ☎ **02/ 9235 1560.**

Quality clothing with a yachting influence is what you'll find at this good-looking store specializing in casual, colorful gear. Open Monday to Wednesday, Friday, and Saturday from 9am to 6pm; Thursday from 9am to 9pm; and Sunday from 11am to 5pm.

WOMEN'S FASHIONS

In addition to the places listed below, head to Oxford Street (particularly Paddington) for more avant-garde designers.

Carla Zampatti. 143 Elizabeth St. ☎ **02/9264 32576.**

There are some thirty Carla Zampatti stores around Australia offering stylish fashions at hard-to-swallow prices. Open Monday to Saturday from 10am to 5pm.

Dorian Scott. 105 George St., The Rocks. ☎ **02/9221 8145.** Fax **02/9251 8553.**

Probably the best place to go for hand-knitted sweaters—called "jumpers" in Australia—Dorian Scott has a wide range of colorful garments from more than 200 leading Australian designers. While some items go for A$80 (U.S.$56), others will set you back several hundred. You'll also find clothing accessories for men, women, and children in this two-story emporium, including Hot Tuna surfware and Thomas Cook adventure clothing. Open Monday to Saturday from 9:30am to 7pm and Sunday from 10am to 6pm. There are also two Dorian Scott stores at Sydney International Airport and another at the Inter-Continental Hotel at 117 Macquarie St.

FOOD

The goodies you'll find in the downstairs food section of the **David Jones** department store on Castlereagh Street (the men's section) will be enough to tempt anyone off their diet. It sells the best of local and imported products to the rich and famous. See "Department Stores," above.

Coles. Wynyard Station, Castlereagh St., Wynyard (directly opposite the Menzies Hotel and the public bus stands). ☎ **02/9299 4769.**

One of the few supermarkets in the city center, this place is a good bet if you want to cater for yourself or are after ready-made food (including tasty sandwiches) and cheap soft drinks. Open daily from 6am to midnight.

Darrell Lea Chocolates. At the corner of King and George sts. ☎ **02/9232 2899.**

This is the oldest location of Australia's most famous chocolate shop. Pick up some wonderful hand-made chocolates as well as other unusual candies, including the best licorice this side of the Kasbah. Open Monday to Wednesday and Friday from 8:30am to 6:30pm, Thursday from 8:30am to 9pm, Saturday from 10am to 6pm, and Sunday from 10:30am to 5pm.

Sydney Fishmarket. At the corner of Bank St. and Pyrmont Bridge Rd., Pyrmont. ☎ **02/9660 1611.**

Finding out about what people eat can be a good introduction to a new country, and, in my opinion, nowhere is this more fascinating than a visit to the local fish market. Here you'll find seven major fish retailers selling everything from shark to Balmain bugs (a kind of squat crayfish), with hundreds of species in between. Watch out for the local pelicans being fed the fishy leftovers. There's also a Doyles restaurant and a sushi bar, a couple of cheap seafood eateries, a fruit market, and a good deli. The retail sections are open daily from 7am to 4pm. Get here by Light Rail (get off at the Fishmarket stop), or walk from Darling Harbour. Parking costs A\$2 (U.S.\$1.40) for the first 3 hours.

GIFTS & SOUVENIRS

The shops at **Taronga Zoo,** the **Oceanarium** in Manly, the **Sydney Aquarium,** and the **Australian Museum** are all good sources for gifts and souvenirs. There are many shops around **The Rocks** worth browsing, too.

✪ **Australian Geographic.** Harbourside Festival Marketplace, Darling Harbour, ☎ **02/9212 6539;** AMP Centerpoint Tower, Pitt St. ☎ 02/9231 5055.

A spin-off from the Australian version of *National Geographic* magazine, this store sells good-quality crafts and Australiana. On offer are camping gadgets, telescopes and binoculars, garden utensils, scientific oddities, books and calendars, videos, music, toys, and lots more. Open Sunday to Wednesday and Friday and Saturday from 10am to 6pm, Thursday from 10am to 7pm.

National Trust Gift and Bookshop. Observatory Hill, The Rocks. ☎ **02/9258 0173.**

You can pick up some nice souvenirs, including books, Australiana crafts, and indigenous foodstuffs here. An art gallery on the premises presents changing exhibits of paintings and sculpture by Australians. There's also a cafe. Open Tuesday to Friday from 9am to 5pm, Saturday and Sunday from noon to 5pm. Gallery open Tuesday to Friday from 11am to 5pm, Saturday and Sunday from noon to 5pm. Closed Monday.

✪ **The Wilderness Society shop.** AMP Centerpoint Tower, Castlereagh St. ☎ **02/9233 4674.**

Australiana is crawling out of the woodwork at this cute little craft emporium dedicated to spending all its profits on saving the few remaining untouched forests and wilderness areas of Australia. You'll find some quality craft items, cute children's clothes, books, cards, and knickknacks.

MARKETS

Balmain Market. On the grounds of St. Andrew's Church, Darling St., Balmain. No phone.

Where to Load up on Olympic Games Gear

A monopoly is good for business, and the organizing committee of the Sydney Olympics has things wrapped up nicely with the outrageously priced **Olympic Store** (☎ 02/9232 3099) in the AMP Centerpoint Tower complex on the Pitt Street Mall. Everything from sweatshirts to socks has the copyrighted Olympic logo on it. Designer T-shirts go for up to A$32.95 (U.S.$23). Low-quality versions cost A$19.95 (U.S.$14).

Active from 8:30am to 4pm every Saturday, this popular market has some 140 vendors selling crafts, jewelry, and knickknacks. Take the ferry to Balmain (Darling Street); the market is a ten-minute walk up Darling Street.

Paddington Bazaar. On the grounds of St. John's Church on Oxford St., on the corner of Newcome St. (just follow the crowds). ☎ **02/9258 0173.**

At this Saturday-only market you'll find everything from essential oils and designer clothes to new age jewelry and Mexican hammocks. Expect things to be busy from 10am to 4pm. Take bus 380 or 389 from Circular Quay.

Paddy's Markets. At the corner of Thomas and Hay sts., in Haymarket, near Chinatown. ☎ **1300/361 589** in Australia or 02/9325 6924.

A Sydney institution, Paddy's Markets has hundreds of stalls selling everything from cheap clothes and plants to chickens. It's open Friday to Sunday from 9am to 4:30pm. Above Paddy's Market is **Market City** (☎ **02/9212 1388**), which has three floors of fashion stalls, food courts, and specialty shops. Of particular interest is the largest Asian-European supermarket in Australia, on level 1, and the **Kam Fook yum cha** Chinese restaurant on level 3, also the largest in Australia.

The Rocks Market. On George St., The Rocks. ☎ **02/9255 1717.**

Held every Saturday and Sunday, this very touristy market has more than 100 vendors selling everything from crafts, housewares, posters, jewelry, and curios. The main street is closed to traffic from 10am to 4pm to make it easier to stroll around.

MUSIC

Birdland. 3 Barrack St. ☎ **02/9299 8527.** www.birdland.com.au.

This is the best store in Sydney for jazz and blues, and it stocks a sizable collection of rare items. The staff is very knowledgeable.

HMV Music Stores. Pitt Street Mall. ☎ **02/9221 2311.**

This is one of the best music stores in Sydney. The jazz section is impressive. CDs in Australia are not cheap, with most new releases costing around A$30 to $35 (U.S.$21 to $24.50).

Red Eye Records. Tank Stream Arcade (downstairs), at the corner of King and Pitt sts. (near Town Hall). ☎ **02/9233 8177** (new recordings), or 02/9233 8125 (second-hand CDs). www.redeye.com.au.

These two shops, tucked away downstairs in a small arcade not far from Pitt Street Mall and the Strand Arcade, are directly across from one another. The larger store sells a wide-range of modern CDs, but the smaller store sells a great collection of quality second-hand and end-of-the-line CDs for around A$20 (U.S.$14) each.

Sounds Australian. In the Argyle Stores department store, The Rocks. ☎ **02/9247 7290.** Fax 02/9241 2873.

Anything you've ever heard that sounds Australian you can find here. From rock and pop to didjeridoo and country, it's all here. Fortunately, if you haven't a clue what's good and what's bad you can spend some time listening before you buy. The management is extremely knowledgeable.

OPALS

ANA House Sydney. 37 Pitt St. ☎ **02/9251 2833.**

When buying good opals, it's always a good idea to bargain, and this is one of the best places to do it in the city. The shop sells some good stones, as well as all the usual touristy trinkets. There's a special VIP viewing room off to the side of the main sales floor if you're interested in buying real quality. Upstairs is a decent souvenir shop.

WINE

Australian Wine Centre. 1 Alfred St., Shop 3 in Goldfields House, Circular Quay. ☎ **02/9247 2755.** Fax 02/9247 2756.

This is one of the best places in the country to pick up Australian wines by the bottle or the case. The shop stocks a wide range of wines from all over Australia, including bottles from small boutique wineries you're unlikely to find anywhere else. Individual tastings are possible at any time, though there are formal tastings every Thursday and Friday from 4 to 6pm.

8

Sydney After Dark

*A*ustralians can be party animals when they're in the mood. Whether it's a few beers around the barbecue, a few bottles of red over a dinner table with friends, or an all-night rage in a trendy dance club, they're always on the lookout for the next event. You'll find that alcohol plays a big part in the Aussie culture.

1 The Performing Arts

If you have an opportunity to see a performance in the ✪ **Sydney Opera House,** jump at it. The "House" is actually not that impressive inside, but the walk back after the show toward the ferry terminals at Circular Quay, with the Sydney Harbour Bridge lit up to your right and the crowd all around you debating the best part of this play or who dropped a beat in that performance—well, it's like hearing Gershwin while on the streets of New York—you'll want the moment to stay with you forever. For details on Sydney's most famous performing arts venue, see section 1 in chapter 6, "Exploring Sydney."

THE OPERA, SYMPHONY & BALLET

Australian Ballet. Level 15, 115 Pitt St. ☎ **02/9223 9522.** www.austballet. telstra.com.au.

Based in Melbourne, the Australian Ballet tours the country with its performances. The Sydney season, at the Opera House, is from mid-March until the end of April. A second Sydney season runs from November to December.

Australian Chamber Orchestra. 50 Darlinghurst Rd., Darlinghurst. ☎ **02/9357 4111;** box office ☎ 02/93681712. www.aco.com.au.

Based in Sydney, this well-known company performs at various venues around the city, from nightclubs to specialized music venues, including the Concert Hall in the Sydney Opera House.

Opera Australia. 480 Elizabeth St., Surry Hills. ☎ **02/9319 6333;** bookings ☎ 02/9319 1088. www.opera-australia.org.au.

Opera Australia performs at the Sydney Opera House's Opera Theatre. The opera season runs January to March and June to November.

| **Where to Find Out What's On** |

The best way to find out what's on is to get hold of the "Metro" section of the Friday *Sydney Morning Herald* or the "7 Days" pullout from the Thursday *Daily Telegraph*.

Sydney Symphony Orchestra. Level 5, 52 William St., East Sydney. ☎ **02/9334 4644;** box office 02/9264 4600. www.symphony.org.au.

Sydney's finest symphony orchestra is conducted by the renowned Edo de Waart. It performs throughout the year in the Opera House's Concert Hall. The main symphony season runs from March to November, and there's a summer season in February.

THEATER

Sydney is blessed with plenty of theaters, many more than I have space for here—check the *Sydney Morning Herald,* especially the Friday edition, for information on what's currently in production.

Belvoir Street Theatre. 25 Belvoir St., Surry Hills. ☎ **02/9699 3444.** Tickets around A$34 (U.S.$23.80).

The hallowed boards of the Belvoir are home to Company B, which pumps out powerful local and international plays upstairs in a wonderfully moody main theater, formerly part of a tomato-sauce factory. Downstairs, a smaller venue generally shows more experimental productions, such as Aboriginal performances and dance.

Capital Theatre. 13–17 Campbell St., Haymarket (near Town Hall). ☎ **02/9320 5000.** Ticket prices vary.

Sydney's grandest theater plays host to major international and local productions like, cough, Australian singing superstar Kylie Minogue. It's also been the Sydney home of musicals such as *Miss Saigon* and *My Fair Lady.*

Her Majesty's Theatre. 107 Quay St., Haymarket (near Central Station). ☎ **02/9212 3411.** Ticket prices average A$55–$75 (U.S.$38.50–$52.50).

A quarter of a century old, this large theater is still trawling in the big musicals. Huge productions that have run here include *Evita* and *Phantom of the Opera.*

Wharf Theatre. Pier 4, Hickson Rd., The Rocks. ☎ **02/9250 1777.** www.sydneytheatre.com.au. Ticket prices vary.

This wonderful theater is situated on a refurbished wharf on the edge of Sydney Harbour, just beyond the Harbour Bridge. The long walk from the entrance of the pier to the theater along old, creaky wooden floorboards builds up excitement for the show. The Sydney Theatre

---

It's a Festival!

If you happen to be in Australia in January, then you should pop along to one of the many events that take place as part of the annual **Sydney Festival.** The festival kicks off just after New Year's and continues until the last week of the month, with recitals, plays, films, and performances held at venues throughout the city, including Town Hall, the Royal Botanic Gardens, the Sydney Opera House, and Darling Harbour. Some of the events are free. "Jazz in The Domain" and "Symphony in The Domain" are two free outdoor performances held in the Royal Botanic Gardens outside the Art Gallery of New South Wales; each event (which generally takes place on the third and fourth weekend in January) attracts tens of thousands of Sydneysiders. For more information on the Sydney Festival, contact **Festival Ticketec** (☎ **02/9266 4111;** fax 02/ 9267 4460). You can also buy tickets and find out about performances on the Web at **www.sydneyfestival.org.au**.

Company is based here, a group well worth seeing whatever production is running. Dinner before the show at the Wharf's restaurant offers special views of the harbor.

2 The Club & Music Scene

ROCK
Metro. 624 George St. ☎ **02/9264 2666.** Cover varies.

A medium-size rock venue with space for 1,000, the Metro is the best place in Sydney to see local and international acts. Tickets sell out quickly.

JAZZ, FOLK & BLUES
✪ **The Basement.** 29 Reisby St., Circular Quay. ☎ **02/9251 2797.** Cover A$9–$10 (U.S.$6.30–$7) for local acts, A$20–$25 (U.S.$14–$17.50) for international performers.

Australia's hottest jazz club also manages to squeeze in plenty of blues, folk, and funk. Pick up a leaflet showing who's playing when at the door. A new Blue Note Bar specializing in jazz opened in July 1998. Acts appear every night.

The Bridge Hotel & Brasserie. 135 Victoria St., Rozelle. ☎ **02/9810 1260.** Cover A$5–$25 (U.S.$3.50–$17.50).

Come on a Sunday afternoon and you're assured of getting the blues. Friday and Saturday nights offer either blues, rock, or house music depending on the whim of the management. The three-level beer garden out the back is nice on a sunny day.

The Harbourside Brasserie. Pier One, Hickson Rd., Walsh Bay (behind The Rocks). ☎ **02/9252 3000.** Cover A$8–$20 (U.S.$5.60–$14) depending on performer.

Eat to the beat of soul and rhythm-and-blues at this not-bad eatery. Comedy nights attract big acts. Drinks are expensive.

Soup Plus. 383 George St. (near the Queen Victoria Building). ☎ **02/9299 7728.** Cover A$5 (U.S.$3.50) Mon–Thurs; A$20 (U.S.$14) Fri and Sat, including 2-course meal.

It seemed such a pity on my last visit to this cavernous jazz bar that the cover charge forced me to eat the bistro-style food on offer, which really was poor. However, some mellow blues cheered our nonplussed group in the end.

DANCE CLUBS

Blackmarket. 111–113 Regent St., Chippendale, at the corner of Meagher St. (5-minute walk from Central Station). ☎ **02/9698 8863.** Cover A$10 (U.S.$7).

This wacky place is known for its Friday night Hellfire Club (from 11pm to 4am), where Sydneysiders of all persuasions hang out to watch jelly wrestling and live sadomasochism shows. It's all in (relatively) good taste, though, with nothing too brutal, and it attracts a fun-loving crowd from students to office workers (about 50/50 male and female). Some people make the effort to dress up. There's some good music on offer, too, in the dark and moody interior. Ravers continue on, or drop in after working the nightshift, at the Day Club, offering dance music from 4am to 2pm on Saturday (you can stay on for free after the Hellfire Club) and 4am to 6pm on Sunday.

Bourbon & Beefsteak Bar. 24 Darlinghurst Rd., Kings Cross. ☎ **02/9358 1144.** Cover A$7.50 (U.S.$5.25) Fri–Sat.

Right in the middle of Sydney's red light district, this 24-hour restaurant and nightspot freaks out to dance music downstairs nightly from 11pm to 5am. It's popular with both young backpackers and the 25-to-35 crowd.

Byblos. 169 Oxford St., Darlinghurst. ☎ **02/9331 7729.** Cover A$10 (U.S.$7).

"Upmarket nightclubbing for the likes of models and beautiful people from the [affluent] north shore of Sydney," is how the manager described this place to me. The interior is pseudo-Roman with lots of pillars. The club offers hard-core club/dance music. Dress code is fashionable, with a shirt collar required for men and no sneakers.

Cauldron. 207 Darlinghurst Rd., Darlinghurst. ☎ **02/9331 1523.** Cover A$10 (U.S.$7).

This intimate and trend-setting nightclub is firmly established as part of "the scene." Tuesday night offers retro music, on Wednesday and Saturday it's house, and on Thursday and Friday it's funk/R&B. A stylish dress code applies.

Mister Goodbar. 11a Oxford St., Paddington. ☎ **02/9360 6759.** Cover A$10 (U.S.$7) Fri and Sat.

A young, trendy, local crowd inhabits Mister Goodbar's two good-size dance floors, which offers reggae on one floor and hip-hop on the other on Wednesdays, and disco and funk other days.

Riche Nightclub. In the Sydney Hilton, 259 Pitt St. ☎ **02/9266 0610.** Cover A$12 (U.S.$8.40) Fri and Sun, A$15 (U.S.$10.50) Sat.

This hot spot for dancing is popular with the local over-25 club set, as well as with hotel guests wanting to shake their booties to typical "dance" music.

GAY & LESBIAN CLUBS

With Sydney having the largest gay community outside San Francisco, it's no wonder there's such a happening scene here. The center of it all is Oxford Street, though Newtown has established itself as a major gay hangout, too. For information on news and events concerning gays and lesbians pick up a copy of the *Sydney Star Observer,* available at art-house cinemas and many cafes and stores around Oxford Street.

✪ **Albury Hotel.** 2–6 Oxford St. (near Barcom Ave.). ☎ **02/9361 6555.** No cover.

An institution, the Albury is a grande dame offering drag shows nightly in the public bar, and knockout Bloody Marys in the cocktail lounge.

✪ **Imperial Hotel.** 35–37 Erskineville Rd., Erskineville (near Union St.). ☎ **02/9519 9899.** No cover.

A couple of minutes' walk from King Street in Newtown, the Imperial is a no-attitude gay venue with a pool and cocktail bar out front and a raging cabaret venue out back. Sydney's best full-production drag shows happen late on Thursday, Friday, and Saturday nights, with dancing in between.

Midnight Shift. 85 Oxford St. (near crown St.). ☎ **02/9360 4319.** Cover A$10 (U.S.$7) Sat.

The beat here is sleazy, groovy, and dance party. A favorite with the denim and leather set, and the odd drag queen, this place gets more energetic as night becomes day. This is the original gay hangout on the Oxford Street strip.

Newtown Hotel. 174 King St., Newtown. ☎ **02/9557 1329.** No cover.

The octagonal bar here is the center of a casual drinking and cruising scene. The place kicks up its heels during late-night drag shows and powerfully camp discos.

77 Night Club. 77 William St., East Sydney. ☎ **02/9361 4981.** Cover A$5 (U.S.$3.50) Thurs, A$7 (U.S.$4.90) Fri, A$6 (U.S.$4.20) Sat, A$5 (U.S.$3.50) Sun.

This basement venue, beneath a tower block and prestige car sales-room, is an odd one out location-wise, but its moody interior is a hot spot for alternative, dance, progressive house, and jungle music.

Taxi Club. 40 Flinders St., Darlinghurst (near Taylor Sq., Oxford St.). ☎ **02/9331 4256.** Cover A$10 (U.S.$7) Fri–Sat.

"Tacky Club," as it's affectionately known, is good for commercial dance music and midweek cabaret shows. It's open 24 hours.

3 The Bar Scene

Most of Australia's drinking holes are known as "hotels," after the tradition of providing room and board alongside a good drink in the old days. Occasionally you might hear them referred to as pubs. You tend to find the term "bar" used in upscale hotels and trendy establishments.

Bondi Hotel. 178 Campbell Parade, Bondi Beach. ☎ **02/9130 3271.** Cover A$5 (U.S.$3.50) Sat only.

This huge, white-washed conglomerate across the road from Bondi Beach offers pool upstairs, a casual beer garden outside, and a resident DJ Thursday to Sunday from 8pm to 4am. There's also a free nightclub on Friday nights. Watch yourself, too much drink and sun turns some people nasty here.

The Friend in Hand. 58 Cowper St., Glebe. ☎ **02/9660 2326.**

In the same location as the fantastically cheap Caesar's No Names spaghetti house, the Friend in Hand offers cheap drinks, poetry readings on Tuesday evenings from 8:30pm, a trivia night on

Thursday evenings from 8:30pm, and the distinctly unusual Crab Racing Party every Thursday from around 8pm. Crab fanciers buy a crustacean for A$3 (U.S.$2.10), give it a name, and send it off to do battle in a race against around 30 others. There are heats and finals, and victorious crustaceans win their owners prizes.

Henry the Ninth Bar. In the Sydney Hilton, 259 Pitt St. ☎ **02/9266 0610.**
This mock-Tudor drinking hole gets very busy on Friday and Saturday nights. They serve up some good ales in an oaky atmosphere. An Irish band whips up the patrons on Thursday and Friday nights, and a cover band does the same on Wednesday and Saturday nights. A good-value happy hour brings beer prices tumbling Monday to Thursday from 5:30 to 7:30pm, Friday from 5:30 to 8:30pm, and Saturday from 8 to 10pm.

Hero of Waterloo Hotel. 81 Lower Fort St., The Rocks. ☎ **02/9252 4553.**
This sandstone landmark, built in 1845, was once allegedly the stalking ground of press gangs, who'd whack unsuspecting landlubbers on the head, push them down a trapdoor out the back, and cart them out to sea. Today, this strangely shaped sandstone drinking hole is popular with the locals, and hosts old-time jazz bands (the musicians are often in their 70s and 80s) on Saturday and Sunday afternoons from 1:30 to 6:30pm, and Irish and cover bands Friday to Sunday evenings beginning at 8:30pm.

Jacksons on George. 178 George St., The Rocks. ☎ **02/9247 2727.** Cover A$5 (U.S.$3.50) for nightclub Fri and Sat after 10pm.
A popular drinking spot, this place has four floors of drinking, eating, dancing, and pool playing, and is a popular haunt with tourists and after-work office staff. Pool is expensive here at A$3 (U.S.$2.10) a game (you'll need to ask the rules, as Australians have their own), and drinks have a nasty habit of going up in price without warning as the evening wears on. The nightclub plays commercial dance, and there's a smart/casual dress code. Happy hour is Monday to Friday from 5 to 7pm, when drinks cost around one-third less than normal.

✪ **Lord Dudley Hotel.** 236 Jersey Rd., Woollahra. ☎ **02/9327 5399.**
The best way to get to this great English-style pub is via the Edgecliff CityRail Station (between Kings Cross and Bondi Junction). From there, it's a five-minute walk up the hill outside the station and then take a right onto Jersey Road. The Lord Dudley has the best atmosphere of just about any drinking hole in Sydney, with log fires in winter, couches to relax in, three bars, and a restaurant.

Cocktails with a View

There's nothing better than a fabulous view rising above the lip of a full cocktail glass. One of the best places in town to drink in the view with your libations is **Horizon,** the cocktail bar at the very top of the multistory ANA Hotel in The Rocks (☎ 02/9250 6000). The views from The Rocks, Circular Quay, and out across Sydney Harbour are spectacular. It's open from noon to 1am daily, except on Sunday when it closes at midnight. Go at night for the city lights.

Another good option is having a cocktail (or a bottle of champagne) in the **Bennelong Bar** in the Sydney Opera House (☎ 02/9250 7548). Sit next to the window and you'll be treated to a very special view of the Opera House sails, the boats coming into Circular Quay, and the best view of the Harbour Bridge in the city. Cocktails here average a steep A$11 (U.S.$7.70). It's open from Monday to Saturday from 5:30 to 11:30pm and Saturday for lunch.

For more dramatic 360-degree sky-high views, head to **The Summit Skylounge,** Level 47, Australia Square, 265 George St. (☎ 02/9247 9777). It's open daily from 6pm to around midnight, and cocktails cost A$12.50 (U.S.$8.75).

The International, 14th floor, Victoria Street, Kings Cross (☎ 02/9360 9080), offers a buzzing art deco cocktail lounge with lots of wood paneling, dim lighting, and leather booths. Cocktails cost A$12 (U.S.$8.40). It's open daily from 5:30 to 11:30pm.

✪ **Lord Nelson Hotel.** At Kent and Argyle sts., The Rocks. ☎ 02/9251 4044.

Another Sydney sandstone landmark, the Lord Nelson rivals the Hero of Waterloo for the title of "Sydney's oldest pub." A drink here is a must for any visitor. The drinks are sold English-style, in pints and half-pints, and the landlord even makes his own prize-winning beers. Of these beers, Three Sheets is the most popular, but if you can handle falling over on your way home you might want to try a drop of Quail (a pale beer), Victory (based on an English bitter), and a dark beer called Admiral. You can get some good pub grub here, too. Upstairs there's a more formal brasserie.

✪ **Marble Bar.** In the Sydney Hilton, 259 Pitt St. ☎ 02/9266 0610.

Once part of a hotel demolished in the 1970s, the Marble Bar is unique in that it's the only grand cafe-style drinking hole in

Australia. With oil paintings, marble columns, and brass everywhere, it's the very picture of 15th-century Italian Renaissance architecture. It's a tourist attraction in itself. Live music, generally jazz or soul, is played here Tuesday through Saturday beginning at 8:30pm. Dress smart on Friday and Saturday evenings. Drinks are normally very expensive, but the happy hour (daily from 7 to 9pm) cuts prices down to what you'd pay during normal drinking hours elsewhere.

The Mercantile. 25 George St., The Rocks. ☎ **02/9247 3570.**

Sydney's original Irish bar is scruffy and loud when the Irish music's playing in the evening, but it's an essential stop on any self-respecting pub crawl in The Rocks. The Guinness is some of the best you'll taste in Sydney. Irish bands kick off every night at around 8pm.

✪ **Watsons Bay Hotel.** 1 Military Rd., Watsons Bay. ☎ **02/9337 4299.**

If it's a sunny afternoon don't waste it, get over to Watsons Bay for the best food you'll find in the sun anywhere. The beer garden serves very good seafood and BBQ meat dishes, while you sip your wine or beer overlooking the harbor. Nearby are the fabulous Doyles Wharf Restaurant and Doyles at the Beach takeaway.

4 The Casino

Star City. 80 Pyrmont St., Pyrmont (adjacent to Darling Harbour). ☎ **02/9777 9000.** No cover. Open 24 hours. Ferry: Pyrmont (Darling Harbor). Monorail: Casino.

This huge entertainment complex, which opened in 1997, has fifteen main bars, twelve restaurants, two theaters—the Showroom, which presents Las Vegas–style revues, and the Lyric, Sydney's largest theater—and a huge complex of retail shops. All the usual gambling tables are here, in four main gambling areas. In all there are 2,500 slot machines to gobble your change.

See also separate Accommodations and Restaurant indexes, below.

ACCOMMODATIONS

RESTAURANTS